Population

Analysis and Models

Louis Henry

Translated by Etienne van de Walle and Elise F. Jones

Academic Press · New York · San Francisco

A Subsidiary of Harcourt Brace Jovanovich, Publishers

Contents

Preface

The Second World War had at least two fortunate windfalls for the science of demography: it led to the creation of the *Institut national d'études démographiques*, and it interrupted Louis Henry's military career. INED resulted in vigorous development of demographic analysis in France and Henry was in the forefront of this research from the beginning. He has emerged among the two or three most original and influential technical demographers of the century. His work on the measurement of natural and controlled fertility (particularly with the help of models), and his pioneering labours in historical demography, have profoundly influenced scholarship in the English language.

So it is that the study of population has remained a field where a reading knowledge of French is necessary to keep abreast of some of the most recent developments in methodology. The translation of the present book gives access to an integrated textbook aimed at the French equivalent of undergraduates. Textbooks in English tend to be much more sociological in orientation and the emphasis on models is unique at this level. Of course, to some extent there has been a separate development of techniques and terminology in the two languages. To one used to the format of vital statistics in the United States, for example, the emphasis on *double classement*, the cross-tabulation of vital events by date of birth and age, may appear as an irrelevant luxury, since the necessary data do not exist in that country. But it should soon become obvious to the reader that for the purpose of understanding and learning, the Lexis diagram which presupposes the double classification is an incomparable tool.

To the translator, the parallel development of demography in the two languages poses certain difficulties. Phrases such as *mariages de la table*, *naissances réduites*, or even *quotients de mortalité*, have no easy equivalent in English. We were as faithful to the original as possible. The only changes either correct mistakes in the French edition, or are justified because some details in the original were too specifically directed to the French student. We must acknowledge Louis Henry's generous assistance in our task.

Etienne van de Walle,   Elise F. Jones,
Population Studies Centre, Office of Population Research,
University of Pennsylvania Princeton University

A*

Foreword

1 What is demography?

If you know a little Greek or are at all cultured, you already know that demography is a science which deals with human populations. But you don't necessarily know anything more about what it involves. To get a more definite idea, imagine that you know by name all the inhabitants of an area—a town, for example; this implies that you know at least the sex of each person. You are then the equivalent of a catalogue or an index, a list or a file of these inhabitants. But if you use this knowledge only in relation to individuals, even though it may be for social or administrative purposes, you are not involved in demography; no more so than when as a child you knew all your classmates by name.

To be involved in demography, one has to ask questions concerning this aggregate of people or collection of individuals, and these are questions to which we are not accustomed since they are rarely asked. The first and simplest is: 'How many people are there?' In reply you must perform a specific operation, i.e. to enumerate the people you know. This is easy if there are not very many of them; but if they are numerous, it is difficult, not to say impossible, without specialized techniques. Thus, the first goal of demography is to determine the size of populations, that is to say the number of individuals who make them up. The preoccupation with numbers is so fundamental to demography that the word population designates both an aggregate of individuals and, at the same time, the size of this aggregate.

Since you know the sex of the inhabitants of your town, you may also wonder about the number of men and the number of women, and whether there are more women than men. Your curiosity could lead you even further and you might formulate your question in this way: 'What are the proportions of men and women in my town?' Then, since the people you know are either children, young people, mature men and women or old people, since some are married and some are not, and since they have different occupations, other questions about the distribution of the population might occur to you. You might consider the age distribution, the distribution by marital status, the distribution according to individual occupation, and so on.

All these questions and the responses they elicit belong in the demographer's domain. But when we talk about distribution we are talking about statistics, so demography means the statistical study of population or, in other words, the application of statistics to human populations. Nevertheless, not every application of statistics to these populations is a part of demography; the statistical study of physical characteristics other than sex and age, such as weight, size, hair or eye colour belongs to biometrics.

The population of your small town does not remain constant and the population you know today is not the same as yesterday's. Some people have died, others have gone away; there are the new arrivals and the newly born. The local press keeps its readers abreast of some of these changes through its births and deaths columns; it may also report arrivals and departures.

Imagine that you always want to be up to date and know all these movements that steadily modify the population of your town. You keep in your head all the information that is included both in the civil or vital registers and in the record of changes of residence, if by good luck your municipality happens to keep one. You still are not involved in demography, however, as long as you lend merely sympathetic or casual attention to these facts, as most people do. As is the case with population structure, population change falls within the scope of demography only when certain questions are asked, such as, 'What proportion of the population died during the year, what proportion departed, what fraction of the population is represented by births and arrivals?' or, 'At what age is marriage most common, at what age do people die on the average, are more boys born than girls?' and so on. As before, these questions call for numerical and statistical answers.

During a period as short as one year, the number of births, deaths, arrivals, and departures is small compared to the total size of the population, which may appear as an almost unvarying whole, where motion but not change takes place. There is no doubt, however, that the population is also the result of these movements, since each one of its members has been born and will die. In whatever way the situation is envisaged, it is certain that there are numerical relationships between the aggregate of inhabitants in a territory at a given moment, and the events—births, deaths, arrivals, departures—which make up population change. The study of these relationships is likewise part and parcel of demography.

These pages of explanation can now be summarized in the definition of demography given by the multilingual demographic dictionary published by the United Nations: 'Demography is the scientific study of human populations, primarily with respect to their size, their structure, and their development.' The French version of the dictionary ends with the phrase 'from a quantitative point of view'. These words are fundamental to the definition for there is no demography without figures and statistics. Thus, with regard to population structure, that is to say the number of inhabitants and their distribution in various categories, demography is the answer to questions concerning this very number and distribution. As to population movement, it is true that demography might have come to include the description of its components—births, deaths and migrations. But this did not happen, either because such events are so well known that there is no need to describe them, or because the study of these events, from the qualitative point of view this time, belongs to other disciplines such as medicine.

One must also remember, although it is not implied in the definition above which is necessarily very condensed, that the study of human populations from a quantitative point of view encompasses demography and sections of other sciences such as biostatistics and population genetics, economics and sociology. The boundaries between these disciplines are not very precise, and it is usage alone which teaches us what belongs to the particular subject matter of each and what belongs to, or can be claimed by, several. It is as well to know from the start, however, that the study of marriage from a quantitative point of view is part of demography, though it was not mentioned above. The reason for this is that in most populations procreation occurs within wedlock more than nine times out of ten and therefore one cannot study fertility without studying nuptiality. Since marriage is broken by divorce, the study of this too (from the quantitative point of view of course) falls within the domain of demography.

2 Events and phenomena

Birth, marriage and death are ordinary words designating everyday *events* that happen to each one of us. For the registrar they become vital events although they are still designated by the same words.

The demographer uses these words also when he talks about the events in question whether as specific events or as registered or tabulated items. But he introduces abstract words when he is talking of the subject matter of demography—natality and fertility for births, nuptiality for marriages and mortality for deaths. In so doing he shows that he is moving from the events of everyday observation to the processes or *phenomena* that are the real object of his study.

These abstract words are mostly used in expressions such as fertility rates, nuptiality index or risk of mortality, which themselves designate well defined ratios either relating vital events to the corresponding population, or relating vital events to each other when one is the consequence of the other, as in the case of birth and marriage for instance. These ratios express a relationship which is something more than just the simple juxtaposition of two numbers. When a crude birth rate of 16 per thousand for 1968 is computed for a country of 50 million inhabitants that has had 800 000 births during that year, we have something more than the two separate numbers representing inhabitants and births. They are put in relation to one another, and this innovation justifies a new word.

3 Analysis and models

Not all the figures provided by observation are usable as such. In most cases one must subject them to detailed analysis in order to interpret them correctly. The analysis can be extended effectively by the use of models, since these shed light on the interaction of phenomena under well defined circumstances and facilitate the search for causal relationships. This is why we have discussed demographic analysis and models in the same book. Nevertheless, we have dealt more fully with analysis, because we wanted to avoid the mathematical proofs which an emphasis on models would entail. This book has been written for the use of students with very diverse backgrounds, some of whom may have scarcely more than an elementary knowledge of algebra.

Part I Analysis

1

Introduction

To analyse (from the Greek 'decomposition') is to decompose a whole into its parts. As familiar examples of analysis, we could cite logical or grammatical analysis, in which one identifies the elements of a sentence, or chemical analysis, in which one looks for the components of a mixture or compound.

1 Demographic analysis

Observation gives us data in their raw state, in the form of absolute numbers of persons or events, distributed into more or less numerous categories. These raw data may look simple to the superficial mind, but they are really the result of very complicated combinations or mixtures, in which many different elements and factors intervene. The purpose of analysis is to unravel the knot, to reduce the complexity, to separate the factors, to isolate the simple phenomena, to eliminate the impurities and extraneous influences. Without this analysis, it would be impossible to understand how demographic phenomena unfold and interact and, hence, to foresee even vaguely their future evolution. Analysis is never finished; the more progress is made, the more new elements and new factors are discovered. Fortunately, this does not always result in additional complication, since one new factor may replace several previously used factors to advantage.

The main directions of analysis

To get an idea of the main directions of analysis, let's take nuptiality as an example. Observation gives us, first of all, absolute numbers of marriages per unit of time (per year). These numbers depend on:
   a) the size of the marriageable population, men and women
   b) their desire to get married
   c) their chances of success.
   It does not take a lot of demography to deduce from observation or reading that various civilizations, various social classes, various periods have placed different values on marriage and celibacy. So the desire to get married depends, at least in part, on a basic cultural and social factor. Circumstances may help or hinder the role of this basic factor and, in order to take this into account, we must introduce a second factor, i.e. outside events of an economic, political, or health-related nature such as depressions, wars and revolutions and epidemics.

The desire to get married and the chances of success vary from one person to another; for the same person, they vary in time, either randomly owing to accident or sickness, or systematically with age. Differences between persons and variations over the life of one person depend on, among other things, demographic characteristics such as age and marital status (single, widowed, or divorced). Thus, the structure of the marriageable population becomes, in the same way as its size, a truly demographic factor.

These considerations permit the replacement of factors (a), (b), and (c) by the following ones which are more manageable:

1   the structure of the marriageable population (size and composition)
2   the cultural and social milieu
3   external events.

One of the tasks of analysis is to separate these three factors and, in particular, to eliminate effects of structure which are always considered as extraneous. It seems as though for a long time this task, in itself difficult enough, was the only one explicitly assigned to demographic analysis.

Simple and compound phenomena

In fact, analysis has another task, which is equally important, but less often mentioned even when it is performed. The phenomena that we observe are not in their pure state, but appear as mixtures; as in chemistry, the job of analysis is to isolate the phenomenon in its pure state.

Let's return to marriage and imagine that we have assembled observations relating to a generation of persons and that we have found from this the proportion of the generation which married at least once. This result, drawn directly from observation, would by no means constitute a good index of nuptiality nor permit comparisons in time and space. Indeed, the number of marriages observed for a generation from the beginning to the end of its life, depends on nuptiality, on mortality and, if the data are collected for one country only, on migration. The higher the mortality, the greater also the number of members of the generation who are prevented from marrying by premature death. As a result, the effect of the phenomenon in which we are interested, nuptiality, is mixed in our observations with the disturbing phenomena, mortality and migration. In order to isolate nuptiality and view it in its 'pure state', one must resort to analysis.

Two essential tasks of analysis

The two essential tasks of demographic analysis are to separate the factors on which the observed phenomena depend and to isolate the phenomena in their 'pure state'. We have introduced these tasks in that order, but they are encountered in the opposite order when one studies a generation. 'Pure' nuptiality for a generation depends, as do the marriages for one year, on various factors—fundamental factors, events, and even structural factors; and it is necessary to break down the combined effect into the specific effects of each factor.

2 Plan of part I

Part I is devoted to analysis and subdivided into two sections of unequal length.

The first section deals with elementary analysis or, if one prefers, with the steps that must precede an analysis of any complexity. It comprises three chapters: after an introduction, chapter 2 is concerned with the analysis of the results of one census or, in other words, with the study of population structure; chapter 3 is a summary presentation of the analysis of population change during a year. These two chapters present no technical difficulty at all, but they already raise some problems of interpretation whose solution demands more extended knowledge. This approach is intended to caution the reader against the frequent temptation to interpret insufficient data too fast and, at the same time, it aims to provide an incentive to go further.

The second section concentrates on the analysis of demographic phenomena—nuptiality, fertility, mortality, mobility (migration) and on the population change that is their result. Roland Pressat's *Demographic Analysis* starts with the study of mortality.[1] He argues correctly that the latter phenomenon, which was the first to be studied by demographers, provides the best introduction to the study of the techniques used to compute indices such as ratios, rates and probabilities utilized in demography. We have followed a different order—nuptiality, fertility, mortality, migration.

Up to the Second World War, demographic phenomena were studied almost exclusively by years or by periods of a few years, that is to say in the form in which the data were collected. Few studies were devoted to the succession of events, births, marriages or deaths through the lifetime of a generation. Just after the war, a few American and English demographers drew attention to the drawbacks of limiting the analysis to the period approach (cross-sectional studies), and to the need for studies based on generations (longitudinal studies). Their point of view has slowly prevailed and longitudinal analysis has now taken over the study of nuptiality and fertility. In contrast, cross-sectional analysis still dominates the study of mortality. The situation in relation to migration remains confused because this sector has been held back by the paucity of data.

It seems interesting to adopt an order which reflects this situation. Moreover, since we believe that longitudinal studies are bound to develop further, we have all the more reason to start with them, and this has the additional advantage of showing exactly what longitudinal analysis has to offer. Only a few years ago, some demographers trained before the war visualized it as merely a balance sheet covering the life history of a generation. It is now clear that the particular aspect of analysis which is aimed at separating one phenomenon from another is even more interesting from the longitudinal than from the cross-sectional angle; in part, this is because the link between population structure and movement becomes clear only through the longitudinal approach.

After a fourth chapter devoted to general issues, chapter 5 is concerned with

---

[1]Roland Pressat, *Demographic Analysis* (New York: *Aldine-Atherton*, 1972; London: Edward Arnold).

nuptiality, both from the point of view of first marriages and from that of marital dissolution and remarriage.

Before any study in depth, demographic phenomena can be classified in two major categories:

1   those which concern events that are non-renewable, either by nature as is the case with death, or in the sense that they have been identified by order (e.g. first marriages)

2   those which concern renewable events which have not been identified by sequence (e.g. births irrespective of order).

Since the study of nuptiality puts the emphasis on first marriages, the chapter which discusses this topic is in this respect a prototype of the longitudinal analysis of phenomena based on non-renewable events.

The study of fertility is the subject of chapter 6. The emphasis here is placed on the study of all birth orders together, so this chapter becomes the prototype for the study of phenomena based on renewable events. The family, considered as the aggregate of a couple and its children, is a complex statistical unit which obviously depends on the fertility of marriages; we devote to it a special chapter, chapter 7.

We could have dealt with the cross-sectional study of nuptiality and fertility in chapters 5 and 6, but the cross-sectional study in this case is really much more oriented towards current events than towards a search for the fundamental characteristics of the phenomenon being investigated. This is why we have discussed the cross-sectional study of nuptiality and fertility in a separate chapter, chapter 8, concerned with all aspects of the cross-sectional approach (except mortality).

Chapter 9 concentrates on mortality, using the cross-sectional approach, since this is an area in which the cross-sectional point of view maintains first place. Chapters 8 and 9 complement chapter 3. These three chapters contain the main technical tools for the study of trends.

Chapter 10 takes up migration. Here, given the current state of development, it is difficult to dissociate observation, which is frequently indirect, from analysis, whether the latter is longitudinal or cross-sectional.

Finally, chapter 11 discusses population change, the consequence of all the phenomena previously studied. The net reproduction rate appears only in that final chapter. Here we treat the properties of populations and of the stationary situation at some length. Knowledge of these properties is a way of avoiding serious errors.

Observation and analysis rarely lead to results which have general validity. In most cases, they provide chronological series which constitute one aspect, and not the least important one, of the history of nations. These results are also of interest in geography, since they refer to various countries at various periods. This being so, a work devoted to analysis cannot attempt to give the student results pertaining to the history of population or to human geography. We have confined ourselves to findings of a general nature—indices that vary little, orders of magnitude, the range of a given rate, evolution in time, the general trend of a phenomenon.

2

Analysis of census data

A census provides a great deal of information about a population. We will confine ourselves here to the analysis of a few interesting population characteristics. The plan of the chapter is as follows:

1. sources—information on the publications where census results are to be found
2. the meaning of the data
3. evaluation of the data
4. analysis of the results.

1 Sources

Special publications are devoted to census results; the published data may be based on either all the census schedules or a sample of the schedules. The latter system is used to obtain provisional results rapidly. For example, preliminary results from the French censuses of 1954, 1962, and 1968 were obtained from one in twenty of the housing sheets and of the individual schedules.

Some census information is also published in statistical and demographic yearbooks such as the United Nations Yearbook. Between censuses, estimates of the population classified by sex, age and marital status may be published at regular intervals. They can be found in statistical yearbooks.

2 The meaning of the data

Age

In some countries, such as France, the persons enumerated are asked their date of birth, in others, for example the United States and Great Britain, their age. When age is asked, it may be specified that it refers to the number of complete years lived (age at last birthday). When not specified, the age reported is often the number of whole years closest to the exact age in years, months and days.

The results may be tabulated by year of birth or by age. These two classifications do not coincide except at the beginning or at the end of the year (1 January or 31 December). The same is true of estimates. In certain cases, the classification may be mixed—by age for children, by year of birth afterwards.

In France, census results are given by year of birth or by group of years of birth, and this is also the case for the one in twenty sample. For estimates given as of 1 January each year, the results are given both by year of birth and by age since the two classifications coincide.

Marital status

Differences of custom, law and convention from country to country are likely to modify the content of any given category. One must ask what type of union has been considered as a marriage: legal marriages only, religious or customary marriages not necessarily having legal sanction, consensual unions and so on. It is not always easy to answer this question. One must also inquire how separated persons have been classified.

Economic activity

This is the area where the risks of mistaken interpretation are greatest if one is not careful. Errors may result either from the definition of economic activity itself or from the classification of the working population.

In a general way, an economically active or working person is one who usually has an occupation or helps a member of his family in the performance of his or her occupation, even if this activity is temporarily interrupted by sickness or unemployment. The wife of a tradesman or a farmer who consistently helps her husband would thus be classified as economically active; a woman who only takes care of her household and her children, on the other hand, would not be classified as economically active. Between the two, there is an entire gamut of intermediate situations where classification is somewhat arbitrary. For men, the problem is less serious. It hinges primarily on the classification of drafted servicemen, and here the practice can, in fact, vary. The working population or labour force includes, in principle, the unemployed, but they are excluded from the employed working population, and it is important to distinguish between the two.

The classification of the working population into categories reflects a variety of concerns and needs. It is important for the person in charge of professional training, for instance, to know specific occupations or trades. The primary concern of the economist may be to know the distribution of the working population among the principal industries. And again for the sociologist, social class membership is the main focus of attention. He gets at this social class by using a socioeconomic classification system which takes into account individual occupation, employment status and industry.

It is easy to see that the situation can become very complicated and that there are marked variations between one country and another. Therefore, it is particularly advisable to be aware of the concepts underlying the statistics when launching into a study of the labour force. It is well to remember from the preceding remarks that, before doing any analysis at all, the titles of the tables and the footnotes must be carefully read; if there are no footnotes, the introductory material at the beginning of the work should be consulted.

3 Evaluation of the data

No census is perfect. There are sure to be counting errors in the sense that certain persons may not have been enumerated, others may have been counted several times, or there may even be entirely fictitious persons among those enumerated. There will also be defects in the reporting: certain information concerning a person may be missing (non-response) or it may be false.

Counting errors

These are often difficult to detect. They are revealed when the census data are compared with statistics from other sources—vital registration, previous censuses and various surveys including, in particular, post enumeration surveys. For example, when there is good birth and death registration, a sizable omission of very young children cannot remain undetected in a population provided that the out-migration of entire families is slight.

Counting errors vary in importance from one category of the population to another. As a result there are inconsistencies, and they are a sign of omissions or deception.

Reporting defects

a) Non-response

The importance of this problem is measured by the size of the 'not specified' or 'unknown' category which must, in principle, be shown in the tables. It is often tempting to distribute the unknowns pro rata and, for instance, to reallocate those with age unknown proportionately to the size of each known age group. The procedure is only justified if the frequency of non-response is the same at all ages; and this is certainly not the case when the non-reporting of age is related, for example, to marital condition. In Greece, in 1951, non-reporting of age occurred for 4 single persons per thousand, for 6 married persons per thousand, and for 9 widows per thousand; in this example, non-response must be more frequent as age increases.

Nevertheless, faulty pro rata distribution leads only to a small degree of error if the relative number of the 'unknown' category is in itself insignificant. Then it is often better to make a faulty distribution than to waste time in search of a better solution.

b) Reporting errors

1) Age
Errors concerning age are frequent, particularly in less developed populations where the notion of duration is rather indistinct. Declared age, or age estimated by the census taker, is likely to be approximate, sometimes very generally so. A round number, such as a multiple of 10 or 5, is often all that is given. There can also be mistakes which are more or less deliberate: women, for instance, have a tendency to report themselves as younger than they are.

The tendency to report age in round numbers, or age heaping, is very clear in distributions by single years of age, as the following table shows.

Table 2.1 Selected ages from the single year distribution: Egypt, census of 1947

Age	Men	Women
55 years	144 352	150 765
56 years	6418	4801
57 years	7151	5149
58 years	8864	7367
59 years	4320	4982
60 years	237 527	288 096
61 years	2210	1483
62 years	6160	5066
63 years	3784	2574
64 years	2339	1586
65 years	75 692	75 490

There are two methods of detecting errors in age reporting even when a distribution by single years is not available:

Examination of the sex ratios:
The sex ratio is defined as the number of men per 100 women. At birth, it is on the order of 105 (a figure worth remembering). In a closed population which has not suffered military losses, this ratio evolves slowly with age. The excess of males is maintained for some time; at older ages, women are more numerous

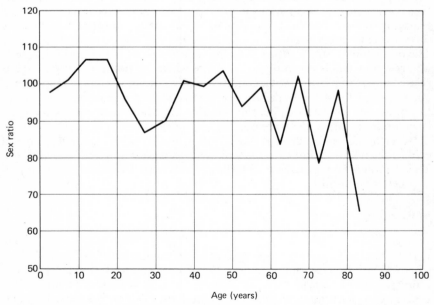

Figure 2.1   Sex ratios in a population with defective age reporting: Egypt, census of 1947

in almost all known populations. When age is badly reported, the variation of the sex ratio with age is erratic and irregular like that shown in table 2.2 and illustrated in figure 2.1.

Table 2.2 Computation of sex and age ratios: Egypt, census of 1947

Age (years)	Numbers in thousands Males	Females	Sex ratio (%)	Number of males (1)	$\frac{1}{2}$ sum of 2 neighbouring age groups (2)	Ratio (1):(2)	Number of females (1)	$\frac{1}{2}$ sum of 2 neighbouring age groups (2)	Ratio (1):(2)
0- 4	1279	1305	98	1279			1305		
5- 9	1209	1191	101·5	1209	1210	1·00	1191	1188	1·00
10-14	1142	1071	107	1142	1097	1·04	1071	1059	1·01
15-19	984	917	107	984	910	1·08	917	888	1·03
20-24	678	706	96	678	835	0·81	706	851	0·83
25-29	686	786	87	686	649	1·055	786	698	1·125
30-34	620	690	90	620	672	0·925	690	720	0·96
35-39	659	654	101	659	595	1·11	654	625	1·045
40-44	569	566	99·5	569	544	1·045	566	535	1·055
45-49	429	415	103·5	429	495	0·865	415	508	0·815
50-54	421	449	94	421	300	1·40	449	294	1·53
55-59	171	173	99	171	336	0·51	173	374	0·46
60-64	252	299	84	252	127	1·98	299	127	2·35
65-69	84	82	102	84	180	0·465	82	218	0·375
70-74	108	137	79	108	54	2·00	137	53	2·60
75-79	23·4	24	97·5	23·4	71	0·33	24	95	0·25
80-84	34·8	52·6	66	34·8			53·6		

Source: Demographic Yearbook of the United Nations, 1955.

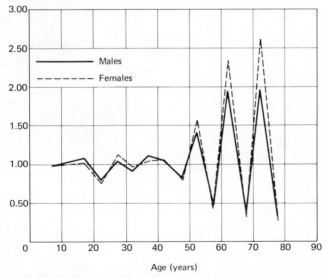

Figure 2.2 Age ratios in a population with defective age reporting: Egypt, census of 1967

Age ratios:

In a population that has not undergone important fluctuations in births, deaths or migration, the size of an age group is about equal to half the total of the adjoining age groups. The ratio of the age group to half that total should be close to 1. If it differs substantially from 1, as in table 2.2 and in figure 2.2, it may be presumed that age is badly reported. This procedure is less general than the preceding one, since it assumes a regular age distribution.

2) Marital status

A situation which attracts disapproval is often concealed. Divorced people, for

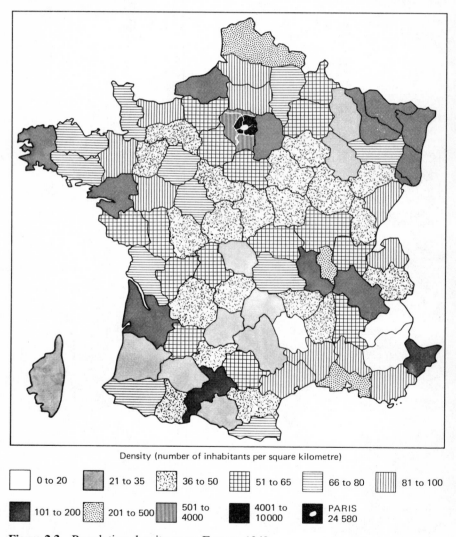

Density (number of inhabitants per square kilometre)

0 to 20	21 to 35	36 to 50	51 to 65	66 to 80	81 to 100

101 to 200	201 to 500	501 to 4000	4001 to 10000	PARIS 24 580

Figure 2.3   Population density map: France, 1948

example, may report themself as widowed. In France, and undoubtedly elsewhere, the resulting error is not inconsiderable; it can be detected by comparison of the census results with divorce statistics or with figures on the marriages of divorced people and on the deaths of divorced people.

4 Analysis of the results

We start with geographical distribution, a little aside from the main topic, and then come to the various analytical approaches required by data classified according to one, two, three or more than three, characteristics.

Geographical distribution

If the only concern is the settlement of a territory, independent of its resources, then geographical distribution is measured by spatial density, i.e. the number of inhabitants per unit of area—per square kilometer (km^2) or per square mile, for instance. Density is only of interest for comparative purposes. In order to obtain variations in density within a country, it is best to descend to the level of small territorial units. In the case of districts for instance, one would compute the density (ratio of the number of inhabitants to land area) for each one, and then draw a map, shading in the area of each district more or less heavily according to its density. The darkest shade would be reserved for urban areas. The density by *département* (as in the map in figure 2.3), or by province or state, gives a more comprehensive view. Other modes of presentation may be used, such as dots which become increasingly concentrated as the density rises. For cities, density is less important than absolute numbers, often represented by circles with an area proportional to the population.

One might try to substitute economic density for spatial density; it would be computed on the basis of the cultivatable area alone rather than of the entire area. Such a measure of economic density would be useful for a population with an agrarian economy. Expansion of this concept to more developed populations would lead to the study of the geographical distribution of resources per inhabitant, a notion which no longer depends on area at all.

Analysis based on one variable

a) Sex

The numbers of both men and women depend on a common factor unrelated to sex—the total size of the population. In this case, the analysis consists of replacing these two absolute numbers by the number of men and women relative to a total taken as one or as a multiple of 10, often 100. Since each of these numbers is the complement of the other, and they add up to 1 or to 100, it is sufficient to consider only one of them. And since we have only two numbers, we can replace the ratio of one of them to their sum by the ratio of one to the other, e.g. the ratio of the number of men to the number of women or the opposite. At birth, it has been customary to consider the number of boys per 100 girls. So, for the sake of consistency, the number of men per 100 women, or the sex ratio, is also preferred to other indices.

Example:
In France, in the census of 1968, the numbers by sex were:
    Males   24 667 000
    Females   25 533 000
    Total   49 800 000
The corresponding sex ratio was 96·6.

b) Age

The enumerated or estimated population is classified by single years of age or by 5-year age groups or, more rarely, by 10-year groups. The size of each group depends on the total population irrespective of age. The analysis consists of replacing the series of totals for each group by a series of proportional numbers adding up to a multiple of 10, such as 1000 or 10000. This series, however, is still too complicated; so the first step in the analysis of an age distribution or age structure, is a division into broad age groups. In practice, the two following distributions are most used:
    0–14, 15–64, 65 years and over (children, persons of working ages, old people);
    0–19, 20–59, 60 years and over (young people, adults, old people).
Table 2.3 presents a few figures for France based on the latter distribution:

Table 2.3 Population distribution in broad age groups: France, selected dates

Age	1776*	1851	1901	1936	1954	1968
0–19 years	428	370	346	302	307	338
20–59 years	500	531	530	551	531	484
60 years and over	72	99	124	147	162	178
Total	1000	1000	1000	1000	1000	1000

  * Estimate

Note the increase in the proportion of old people, and the simultaneous decrease in the proportion of young people up to 1936; this is the phenomenon of ageing which occurs when the birth rate of a population is declining. We will come back to this later.

c) The Age pyramid

The graphical presentation called the 'age pyramid' gives a good overall view of the age distribution of a population. We plot age on the vertical axis, and numbers on the horizontal axis (there are two horizontal readings, for males on the left, and for females on the right). The numbers refer to a specified age interval, most often one year. Each age interval, whether one year or more, is represented by a rectangle with an area proportional to the size of the group. The height of this rectangle is proportional to the number of years in the age interval, and the length is proportional to the size of the group divided by the same number of years.

Suppose, for example, that we must present the age distribution of the French population on 1 January 1968, assuming that it is given by single years up to 19 years of age and by 5-year age groups for ages 20 and over (the figures are taken from table 2.4). The number of boys less than 1 year old is 422 283; we shall represent this by a rectangle with a height of one and a length equal to 422 283 or, in round numbers, 422 000 on the scale adopted. The number of men aged 20–24 years is 1 814 075; we shall represent this group by a rectangle having a height of 5 (5 years of age) and a length to scale of 1 814 075 divided by 5, or, in round numbers, 363 000. It would be a serious mistake to represent this group by a rectangle of the same height, and of a length to scale of 1 814 000. This error is sometimes encountered, however, as figure 2.4 illustrates. It gives the two sides of the pyramid corresponding to the distribution above, based partly on 5-year age groups, partly on 10-year age groups. The left hand side is constructed correctly, while on the female side, the sort of mistake which we mentioned has been made.

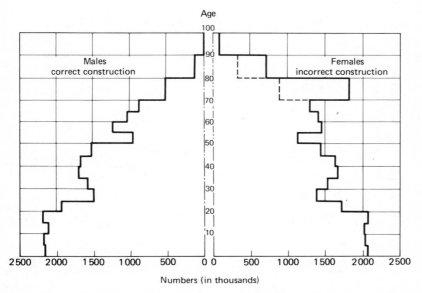

Figure 2.4 Age pyramid with unequal age categories, correct and incorrect construction: France, 1 January 1968

The irregularities of the age pyramids reflect the history of the previous seventy years (beyond that the influence of events is hard to perceive). For the European countries which participated in the two world wars, the pyramids are extremely irregular. Hollows on the male side caused by military losses can be identified; also, there are troughs common to both sexes owing to the decline in births during wartime. In this respect, figure 2.5 is particularly illuminating. It shows the population of France on 1 January 1968, classified by year of birth (the equivalent of a distribution by single years of age).

Table 2.4 Total population by sex and age (based on the results of the census of March 1968): France, 1 January 1968

Year of birth	Age in completed years	Both sexes	Males	Females
1967	0	826 345	422 283	404 062
1966	1	847 106	432 450	414 656
1965	2	851 271	434 786	416 485
1964	3	864 915	441 456	423 459
1963	4	856 428	435 975	420 453
1967–1963	0–4	4 246 065	2 166 950	2 079 115
1962	5	829 833	423 269	406 564
1961	6	843 558	429 979	413 579
1960	7	825 866	420 681	405 185
1959	8	838 284	426 897	411 387
1958	9	822 769	418 787	403 982
1962–1958	5–9	4 160 310	2 119 613	2 040 697
1957	10	828 478	421 686	406 792
1956	11	822 631	418 770	403 861
1955	12	822 094	418 452	403 642
1954	13	827 382	421 139	406 243
1953	14	816 946	415 937	401 009
1957–1953	10–14	4 117 531	2 095 984	2 021 547
1952	15	835 804	425 597	410 207
1951	16	830 885	423 098	407 787
1950	17	863 864	440 198	423 666
1949	18	864 732	441 091	423 641
1948	19	869 755	444 194	425 561
1952–1948	15–19	4 265 040	2 174 178	2 090 862
1947	20	861 960	441 141	420 819
1946	21	819 370	420 271	399 099
1945	22	623 521	320 228	303 293
1944	23	616 917	317 225	299 692
1943	24	612 012	315 210	296 802

Age in completed years	Year of birth	Both sexes	Males	Females
50	1917	329 287	160 695	168 592
51	1916	312 000	151 809	160 191
52	1915	386 972	187 813	199 159
53	1914	573 109	277 441	295 668
54	1913	577 665	278 992	298 673
50–54	1917–1913	2 179 033	1 056 750	1 122 283
55	1912	583 132	280 947	302 185
56	1911	542 674	260 830	281 844
57	1910	571 611	273 626	297 985
58	1909	561 159	267 472	293 687
59	1908	560 478	265 684	294 794
55–59	1912–1908	2 819 054	1 348 559	1 470 495
60	1907	536 856	252 800	284 056
61	1906	537 255	251 764	285 491
62	1905	527 214	245 533	281 681
63	1904	517 458	238 941	278 517
64	1903	504 044	230 576	273 468
60–64	1907–1903	2 622 827	1 219 614	1 403 213
65	1902	503 361	227 737	275 624
66	1901	484 913	216 505	268 408
67	1900	454 394	198 748	255 646
68	1899	434 767	186 520	248 247
69	1898	405 460	168 680	236 780
65–69	1902–1898	2 282 895	998 190	1 284 705
70	1897	389 631	156 172	233 459
71	1896	371 085	142 994	228 091
72	1895	321 416	119 402	202 014
73	1894	312 236	112 200	200 036
74	1893	296 404	104 141	192 263

Left block — Age groups 20–49:

Period	Year of birth	Age	Total	Males	Females
1947–1943		20–24	3 533 780	1 814 075	1 719 705
	1942	25	574 769	296 129	278 640
	1941	26	523 420	269 954	253 466
	1940	27	558 985	288 322	270 663
	1939	28	603 016	311 197	291 819
	1938	29	602 064	309 546	292 518
1942–1938		25–29	2 862 254	1 475 148	1 387 106
	1937	30	609 176	312 443	296 733
	1936	31	622 373	318 332	304 041
	1935	32	622 037	317 574	304 463
	1934	33	651 248	332 162	319 086
	1933	34	644 941	328 745	316 196
1937–1933		30–34	3 149 775	1 609 256	1 540 519
	1932	35	677 016	345 090	331 926
	1931	36	673 183	342 964	330 219
	1930	37	698 935	355 854	343 081
	1929	38	666 275	338 804	327 471
	1928	39	672 159	340 661	331 498
1932–1928		35–39	3 387 568	1 723 373	1 664 195
	1927	40	664 560	335 655	328 905
	1926	41	669 761	336 915	332 846
	1925	42	668 550	334 892	333 658
	1924	43	655 012	327 129	327 883
	1923	44	655 771	326 264	329 507
1927–1923		40–44	3 313 654	1 660 855	1 652 799
	1922	45	656 967	325 845	331 122
	1921	46	673 437	332 912	340 525
	1920	47	690 809	341 373	349 436
	1919	48	419 820	206 538	213 282
	1918	49	371 126	181 866	189 260
1922–1918		45–49	2 812 159	1 388 534	1 423 625

Right block — Age groups 70–95 and over:

Period	Year of birth	Age	Total	Males	Females
1897–1893		70–74	1 690 772	634 909	1 055 863
	1892	75	266 981	92 697	174 284
	1891	76	254 208	87 468	166 740
	1890	77	230 211	77 852	152 359
	1889	78	221 276	73 773	147 503
	1888	79	200 443	65 863	134 580
1892–1888		75–79	1 173 119	397 653	775 466
	1887	80	180 541	58 265	122 276
	1886	81	157 970	50 114	107 856
	1885	82	142 562	44 245	98 317
	1884	83	123 921	37 719	86 202
	1883	84	102 404	30 565	71 839
1887–1887		80–84	707 398	220 908	486 490
	1882	85	90 055	26 289	63 766
	1881	86	72 352	20 753	51 599
	1880	87	59 355	16 655	42 700
	1879	88	46 357	12 719	33 638
	1878	89	36 807	9 872	26 935
1882–1878		85–89	304 926	86 288	218 638
	1877	90	27 841	7 293	20 548
	1876	91	21 361	5 086	16 275
	1875	92	14 880	3 478	11 402
	1874	93	11 516	2 594	8 922
	1873	94	7 266	1 648	5 618
1877–1873		90–94	82 864	20 099	62 765
1872 and before		95 years and over	12 048	2 430	9 618

	Total	Males	Females
Total population	49 723 072	24 213 366	25 509 706
Under 20 years	16 788 946	8 556 725	8 232 221
20 to 64 years	26 680 104	13 296 164	13 383 940
65 years and over	6 254 022	2 360 477	3 893 545
Under 15 years	12 523 906	6 382 547	6 141 359
60 years and over	8 876 849	3 580 091	5 296 758

Source: INSEE.

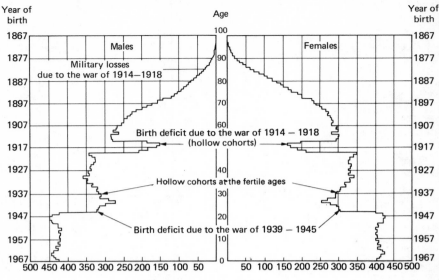

Figure 2.5   Age pyramid by single years of age: France, 1 January 1968

Table 2.5 Computation of the sex ratio (males per 100 females) by age* of the native population: France, 1926

Year of birth	Approximate age	Total number in thousands		Sex ratio
		Males	Females	
1921–1926	0– 4 years	1745	1717	101·6
1916–1920	5– 9 years	1085	1060	102·4
1911–1915	10–14 years	1477	1458	101·3
1906–1910	15–19 years	1617	1612	100·3
1901–1905	20–24 years	1480	1591	93·0
1896–1900	25–29 years	1409	1523	92·5
1891–1895	30–34 years	1093	1428	76·5
1886–1890	35–39 years	1131	1410	80·2
1881–1885	40–44 years	1137	1368	83·1
1876–1880	45–49 years	1175	1321	88·9
1871–1875	50–54 years	1120	1201	93·3
1866–1870	55–59 years	974	1080	90·2
1861–1865	60–64 years	842	958	87·9
1856–1860	65–69 years	655	795	82·4
1846–1855	70–79 years	714	967	73·8

*The first age group includes 5 years of births, but 1926 includes only children born before 7 March. Ages refer approximately to 1 January 1926, except of course, for children born at a later date.
Source: Résultats statistiques du Recensement général de la population, éffectué le 7 mars 1926 I, p. 20.

Analysis using two variables

Up to now, the tabulations have used only one variable, first sex, then age. It is true the age pyramid was constructed for both sexes; but what was involved was only repeating the same computations separately for each sex.

a) Sex and age

Let us now look at how one deals with the two variables sex and age combined, using the data of table 2.5. We will still convert the absolute numbers in this table into proportional numbers and this can be done in several ways.

1 One can replace each absolute number, (e.g. the number of men aged 30–34 which is 1093) by the number of men of that age per 10 000 inhabitants, that is 294 (1093/37 143 × 10 000).
2 One can also replace 1093 by the number of men 30–34 years old per 10 000 French males, which comes to 619 (1093/17 654 × 10 000).
3 Finally, one can replace 1093 by the number of men aged 30–34 per 10 000 persons, men and women, of that age, or 4336 (1093/2521 × 10 000).

The only purpose of (1) is to permit the construction of age pyramids by proportional numbers; they are easier to compare than those in absolute numbers. But a pyramid, whether it is in absolute or in proportional numbers, only gives a very summary view of the balance (or imbalance) of the sexes and of its variation from one generation to another. Distribution (2) is never used; it amounts to repeating for each sex the analysis of the age distribution that had already been done for the combined sexes, without taking into account the proportion of each sex relative to the whole. This would reveal differences between the two proportional distributions and, in order to explain them, we would have to bring in the variation in the sex distribution with age. In contrast, the relative numbers computed in (3) give for each age the

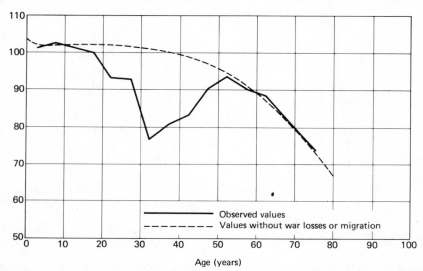

Figure 2.6 Sex ratio by age in the native born population: France, census of 1926

distribution of men as a proportion of all persons of the same age; all these numbers together allow us to examine how this proportion changes among the successive generations enumerated. In other words, we have proceeded with each age in turn in the same way as was done for the ages together in the analysis with one variable, sex. Analysis using two variables can thus be reduced to a series of analyses with one variable, a series which can be visualized in its entirety in a graph.

In the case of sex, it is better to use an index other than the proportion of males, or index of masculinity. This other index is the sex ratio, already defined. The solid line in figure 2.6 illustrates the right hand column of table 2.5

Analysis using three variables

Distributions using three variables most often combine sex, age, and some other characteristic; one then treats the two sexes separately, reducing the problem for each to an analysis by two variables, of which one is age. The procedure is shown in the following examples and, in every case except the last, the title indicates the characteristic other than sex and age.

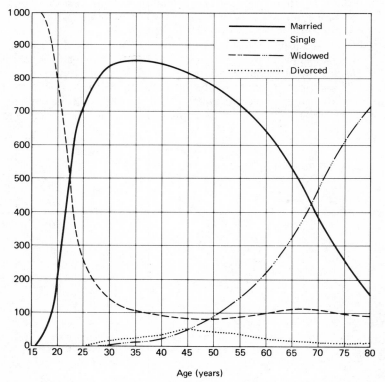

Figure 2.7   Proportion single, married, widowed and divorced per thousand females by age: France, 1 January 1962

Table 2.6 Distribution of women by age and marital status in absolute numbers and proportions per 1000 of the same age: France, 1 January 1962 (results from the 1 in 20 sample)

Age	Single	Married	Widowed	Divorced	Total
15	392 785	817			393 602
	998	*2*			*1000*
16	293 904	3168		4	297 076
	989	*11*			*1000*
17	282 755	10 458		6	293 219
	964	*36*			*1000*
18	262 988	25 945	40	6	288 988
	910	*90*			*1000*
19	219 260	48 484	41	90	267 875
	819	*181*			*1000*
20	169 795	70 463	111	180	240 549
	706	*293*		*1*	*1000*
21	146 180	107 243	178	443	254 044
	575	*422*	*1*	*2*	*1000*
22	129 946	149 264	308	659	280 177
	464	*533*	*1*	*2*	*1000*
23	103 602	174 741	459	1066	279 868
	370	*624*	*2*	*4*	*1000*
24	82 661	198 426	510	1490	283 087
	292	*701*	*2*	*5*	*1000*
25	69 584	217 464	829	1997	289 874
	240	*750*	*3*	*7*	*1000*
26	60 771	226 496	977	2740	290 984
	209	*779*	*3*	*9*	*1000*
27	54 035	248 378	1183	3406	307 002
	176	*809*	*4*	*11*	*1000*
28	48 709	250 547	1370	3886	304 512
	160	*823*	*4*	*13*	*1000*
29	46 640	268 584	1608	4825	321 657
	145	*835*	*5*	*15*	*1000*
30–34	190 128	1 377 839	14 854	33 269	1 616 090
	118	*852*	*9*	*21*	*1000*
35–39	161 627	1 389 531	29 660	48 564	1 629 382
	99	*853*	*18*	*30*	*1000*
40–44	112 082	1 039 177	43 342	55 122	1 249 723
	90	*831*	*35*	*44*	*1000*
45–49	108 750	1 002 350	88 396	62 548	1 262 044
	86	*794*	*70*	*50*	*1000*
50–54	133 703	1 114 815	168 471	65 201	1 482 190
	90	*752*	*114*	*44*	*1000*
55–59	143 526	996 686	261 883	50 883	1 452 978
	99	*686*	*180*	*35*	*1000*
60–64	142 662	786 495	365 690	37 372	1 332 219
	107	*590*	*275*	*28*	*1000*
65–69	134 529	538 224	453 956	27 067	1 153 776
	117	*466*	*393*	*24*	*1000*
70–74	104 335	303 889	512 371	19 594	940 189
	111	*323*	*545*	*21*	*1000*
75–79	70 051	148 300	472 217	13 716	704 284
	99	*211*	*671*	*19*	*1000*
80–84	39 849	49 659	322 828	1135	419 471
	95	*118*	*770*	*17*	*1000*
85–89	17 325	11 630	151 286	2113	182 354
	95	*64*	*830*	*11*	*1000*
90 and over	4531	1296	41 634	237	47 698
	95	*27*	*873*	*5*	*1000*

Note: Proportions in italics.

a) **Marital status**

The distribution according to marital status is computed separately for each sex and age, by single years or by age group. At young ages, this distribution changes extremely rapidly. It is interesting, therefore, to compute it by single years of age up to age 30 (for women) or 35 (for men). Table 2.6 gives both the absolute and the relative numbers of single women, married women, widows and divorced women in France on 1 January 1962; these data are illustrated in figure 2.7

b) **Labour force participation**

The labour force participation rate, i.e. the ratio of the working population to the total population, is computed separately for each sex and age, by single years or by age group. (See table 2.7 for an example.) Once the analysis has been made for each sex, the two series of results must be compared. This is usually done by using one or more graphs. Figure 2.8, for instance, allows us to compare the labour force participation rates of men and women.

Table 2.7 Labour force participation rates:* France, census of 1968 (provisional results from the 1 in 20 sample)

Age (years)	Males	Females	Age (years)	Males	Females	Age (years)	Males	Females
15	117	40	25–29	*950*	*506*	60	760	375
16	351	209	30–34	*973*	*424*	61	687	341
17	426	299	35–39	*973*	*413*	62	645	318
18	565	438	40–44	*965*	*434*	63	611	302
19	668	559	45–49	*954*	*453*	64	574	275
15–19	*429*	*314*	50–54	*914*	*451*	*60–64*	*657*	*323*
20	742	621	55	884	445	65	508	239
21	798	646	56	832	429	66	296	149
22	849	645	57	810	422	67	251	131
23	877	616	58	801	418	68	229	112
24	903	579	59	790	399	69	211	94
20–24	*826*	*624*	*55–59*	*824*	*423*	*65–69*	*305*	*147*
						70–74	*149*	*74*
						75 and over	79	33

*Working population including drafted service men and persons looking for work, per thousand of same sex and age.

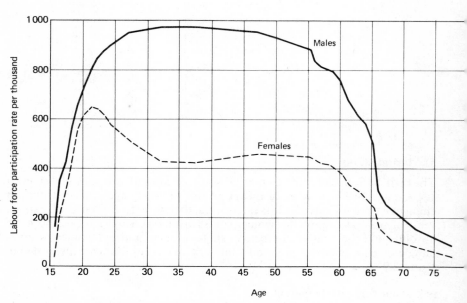

Figure 2.8   Labour force participation rates by sex and age: France, census of 1968

c) School attendance

In the case of school attendance, with children, adolescents and young adults considered together, the classification distinguishes those not in school from those attending school, the latter divided according to their level of education.

The analysis can also be done in two stages: first, determining the proportion attending school; then, for those attending school, computing the proportional distribution by level of education. Table 2.8 gives the absolute numbers and the two series of proportional figures for the male sex.

Table 2.8 Distribution of boys by year of birth and type of instruction in absolute numbers and proportions per 1000 of the same year of birth: France, school year 1957–8

Year of birth	Age on Jan. 1 1958	Pre-school	Primary school	General secondary school	Technical secondary school	Higher education	Subtotal	Other and not in school	Total
1952–54	3–5	663·3	77·3				740·6	448·4	1189
		896	*104*				*1000*		
		558	*65*				*623*	*377*	*1000*
1951	6		392·3				392·3	2·7	395
			1000				*1000*		
			993				*993*	*7*	*1000*
1950	7		412·7				412·7	3·3	416
			1000				*1000*		
			992				*992*	*8*	*1000*
1949	8		417·2				417·2	3·8	421
			1000				*1000*		
			991				*991*	*9*	*1000*
1948	9		414·8				414·8	4·2	419
			1000				*1000*		
			990				*990*	*10*	*1000*
1947	10		393·3	18·5			411·8	4·2	416
			955	*45*			*1000*		
			946	*44*			*990*	*10*	*1000*
1946	11		302·2	92·6	2·2		397·0	6·0	403
			761	*23*	*6*		*1000*		
			750	*230*	*5*		*986*	*15*	*1000*
1945	12		194·0	97·2	6·7		297·9	6·1	304
			651	*326*	*23*		*1000*		
			638	*320*	*22*		*980*	*20*	*1000*
1944	13		184·1	89·2	13·8		287·1	6·9	294
			641	*311*	*48*		*1000*		
			626	*303*	*47*		*976*	*24*	*1000*
1943	14		38·1	87·6	61·5		187·2	108·8	296
			204	*468*	*328*		*1000*		
			128	*296*	*208*		*632*	*368*	*1000*
1942	15		3·7	64·2	58·3		126·2	148·8	275
			29	*509*	*462*		*1000*		
			14	*233*	*212*		*459*	*541*	*1000*
1941	16		0·9	42·5	52·7		96·1	150·9	247
			9	*442*	*549*		*1000*		
			4	*172*	*213*		*389*	*611*	*1000*
1940	17		0·4	30·1	32·0	2·3	64·8	198·2	263
			6	*465*	*494*	*35*	*1000*		
			1	*114*	*122*	*9*	*246*	*754*	*1000*
1939	18		0·7	22·0	12·8	7·7	43·2	245·8	289
			16	*510*	*296*	*178*	*1000*		
			2	*76*	*44*	*27*	*149*	*851*	*1000*
1938	19			11·7	4·9	13·0	29·6	236·2	293
				395	*166*	*439*	*1000*		
				40	*17*	*44*	*101*	*899*	*1000*

Note: Proportions in italics
Source: Bureau universitaire de statistiques

Table 2.9 Male working population* by age and socioeconomic category: France, census of 1954 (results from the 1 in 20 sample)

	Under 20 years		20–24 years		25–34 years		35–44 years		45–54 years		55–64 years		65 years & over	
	Absolute number (thousands)	Prop. per thousand	Absolute number (thousands)	Prop. per thousand	Absolute number (thousands)	Prop. per thousand	Absolute number (thousands)	Prop. per thousand	Absolute number (thousands)	Prop. per thousand	Absolute number (thousands)	Prop. per thousand	Absolute number (thousands)	Prop. per thousand
Farmers	197·4	230	190·6	165	422·0	135	316·8	139	537·9	192	379·1	242	297·4	410
Farm labourers	118·5	138	110·9	96	268·9	86	159·2	70	182·8	65	101·3	65	38·9	54
Owner-operators in manufacturing and commerce	26·5	31	52·0	45	251·6	81	292·5	128	418·5	150	204·1	169	135·1	187
Professionals, managers and officials—upper rank	0·3		6·6	6	119·5	38	115·1	50	133·4	48	77·4	49	28·4	39
Managerial workers—middle rank	8·0	9	53·5	46	222·5	72	150·5	66	156·3	56	90·3	58	30·3	42
White-collar workers	53·3	62	87·2	75	281·0	90	196·7	86	215·3	77	118·6	76	34·2	47
Blue collar workers	431·1	502	605·3	523	1394·5	448	920·5	403	1042·3	372	475·8	304	119·9	166
Service workers	10·3	12	11·7	10	36·7	12	32·8	14	47·2	17	38·1	24	20·8	29
Other categories of workers	13·9	16	39·2	34	119·3	38	101·6	44	63·5	23	21·2	14	19·1	26
All workers*	859·3	1000	1157·0	1000	3116·0	1000	2285·5	1000	2797·1	1000	1565·9	1000	724·2	1000
Total population	1699·6		1487·4		3224·0		2355·7		2935·0		1909·8		2006·2	

*Including the unemployed looking for work, excluding drafted service men.

Source: Recensement de 1954, résultats du sondage au 20ᵉ, France entière, 1956, pp. 28 and 35.

d) Socioeconomic status

Within each sex and age group, the working population, total or non-agricultural, can be distributed proportionally among the broad social status categories. The results shown in table 2.9 are those for the male population.

e) Another case

Table 2.10 is excerpted from a series of tables for which the classification criteria were the age at marriage of the woman, the year of marriage, and the number of children born alive to this marriage. In a case like this, one is once again reduced to the analysis of a series of tables, similar to table 2.10, based on two variables.[1] In each one, the absolute numbers of each row are replaced by relative numbers adding up to 1000 or 10 000.

Because the number of children in a family can assume a large number of different values, comparisons within a table and, even more, between tables, are difficult. Since the variable being analysed, i.e. the number of children, is quantitative, one may resort to statistical simplifications. Instead of comparing two or more entire distributions, we compare essential characteristics of which the most important would be the mean. It is given in the right hand column of table 2.10.

More than three variables

The solution is always the same: one must reduce analysis to a series of tables based on two characteristics in combination. Of course, comparisons between tables can be very complicated and very often the study has to be subdivided into several parts.

For instance, let us consider labour force participation rates according to sex, age, and industrial category (here simply agricultural and non-agricultural population).[2] We know already that there are very marked differences between men and women, and we want to know whether this is also true within each category. To begin with, we analyse the table for each sex separately, thus reducing the problem to three variables; then we use graphs to compare the labour force participation rates by age for men and women within the same category. In brief, one does two analyses based on three variables.

5 The problem of interpretation

Up to now we have contented ourselves with replacing absolute numbers by relative numbers according to certain rules. The goal was to separate by this means that which proceeds from the size of a population from that which is not dependent on size. We must now ask what the transformed results mean. Let's take as an example the non-agricultural working population according to the census of 1954. This census was the first one to yield results of this nature, and

[1] The layout of the tables is largely imposed from outside. In the present instance, each table could very well refer to a marriage cohort (the marriages during a calendar year), and each line could refer to an age at marriage. This yields the same overall distribution of children.
[2] Agricultural households are those whose head is, or was formerly, either a farm operator or an agricultural labourer.

Table 2.10 Distribution of women married at age 20 and 21 by year of marriage and number of live born chidren ** from that marriage in absolute numbers and proportions per 1000 married in the same year: Norway, census of 1920

Year of marriage		Number of live born children from the marriage																			Total	Mean number of children
		0	1	2	3	4	5	6	7	8	9	10	11	12	13	14	15	16	17	18 and over*		
1920	absolute number	823	1067																		1890	
	proportion	435	565																		1000	0·46
1919	absolute number	288	1702	115																	2105	
	proportion	137	808	55																	1000	0·92
1918	absolute number	229	1774	814	43																2860	
	proportion	80	621	284	15																1000	1·23
1889	absolute number	23	17	32	56	51	55	69	74	92	80	80	60	36	28	6	3	2	1	1	766	
	proportion	30	22	42	73	67	72	90	97	120	104	104	78	47	37	8	4	3	1	1	1000	7·27
1888	absolute number	22	15	30	34	47	61	70	59	70	78	93	67	28	15	5	5	1	1	1	702	
	proportion	31	21	43	49	67	87	100	84	100	111	133	95	40	21	7	7	2	1	1	1000	7·35
before 1888	absolute number	260	252	358	407	545	664	768	939	1097	1295	1306	888	603	296	119	57	20	9	3	9884	
	proportion	26	26	36	41	55	66	78	95	111	131	132	90	61	30	12	6	3	1		1000	7·73

* In 1889: 21: in 1888 : 18 : before 1888 : 18.

**Women with number of children not stated are not included.

Source: *Folketelling i Norge VI, Norges offisielle Statistich* VII. p. 97.

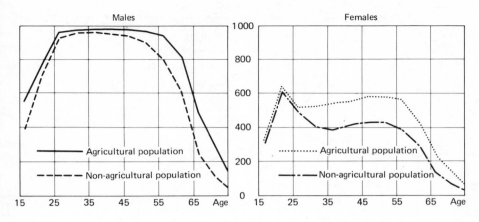

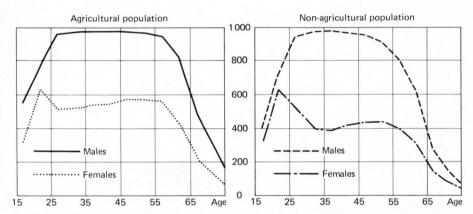

Figure 2.9 Labour force participation rates for the farm and non-farm population by sex and age: France, census of 1968

therefore the problem of the interpretation of these first results cannot be dodged by implicit reference to other censuses. We must remember just two essential features of these results: as we move from the youngest toward the oldest enumerated persons, the proportion of manual workers decreases, and the proportion of employers in manufacture and commerce increases.

Several explanations come naturally to mind:

a) Many men start as manual labourers (and, in this case, they become economically active younger than others); but among them many leave to become craftsmen, tradesmen, or office workers; such changes exceed by far the number of craftsmen, tradesmen, or office workers who shift to manual labour.

b) It is rare to be an employer at 20 years of age, but one can become one in various ways such as by establishment on one's own as a craftsman or a tradesman, or by inheritance. An employer who retires from professional life does so, on the average, later than a manual labourer.

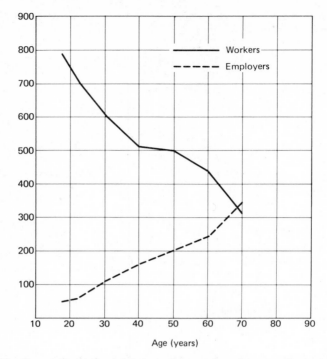

Figure 2.10   Proportions of employers and manual workers per thousand non-farm males in the labour force: France, census of 1954

These explanations drawn from common observation are not necessarily false, but they are expressed as if the transformed data were related to a generation (the people born during the same year) followed throughout its active life. However, this is not the case; we have actually observed several generations at different times in their life. So, leaving aside common knowledge about the present, one could just as well arrive at the following interpretation:

a)   The proportion of manual workers increases as we go from the earliest to the more recent generations.

b)   The proportion of employers decreases during the same span of time.

We could even resort to some ad hoc combination of these two interpretations.

Let us now examine the conditions under which each type of simple explanation is true.

1   If there is no change at all from one generation to another, the same proportion as was observed at, say, age 30 for persons born in 1924 will be observed in 1964 for persons born in 1934, who were 20 years old in 1954, and will be 30 years old in 1964. The difference observed in 1954 between the generation of 1934 and that of 1924 is thus identical to that which one would observe between age 20 and age 30 for either one of these generations. In other words, *if each generation has the same life history*, then the proportions observed in a single census classified by age are equivalent to those that would be obtained from continuous observation of one

generation. In this instance, cross-sectional observation at one point in time, achieved in a census, is equivalent to the continuous or longitudinal observation of a generation.

2 If there is no change of socioeconomic status at all during the lifetime of any individual, then observed differences must be the differences between cohorts, at least after the point when differences in age of entry in the labour force cease to have an influence.

Everyday observation tells us that the assumptions of the latter interpretation are not fulfilled: we know that there are changes of occupation and of socioeconomic condition during the individual's lifetime. Since, on the other hand, we live in a time of great upheaval, we have reason to believe that the history of generations changes fast enough so that the assumptions of the first interpretation are not met either. Differences between generations and changes of occupation during individual lifetimes combine to give the proportions actually observed in the census. The analysis must therefore be extended if we want to separate the two components.

What has just been said concerning one of the examples of the preceding section has a more general application. The utmost caution is necessary when we are tempted to translate the observations of one census into the life history of a generation. Sometimes there are anomalies in the transformed data which prevent us from making a false interpretation. For instance, the proportion of single people cannot increase with age in the same generation, while this often happens in a cross-sectional series. This happens in table 2.6 between ages 45–49 and 65–69. But we are not always lucky enough to have such a danger signal.

Nevertheless, it is worth mentioning some situations where the results of a single census can be interpreted without too much risk.

a) In dealing with a characteristic which changes very little after a certain age, for instance educational achievement, marked changes in this characteristic with age can only be the result of differences between generations—e.g. the progressive dwindling of illiteracy. But if the changes are moderate, we must question whether they could not be the result of selection by mortality or migration, that is to say, of higher death or mobility rates among certain subgroups than among others.

b) There may be serious reason to believe that traditional customs of the population in question have not been modified and that each generation continues to have the same life history as previous ones. The nuptiality of certain non-European populations has thus been studied on the basis of one single census. But one must verify the hypothesis as soon as another census becomes available.

Conversely, there are characteristics that we cannot attempt to approach if we have no information other than one single census; mortality is a good example.

3

Summary analysis of population change during one year

This kind of analysis stresses current events; the aim is to delineate those features which distinguish the year in question from the preceding years.

1 Sources

Final and complete statistics on population movement are usually presented in a special publication, and several years can elapse between the year for which the statistics are given and their publication. In France a major portion of the final statistics is published approximately one year after the close of the year in question. Provisional statistics, necessarily in condensed form, are published in monthly or quarterly bulletins. Statistical and demographic yearbooks likewise contain data on population change; the United Nations Yearbook is particularly useful.

The final statistics are usually confined to the natural movement of the population, i.e. births, marriages, divorces and deaths. Statistics on migration are published in a less systematic fashion, and one often has to hunt for them. However, they are usually summarized in the yearbooks. For divorces, judicial sources may also be consulted.

2 The meaning of the data

The following is information pertinent to France.

Place of registration and place of residence

To begin with, we need to know that births, marriages and deaths are registered at the town hall of the commune where they occur. The result is that many local statistics reflect registered events rather than events actually occurring to the people residing in the administrative unit under consideration. Unless caution is exercised, serious errors of interpretation will be made. One could, for instance, conclude that infant mortality is higher in the countryside, whereas in fact higher mortality is characteristic of cities—this mistake has actually been made. Such risks are not encountered when the statistics are compiled according to place of residence. This classification is available for France from 1951 on.

Births

In France, children born alive who die before the birth is registered are classified as stillbirths. As far as the birth statistics go, the error is usually not corrected since it is rather small.

Divorces

Vital statistics pertain only to those divorces which have been entered in the official records. A variable amount of time elapses, about a year on the average, between the decree itself and the recording of the event; in addition, some of the decrees are never recorded either because one of the partners dies or through oversight. The statistics of the Ministry of Justice give the number of requests for divorce which have been granted (divorce decrees), the number of separation requests and the number of ordinances of non-conciliation. Among the decrees granted, it distinguishes between direct divorces and divorces which follow a judicial separation. Experience suggests that there is room for confusion.

Deaths under one year

These do not include children born alive who die before their births are registered (also called 'false stillbirths'). In the final statistics, however, a distinction is made between true stillbirths and those which were really infant deaths, i.e. between those who did not breathe and those who did; then the infant mortality rates are corrected on this basis and thus two series of rates exist (uncorrected and corrected). These examples show that one must look in detail into the meaning of published data. The institution publishing the data should give all the necessary information, although this does not always happen.

3 Evaluation of the data

It is generally accepted that birth, marriage, and death statistics in Western Europe are virtually free of counting error and that registration is just about complete. This is not necessarily the case with judicial statistics on divorce which in France remain far from perfect. In developing countries, on the other hand, vital registration is very often deficient. This can sometimes be seen when, for instance, many more very young children are enumerated in a census than there are births for the corresponding years, even though the census itself is known to be underenumerated.

4 Yearly balance

The first step is to set up a balance sheet for the year. This is often done before the year is ended and the result is then a provisional balance sheet based on estimates.

Estimates

We will take the case of France. At the time when the provisional balance sheet is made up, the results of the first three quarters of the year are available. For births and marriages, these three quarters are taken to represent the same proportion of the whole year as was the case in preceding years. For deaths, it is more correct to add an absolute number of deaths equal to those of the fourth quarter of a recent normal year; the risk of significant error is very slight, since epidemics and major cold spells are exceptional in the fourth quarter.[1]

Example for births:

1957 :	first 3 quarters	614 000 births
1955–6:	first 3 quarters	610 000 „
	whole year	803 000 „

On the basis of these data, we estimate the total number of births in 1957 as follows:

$$\frac{614\,000 \times 803\,000}{610\,000} = 808\,000$$

Example for deaths:

1953 :	423 000 deaths during the first 3 quarters.
1951–2:	The number of deaths in the fourth quarter has been in the neighbourhood of 130 000. Hence, the estimate for 1953 is: 423 000 + 130 000 = 553 000.

The data for all or part of the fourth quarter may be available for sectors of the country, such as the Seine *département* and 110 cities before 1968. This may be used to make estimates for the whole of France, provided we know the ratio of France as a whole to Seine + 110 cities for each category of events. One would then have had to make a preliminary study of the evolution of this ratio in the recent past.

In the case of marital dissolution, provisional results have been obtained for some years simply by multiplying by 4 those of Seine that became available immediately.

Presentation of the balance sheet

The balance sheet for a given year may be presented in several ways; however it is done, it should be accompanied by the data for a few preceding years and periods of time. Examples are the provisional balance sheet for 1957 (table 3.1) and the table on natural population change for 1967 (table 3.2).

The first balance sheet includes officially sponsored migration, which is all that is recorded in France; the other one does not include migration and is more like a balance sheet limited to natural increase. If all migratory movements were known, it would be best to make just one table showing all the components of the population movements in absolute numbers and, if necessary, to make a separate table for the rates.

---

[1]This rule applies also to the southern hemisphere; the risk of error is even smaller as the fourth quarter corresponds to spring.

Table 3.1 Provisional demographic balance sheet (numbers in thousands):
France, 1957

	1934–1938	1953	1954	1955	1956(a)	1957(a)
Marriages	282	308	314	313	294	*310*
Dissolutions of unions(b)	34	45	45	44	*43*	*44*
Live births	636	801	807	802	804	*810*
Deaths, all ages	642	553	515	523	542	*525*
Deaths under one year(c)	42·8	30·2	29·5	27·5	25·5	*24*
Excess of births	−6	248	292	279	262	*285*
Controlled immigration(d)						
Non-seasonal workers	−	15	12	19	65	*110*
Dependents	−	5	4	5	6	*9·5*
Algerians (net immigration)	−	12	25	28	3·5	20
Population present on 30 June	41 200	42 650	42 950	43 300	43 600	44 000
New citizens (France only)	30	9·5	24·5	26	22·5	23

Note: Numbers in italic are estimates.
   (a)   Probably the final numbers for marriages, births and deaths.
   (b)   Including ordinances of non-conciliation. Estimates on the basis of 4 ×
          the numbers observed in Seine.
   (c)   Not including children dead before registration (false stillbirths)
   (d)   Workers entering under sponsorship of the National Office of
          Immigration.

5 Crude rates

The absolute number of events lends itself poorly to comparisons of different
populations, whether in time or in space. One almost always adds the crude
birth, marriage, and death rates and also the infant mortality rates which will
be discussed in chapter 9. The crude birth rate and the crude death rate are
obtained by dividing the number of births or deaths respectively, in a year, by
the average population for the year.

Example: There were 837 500 live births in France in 1967, and 49 886 000
inhabitants at mid year; the corresponding crude birth rate is:

$$\frac{837\,500}{49\,886\,000} = 16\cdot8 \text{ per thousand.}$$

The crude marriage rate has two different definitions: it is either the ratio of
the number of marriages during the year to the average population, or the ratio
of the number of newly married persons (twice the number of marriages) to the
average population. The first definition is that used in the United Nations
Demographic Yearbook. The second is the one currently used in France.
These rates are given per thousand with one decimal point, or without the
decimal, per 10 000. The crude rates for France are given in the right hand
columns of table 3.2 .

Table 3.2 Natural population change: France, 1930 to 1967

Period	Population at middle of period	Numbers in thousands										Rate per 1000					
		Marriages	Divorces finalized	Live births		Still births		Total Deaths	Deaths under age one	Excess of births over deaths		Nuptiality (newly married people per 1000 inhabitants)	Natality (live births per 1000 inhabitants)	Mortality (deaths per 1000 inhabitants)	Natural increase (excess of births per 1000 inhabitants)	Infant mortality (deaths under age one per 1000 live born children)	
				Total	Legi-timate	Total	Who drew breath (a)									Unad-justed rate (b)	Ad-justed rate (c)
1930–1932	41 800	327·9	23·9	735·4	676·6	25·7	3·9	662·6	56·6	+72·8		15·7	17·6	15·9	+1·7	76·9	81·8
1935–1937	41 200	279·8	25·3	629·8	587·8	21·6	3·4	643·4	42·3	−13·6		13·6	15·3	15·6	−0·3	66·4	71·4
1946–1950	41 100	397·4	48·3	860·1	795·7	21·9	3·9	537·2	49·8	+322·9		19·4	20·9	13·1	+7·8	59·1	63·4
1951–1955	42 800	313·8	31·8	810·4	756·6	18·6	3·7	534·9	31·7	+275·5		14·7	18·9	12·5	+6·4	38·9	43·3
1956–1960	44 800	311·4	30·7	813·2	763·1	17·8	3·7	518·0	22·1	+295·2		13·9	18·2	11·6	+6·6	27·3	31·7
1961–1965	47 700	333·0	32·4	853·2	802·8	17·2	3·5	529·1	17·4	+324·1		14·0	17·9	11·1	+6·8	20·5	24·5
1962	46 998	316·9	30·6	828·9	779·9	17·1	3·4	537·7	18·0	+291·2		13·5	17·6	11·4	+6·2	21·7	25·7
1963	47 854	339·5	30·3	865·3	814·3	17·7	3·5	554·3	18·6	+311·0		14·2	18·1	11·6	+6·5	21·7	25·6
1964	48 411	347·5	33·3	874·2	822·6	17·4	3·6	516·5	16·9	+357·7		14·4	18·1	10·7	+7·4	19·4	23·4
1965	48 919	346·3	34·9	862·3	811·4	16·7	3·4	540·3	15·6	+322·0		14·2	17·6	11·0	+6·6	18·1	21·9
1966	49 400	339·7	36·5	860·2	809·1	16·4	3·3	525·5	15·5	+334·7		13·8	17·4	10·6	+6·8	18·0	21·7
1967	49 866	345·6	37·2	837·5	786·1	15·6	3·1	539·9	14·4	+297·6		13·9	16·8	10·8	+6·0	17·1	20·7

(a) Infants born alive, but dead before civil registration.

(b) The deaths under age one during a given year are related to the corresponding births (births of the year considered and the preceding year).

(c) Rate calculated like the preceding one, but the stillborn children who drew breath are added to the numerator and to the denominator.

The order of magnitude of crude rates

a) The crude birth rate

The crude birth rate of primitive populations, that which prevailed for thousands of years before the introduction of birth control, was between 35 and 55 per thousand with very few exceptions.[2] Rates of this order still exist in numerous countries of Africa, Latin America, and Asia. By 1960, the only country of Europe with a crude birth rate in excess of 40 per thousand was Albania; Iceland and Malta were between 25 and 30 per thousand; all the other countries had rates of less than 25 per thousand, among which two, Hungary and Sweden, were a little under 15 per thousand and relatively few (Spain, Ireland, the Netherlands, Poland, Portugal, and Yugoslavia) exceeded 20 per thousand.

Since that time, the crude birth rate has gone down markedly in Albania (34 per thousand in 1966) and it has gone up considerably in Romania (27 per thousand in 1967 against 14·3 per thousand in 1966) as a result of sweeping changes in abortion laws. Among other countries, only Spain, Ireland, Iceland and Portugal now (1968) exceed 20 per thousand, and then usually by very little; none is as high as 25 per thousand. At the other end of the spectrum Belgium, Luxembourg and Sweden in western Europe and East Germany, Hungary and Czechoslovakia in eastern Europe are below 15 per thousand or very close to that value. In France, the rate is 16·6 per thousand. In 1967, the birth rate was 17·8 per thousand in the United States and 17·5 per thousand in the Soviet Union.

b) The crude death rate

It is believed that under primitive conditions the crude death rate was between 30 and 40 per thousand in a normal year; beyond that there were catastrophic years (epidemics, famines) where mortality was several times higher, e.g. in Amsterdam, 140 per thousand in 1636, 125 per thousand in 1655, 170 per thousand in 1664. Little is known of present levels of mortality in many parts of the world, but it is likely that it is lower than the normal primitive mortality almost everywhere. The great peaks at least have disappeared, although quite recently rates of the order of 30 per thousand have been reported for rural Africa. But 15 to 20 per thousand no doubt corresponds better to the intermediary situation characteristic of numerous populations of Africa, Latin America and Asia. Some already have much lower rates, such as Ceylon where the crude death rate was 8·2 per thousand in 1967.

In Europe, in 1967, the crude death rate ranged from 8·2 per thousand in the Netherlands to 13·0 per thousand in Western Germany; it was 11·0 per thousand in France. In 1967, it was 9·4 per thousand in the United States and 7·6 per thousand in the USSR. One should never forget that this crude rate is heavily influenced by the age distribution; thus, when health conditions are equal, the country with the most old people has the highest mortality.

[2] At the beginning of the eighteenth century, Iceland had a crude birth rate of less than 25 per thousand owing to an abnormally high proportion of single people, resulting from very unfavourable economic conditions at the end of the seventeenth century.

c) The marriage rate

This rate is known only for European populations or for populations of European origin living outside Europe. In Europe, the number of marriages per thousand inhabitants varied in 1967 between 6·1 in Ireland and 9·4 in Hungary; it was 6·9 in France.

Note:
Converting the absolute number of events to a base of 1000 or 10 000 people is a kind of preliminary spadework. Other ways of accomplishing this task have been proposed, such as relating the number of births to the number of women aged 15–49 years (or 15–44, 20–44, 20–49 years), i.e. to the number of women at childbearing ages; this would seem to make more sense. But this rate, which is called the general fertility rate, is in itself very superficial. When it is a question of choosing among summary rates, the simplest, the crude birth rate, is to be preferred. The ratio between the two rates, moreover, fluctuates only a little: the general fertility rate for women aged 15–44 years is between 4·5 and 4·8 times the birth rate; it ranges somewhere between 55 per thousand and 250 per thousand.

6 Population movements by month and by quarter

The study of the year is not restricted to overall results; one can investigate what happens during each month or quarter either in retrospect or as it occurs.

Correction for the unequal length of the months

In order to compare months or quarters easily, the observations must be equalized in duration. This is done by computing the daily average of events for the month or quarter, i.e. by dividing the number of events for the month or quarter by the number of days (always remembering leap years).

Annual rates

It is possible to compute a crude birth rate, for instance, for each month or each quarter but, in order to make comparisons easier, it is best expressed as a yearly rate. This is done by multiplying the average daily number of events by the number of days in the year (365 or 366) and dividing the result by the average population for the relevant period.

Example:
France, first quarter, 1956:

Births	204 200
Number of days in the quarter	91
Mean population	43 500 000
Number of days in the year (leap year)	366

Yearly rate $\dfrac{204\,200}{91} \times \dfrac{366}{43\,500\,000} = 18\cdot9$ per 1000

It would also be possible to use an ordinary year of 365 days consistently; this solution would be preferable in certain respects, but the results for leap years would then have to be adjusted by multiplying them by the ratio of 365/366.

Seasonal component

Demographic phenomena for a part of a year are, like other phenomena, the result of diverse influences:

the long-term evolution or secular trend;

cycles, such as economic cycles, which are vaguely recurrent, but over a period longer than the year;

the seasonal rhythm of weather, of work and of religious practice; this is the basis of the seasonal component;

the structure of the part of the year under consideration; this factor plays a major role with respect to marriage for certain days of the week (Saturday in France) are preferred for weddings and the number of those days varies between 4 and 5 in any month; moreover, certain holidays preclude the celebration of marriages on the days when they fall;

chance events, responsible for variations that cannot be explained by previous factors; since daily events, fluctuations in the weather, for instance, present themselves in a haphazard way, this residual factor can be assimilated to a random factor, except in extreme cases.

When we study population movements over a certain month of a certain year, we try to bring out the characteristics which distinguish that specific period as opposed to those traits which it shares with months of the same name in adjacent years, since these latter common traits are precisely those that make up the seasonal component. Moreover, the existence of seasonal change makes it difficult to compare the various months within the same year. For those reasons, the crude results for each month are corrected by dividing them by the appropriate seasonal adjustment factor. The following is an example.

Table 3.3 Seasonal adjustment of the infant mortality rate: Seine *département*, 1947

Year	Month	Seasonal coefficient	Infant mortality rate per thousand	
			Crude	Corrected
1947	January	1·19	84	70·5
	February	1·22	86	70·5
	March	1·25	82	65·5
	April	1·20	69	57·5
	May	1·07	63	59·0
	June	0·92	52	56·5
	July	0·82	50	61·0
	August	0·80	49	61·0
	September	0·72	50	69·5
	October	0·78	60	77·0
	November	0·88	64	72·5
	December	1·15	58	50·5

The fluctuations of the corrected series in the table reflect the peculiarities of each month of the year 1947, beyond those which are common to all the months of the same name, January, February and so on, within a more or less extended period around 1947.

7 The interpretation of population change for one year

We have discussed the presentation of data relating to one year, its comparison with preceding years and the verification of the differences. It remains to give an interpretation and explanation. These, however, require us to draw on the entire arsenal of demography and we shall therefore have to return to them later. For the moment, let's be content to formulate the problem: a difference between two years has been documented; the result may be expected if the observed figure is that which would have been predicted in view of the population structure and of the trend in behaviour or health conditions; or it may represent a significant divergence from the expected. If so, we shall have to investigate what peculiarities of the year can explain the discrepancy. The answer may lie in

epidemics (influenza in particular);

the weather (severe winters, hot summers);

the economic situation (unemployment or threat of unemployment, recovery after a crisis);

the political situation (total or partial mobilization, a war).

8 Appendix: computation of the seasonal adjustment factor

The seasonal component is cyclical, with a periodicity equal to one year and it therefore disappears in averages of 12 months; the effect of chance is eliminated by averaging several years together. The factor of structure does not influence births or deaths; they are classified according to the day when they occur, and the number of these events during one month is not dependent on the number of days when civil registration offices are open.

First method

The seasonal component for one month, let us say February, can be isolated by comparing several years' results for February with an average of 12 months centred on the middle of February. This method is thus based on deviations from the 12 months' moving average. It assumes that the long-term trends are sufficiently linear over a period of 12 months for the average of those 12 months to remain on the trend line.

To describe the method in more detail, let's take the example of infant mortality in the Seine: the annual rates per 10 000 are given in table 3.4, column 1.

For the month of February 1956, column 2 gives the mean for the 12 months centred on 1 February, that is the six months before February 1956, the month of February, and the five following months. Column 3 gives the mean for the 12 months centered on 1 March, that is from September 1955 to August 1956. The average of those two means is the mean centered on the middle of the month, as are the monthly observations themselves.

Table 3.4 Computation of the seasonal coefficient by the moving average method: infant mortality of Seine, 1955–6

Year	Month	Rate per 10 000 (1)	Backward mean (2)	Forward mean (3)	Centred mean (4)	Ratio (1)/(4) (5)
1955	June	232				
	July	182				
	August	156				
	September	168				
	October	195				
	November	204		222·3		
	December	299	222·3	220·6	221·5	1·35
1956	January	260	220·6	220·3	220·5	1·18
	February	302	220·3	219·3	219·8	1·37
	March	234	219·3	220·7	220·0	1·05
	April	211	220·7	220·2	220·4	0·96
	May	225	220·2	222·7	221·5	1·02
	June	211	222·7	217·3	220·0	0·96
	July	179	217·3			
	August	144				
	September	185				
	October	188				
	November	235				
	December	234				

The rate in column 1 is divided by the centred mean in column 4 and the resulting ratio in column 5 is 1·37 for February 1956. This computation must be carried out for a series covering at least ten years so that at least ten ratios will be available for each month. Then, after eliminating exceptional cases if necessary,[3] the mean of the ratios is calculated; alternatively one could take the median.

Finally, the means or medians are summed over the year. If the result is equal to 12, the figures stand as the wanted seasonal component for each month but, if not, they are all modified proportionately to bring the total to 12 (or to 1200 if the adjustment factor is based on an index of 100).

Example:

	Jan.	Feb.	Mar.	Apr.	May	June	July	Aug.	Sep.	Oct.	Nov.	Dec.	Sum
Ratio × 100	143	122	115	98	92	88	84	75	80	94	107	120	1218
Seasonal component	141	120	113	96	91	87	83	74	79	93	105	118	1200

In this example, the seasonal factors are obtained from the ratios by multiplying the former by 1200/1218 and rounding off the results.

[3]Examples: December 1879—exceptionally cold; October 1918—an exceptionally serious influenza epidemic.

Alternative method

The method just described is unfortunately rather long. It is possible to proceed faster by simply relating the result for each month to the average for the year, for instance by taking the ratio of the rate for February 1956 to the average rate for 1956 which is 217·3. This ratio is equal to 1·39 instead of 1·37.

These ratios are then treated in the manner described for the preceding method. But it may be necessary to introduce a correction. Let us assume that there is a general trend towards a decrease of 2% per year; the month of December, centred on the middle of December, is 5-1/2 months away from the 1st of July, the middle of the year; so in the absence of seasonal movement, the rate for December would be lower than the average for the year by an amount equal to $2 \times 5·5/12 = 11/12$ which is not the same thing as 1. The seasonal adjustment factor for December obtained on the basis of the average for the year thus has to be corrected: it must be increased by 1% or divided by 0·99. By the same reasoning, the January adjustment factor should be decreased by 1% and so on. For practical purposes, this correction is only useful if the trend is very marked.

When the trend is slow, a modification of this procedure can be used that consists of adding up the observations for each month for the period of ten, twenty, or fifty years over which seasonal movement is studied. This sum is then divided by the number of days in the month; the 12 ratios thus obtained are added and this total is adjusted to 1200. Do not forget that the number of days in February can vary; the average number of days in February for the period under investigation must be used. If the period is fairly long, this number is equal or very close to 28·25.

Note:

Insofar as it reflects customs and habits, seasonal change is a subject for study in itself. The techniques that we have just given thus go beyond the framework of the analysis of population movement during one year.

The case of marriage

In demography, we study seasonal movement by month or sometimes by quarter, but never by week. The structure of the month intervenes in two ways:

1 Any given day, let's say Saturday, occurs more or less often in one month; these are normal fluctuations in structure.
2 A fixed holiday reduces marriages on that day to almost nothing and disturbs the normal situation.

This disturbance is difficult to eliminate; the marriages which would have taken place on that day will either have been advanced or postponed in an unsystematic way. This is probably not very important when Bastille Day, 15 August or even Armistice Day fall on a Saturday, since the averted marriages would still be celebrated in July, August, or November, but the same cannot be said when 1 January or May Day is a Saturday. So let's simply investigate, without getting into too much detail, how the normal variations of the structure of the month can be eliminated.

If we know the number of marriages per day, we can compute the average number of marriages by day of the week for each month and for the year. The seven numbers in each of these series are then added up, and the ratio of the first, that of the month, to the second, that of the year, is taken. The computations are continued as for births and deaths.

Example:

Between 1966 and 1967, there was a difference in the number of Saturdays in January and December on the one hand, and in September and October on the other, but since 1 January 1966 fell on a Saturday, the change during that month was further disturbed. Comparison of September and October is thus better suited to our purpose, which is the elimination of the normal effect.

Since the National Institute of Statistics has given the distribution of marriages by day for these two years, the following table can be drawn up:

Table 3.5 Number of marriages taking place on a Monday, Tuesday, Wednesday, Thursday, Friday, Saturday or Sunday, and number of Mondays, Tuesdays, Wednesdays, Thursdays, Fridays, Saturdays and Sundays: France, selected months

	September 1966		October 1966		September 1967		October 1967	
	Marriages	Days	Marriages	Days	Marriages	Days	Marriages	Days
Monday	2 716	4	2 591	5	2 698	4	2 934	5
Tuesday	1 079	4	879	4	1 173	4	1 053	5
Wednesday	1 085	4	813	4	826	4	725	4
Thursday	2 298	5	1 468	4	1 742	4	1 497	4
Friday	3 664	5	2 387	4	3 907	5	2 486	4
Saturday	21 509	4	23 729	5	26 982	5	20 314	4
Sunday	46	4	50	5	35	4	38	5
Total	32 397		31 917		37 363		29 047	

The average number of marriages by day of the week is computed and added to make an average week:

Table 3.6 Mean number of marriages per day of the week and in an average week: France, selected months

	1966		1967	
	September	October	September	October
Monday	679	518	675	587
Tuesday	270	220	293	211
Wednesday	271	203	206	181
Thursday	460	367	435	374
Friday	733	597	781	622
Saturday	5377	4746	5396	5078
Sunday	11	10	9	8
Total	7801	6661	7795	7061

In 1966, there were 339 746 marriages in 52 weeks plus a Saturday; the average number of marriages on a Saturday having been 4301, the number of marriages for the 52 weeks amounted to 335 445, or 6451 per week. In 1967, there were 53 Sundays and a similar computation gives 6646 marriages per week.

The ratio of each month to the average of the year is computed by dividing the number of marriages of the average week of the month by 6451 in 1966, 6646 in 1967. This gives:

	1966	1967
September	1·21	1·17
October	1·03	1·06

If we had not taken the structure of months into account, we should have obtained the following ratios:

	1966	1967
September	1·16	1·32
October	1·11	0·99

The influence of the change in the structure of the month is thus very obvious; the ratios based on the average for the year vary much more for the same month in the latter table than in the former.

4

General overview of the analysis of demographic phenomena

1 Introduction

Consider a given person: he or she has a biography, an individual history, of which a good portion concerns demography and sociology; it is made up of events—births, marriages, deaths, moves, illnesses, religious ceremonies, assorted activities and circumstances. The whole can be expressed in tabular form like the following biography of an imaginary woman, whom we will call Jeanne Seillé. This biography is composed essentially of a series of dates; for each date a place is given and an event, vital or otherwise, to which the date and place apply. The events fall under different headings according to whether they are purely demographic or whether they concern health, education and occupation, religion, police record etc; the demographic items are on the left and a mixture of sociology and demography are on the right.

We can infer from this biography a certain number of demographic characteristics of the person in question: she married at such and such an age, she had so many children, she became a widow at a given age, remarried after so many years of widowhood, and died at such and such an age from a certain disease; the same thing could be done for her health history, her education and occupation, etc. The biography is of interest to the demographer only as one element in the collective history of the group to which an individual belongs. This group, or *cohort*, can be defined simply by the data from the chronological sequence; for instance, it could be the group of women born in Ariège during the period 1905–9.[1] Other characteristics such as the social class into which the individual was born, his own or his parents' physical or psychological characteristics, may be added. We could add information on personal characteristics to the biography, possibly much more than that which has been included in the biography of Jeanne Seillé. As of now, the groups studied in demography are defined only by demographic and social characteristics. Physical traits, aptitudes and personality are not included, but since this situation could change it seems important to mention that the definition of a cohort may involve criteria other than those in use now.

The collective history which concerns the demographer, for instance the history of the group of which Jeanne Seillé is a member, can be told in statistical form. It is not a question of reviewing every fact of local, regional or even national history in which this group has been to some extent involved, but

[1]One of the *départements*, or administrative units of France (translator's note).

Table 4.1 Biography of Jeanne Seillé

Dates	Place	Pure demography	Health	Studies and occupations	Religion	Legal affairs
20 March 1905	Lescure (Ariege)	Birth				
25 April 1905	—				Baptism	
October 1911	—			Kindergarten		
1912	—		Measles			
1916	—				Communion	
1917	—			Graduation from primary school		
1919	—		Puberty			
April 1920	St Girons	Migration		First job (hotel maid)		
3 February 1926	—	Marriage				Marriage
December 1926	—			Leaves employment		
13 April 1927	—	Birth of son	Delivery			
25 September 1930	—	Birth of daughter	Delivery			
3 February 1932	—	Spontaneous abortion				
14 June 1940	—	Widowhood				
July 1940	—			Resumes employment (maid)		
July 1946	—			Leaves employment		
13 August 1946	—	Remarriage				
August 1946	Toulouse	Migration				
October 1954	—		Menopause			
January 1975	—		Influenza			
20 January 1975	—	Death (from influenza)				

Father's occupation: Farmer
Husband's occupation: Labourer
Health of parents: Good
Religious practice of individual: Almost none

of telling, for each demographic fact such as a marriage, the frequency with which it has been observed and how the age at marriage of the women involved was distributed. Often it is not enough for the demographer to know what the statistical history turned out to be. In real life, an event other than the one being studied, like death, may have prevented the event of interest, such as marriage, from occurring. The phenomenon of nuptiality is not observed in its pure state; it has been influenced by the phenomenon of mortality and it is up to analysis to eliminate disturbing effects and to isolate each phenomenon in its pure state. In doing this, a history which is partly fictitious is substituted for the real history.

2 Choice of demographic indices

Demographic statistics provide us with a large number of more or less commonly used indices to measure each demographic phenomenon. The choice of the right index should be a constant preoccupation of the analyst. Of course, the best choice may not be possible unless the required data are available. Here is a generally applicable example of good indices. A group is selected consisting of all individuals having experienced an event A, say the delivery of a second baby during a given year, 1948 for example; we are investigating an event B, say a third delivery among members of this group. We must determine:

a) the proportion of the group experiencing event B

b) the distribution of the time interval between events A and B.

In our example, (a) refers to the proportion of the women giving birth to a second child in 1948 who proceed to have a third child; (b) denotes the distribution of intervals between the second and the third births, usually in months. These indices can be relative either to the real history or to the fictitious history of the cohort.

Answering these two questions does not exhaust the subject, of course; other aspects of the phenomenon are worthy of interest. But by posing the problem in these terms, one is assured of avoiding mistakes and of covering the essentials. Furthermore, the results obtained answer not only the questions we have asked but others as well.

3 Some terminology

When we study the sequence of events over time within a well defined group, or cohort, we are involved in *longitudinal analysis*, also called *cohort analysis*. Entry into a cohort occurs at a certain date, and the cohort is always defined by the period of one or more years of entry (thus the marriage cohort of 1936 refers to all marriages celebrated in 1936). A cohort may be called a generation when it is composed specifically of individuals born during the same calendar year.

We are involved in *cross-sectional analysis*, or *period analysis*, when we study the observations of one given year, or one given period, covering different cohorts. We shall discuss this in chapters 8 and 9. Chapters 5, 6 and 7 are devoted exclusively to longitudinal analysis.

4 Lexis diagram

The Lexis diagram (figure 4.1) is a tool which is useful and frequently indispensable in the study of demographic phenomena.

We first draw a grid with fairly large squares and add the diagonals which join the intersections of the squares from the lower left to the upper right.

Since a *cohort* is defined as the sum of persons who were born, were married, entered the labour force, etc. during the same year, the horizontal lines distinguish ages, duration of marriage or lengths of time spent in the cohort in years elapsed. The bottom horizontal line corresponds to birth, marriage and, in general, to entry into the cohort; each successive horizontal line upwards

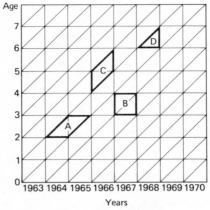

Figure 4.1   Lexis diagram

corresponds to a subsequent anniversay of the entry. Vertical lines distinguish the calendar years and correspond to 1 January at 0 a.m. or more conventionally, to 31 December at 12 p.m. The diagonals separate the cohorts of people born during the same year, marrying during the same year, etc.

Each event concerning a member of the cohort, a death to give a concrete example, is located by its date and by the exact age or date of birth of the deceased. All deaths occurring on the same date are on the same vertical line, all deaths occurring at the same age are on the same horizontal line, and all deaths of persons born on the same date are on the same diagonal line.

The deaths occurring at a certain age, in completed years, among the persons of a certain generation, are located in a parallelogram bordered by horizontal and diagonal lines (parallelogram A on the graph); this parallelogram lies astride two calendar years. The deaths occurring at a given age during a given civil year are located in a square (square B on the graph); they pertain to two different generations. The deaths occurring during a certain year among the persons of a certain generation are located in a parallelogram bounded by vertical and diagonal lines (parallelogram C on the graph); this parallelogram lies astride two different ages. Finally, the deaths common to a given civil year, a given generation and a given age, are located in a single triangle such as D.

5
Nuptiality

1 Introduction

In contrast to death, marriage is not an inevitable demographic event since some people never marry, even though they live long enough to have the opportunity. However, first marriage is a non-renewable event, similar to any event that can be differentiated from like events by its order. Thus, the study of first marriages is our introduction to the analysis of events that are neither inevitable nor renewable. The analytical approach we use is applicable to all evitable events provided we order those which would appear at first sight to be renewable. We shall describe this approach without going into the particular problems of nuptiality. These have not yet been resolved in a satisfactory way.[1]

[1]Since it takes two to marry, marriage is distinguished (as a demographic event) in that it simultaneously concerns two individuals of different sex. It follows that nuptiality is affected by the balance or imbalance in the number of boys and girls available and by the conformity or nonconformity of their age distribution to prevailing tastes and customs. This is obvious when we think about extreme cases, either a few girls to go with a great many boys, or an approximate balance of the sexes with a great disparity in age. Whether there is balance or imbalance, conformity or disparity in ages, both are closely linked to the structure of the population and to irregularities which originate in past fluctuations of demographic phenomena unrelated to nuptiality such as the birth rate (in this case, both sexes are affected at the same time), or migration and mortality (one sex may then be affected more than the other one). An example is the nuptiality of generations born in France in 1946 or later, which was influenced by the great imbalance between these generations and the immediately preceding ones, originating in the recovery of the birth rate. In contrast the nuptiality of French women born in 1896–1900 was primarily affected by the war losses of 1914–18 which were restricted to the masculine sex. The nuptiality of one sex can be disturbed by migration and mortality for that sex, like all demographic phenomena, and beyond that by migration and mortality among the opposite sex, as well as by fluctuations in the birth rate when the situation arises. Analysis aims at eliminating these disturbing influences so as to reach a fundamental understanding of nuptiality, independent of structure. Up to now this aim has not been achieved and, for lack of the means to do better, nuptiality continues to be treated as if it were related to each sex separately. In the routine cases, that is to say in the absence of sharp fluctuations in the age pyramid, this involuntary simplification is equivalent to the assumption that the removal of disturbing phenomena, and most of all the elimination of mortality, would not markedly modify the ratio of the marriageable number of the sex being studied to that of the other sex. When this hypothesis can be approximately verified, the simplification into which we have been forced is less alarming. Note that the ratio of women to men is only one example of the numerical relationships between one human group and the rest of the world. Such relationships may indeed depend on disturbing phenomena, so the problem which nuptiality raises is perhaps not as uncommon as it looked at first sight. We will come back to this in chapter 17, 'Nuptiality models'.

2 First marriages

The purpose of the analysis

Observation provides us at best with the number of first marriages by age in a given country over the life of a generation. These numbers depend in the first place on the actual number of single persons, and that in turn depends on the initial size of the generation, on the diminution in size due to marriage, death and out-migration, and on the augmentation in size due to in-migration. Initial size, deaths, and moves are matters which are foreign to the phenomenon under study, i.e. nuptiality, and the aim of demographic analysis is precisely to distinguish the influence of nuptiality from that of the intervening phenomena, mortality and migratory movements. In other words, demographic analysis tries to present nuptiality in its pure state. This analysis can be done on the basis of single generations or by group of generations.

According to the general rules presented in chapter 4, the analysis must allow us to determine, in the absence of mortality and migration (for each generation studied):

    a) the proportion of members of a generation who would marry at least once, a proportion which can be designated the probability of first marriage

    b) the distribution of age at first marriage.

In the case of nuptiality, however, it is customary to focus on the proportion of persons who do not marry rather than on that of persons who marry at least once. Furthermore, the single condition is considered definitive by a certain age, usually 50 years.

The problem which analysis must resolve can thus be phrased as follows: in the absence of mortality and migration, what would be

    a) the proportion of women single at age 50 for a given generation in a given country and

    b) the distribution by age at first marriage for the first marriages of this generation concluded before the age of 50?

To avoid any confusion between the observed proportions and the proportions that would be realized if nuptiality were not disturbed by mortality and migration, it is preferable to use a different term in each case. From now on the term 'proportion single' will apply only to observed proportions. Those which would exist in the absence of mortality and of migration will be designated by the term 'probability of remaining single'. The proportion of persons who will never marry becomes the 'definitive probability of remaining single'; the proportion of persons who would not be married by age x (still in the absence of mortality and migration), becomes the 'probability of remaining single at age x'. For the sake of convenience, the probability of remaining single at age 50 is substituted for the definitive probability of remaining single.

The classical approach: computation of probabilities

We can simplify the discussion by setting migration aside, thus eliminating superfluous difficulties and avoiding the risk of false conclusions.[2] Premature

[2]Immigration introduces alien people into the group defined by year and country of birth; in

death prevents single people from marrying; this is the mechanism by which mortality affects nuptiality. To eliminate this influence, we would need to know (for single women who died before age 50) what their marriage pattern would have been if they had lived. Since we don't know this, we have recourse to an hypothesis: we assume that those who died single at a certain age a, would have married in the same way as those who did not die at this age if they had lived beyond age a.[3] Let us therefore consider single persons who reach a certain exact age x and let us imagine that we have been able to compute the proportion n_x of those single persons who would marry between age x and age y (age y greater than age x) in the absence of mortality. As a consequence of the preceding hypothesis, this proportion is the same as that which would prevail in the absence of mortality up to age x, that is to say, if instead of having only the surviving single people at age x, we had all the persons who, in the absence of mortality, would not have been married by age x. The complement of n_x, $1 - n_x$, represents the proportion remaining single at age x that would still be single at age y in the absence of mortality. So, knowing n_x, we are able to pass from the probability of remaining single at age x to the probability of remaining single at age y. But if we can go from one age to the next, we can go progressively from the minimum age at marriage, where the probability of remaining single is equal to one, to age 50 years and hence answer the first question raised above. The problem is to compute n_x.

a) Computation of the probability of marrying

The index n_x which we have to calculate is a probability of marrying; the word probability is reserved for indices where we start with the number of people at the beginning of a period, while we talk about rates when the figures are based on the average of the population during the period.[4]

---

principle they should be excluded but this is not always possible. For people who emigrate, it is tempting to substitute their nuptiality abroad for that which they would have had if they had stayed, although their nuptiality abroad depends on conditions which may be very different.

[3]It is very unlikely that this hypothesis is true, at least for the population as a whole. On the one hand, there are social and regional differences which affect both nuptiality and mortality. To simplify the situation, let's imagine that there are only two classes, class A with a high mortality and a low definitive probability of remaining single and class B with low mortality and high definitive probability of remaining single, and that in each class the above hypothesis is true; it will not be true for the whole since at each age class A would be comparatively larger without mortality than it is with it.

On the other hand, it is also doubtful that the hypothesis would be true within a class or a region, since certain illnesses diminish the chance of marrying and increase the risk of death.

We could nevertheless consider the hypothesis as likely for groups of persons having in common several characteristics which are related both to nuptiality and to mortality, e.g. social class, geographical region, health conditions, etc.

This hypothesis should not be confused with the additional hypotheses concerning differences in mortality between the single population and the whole population mentioned later on. In this first hypothesis, it is unimportant whether the single and the whole population have the same age pattern of mortality or not.

[4]More generally, the probability that A will occur is the ratio of the events A, which are non-renewable, happening between age x and y in a cohort, to the number of members of that cohort who reached age x (time elapsed since the origin of the cohort) without having undergone the event.

Let us designate C_x the number of members of a given generation who are still single at exact age x:[5] M_x will be the number of first marriages, D_x the number of deaths of single people, both between exact ages x and y. In the absence of mortality, there would be more than M_x marriages, since we would have to add the marriages between ages x and y among the single people who died between these ages; let us call e_x the number of these additional marriages. We now define n_x by the relation:

$$n_x = \frac{M_x + e_x}{C_x}.$$

The proportion single who would have married between ages x and y would be very close to n_x for those among them who died at an age close to x, as a consequence of the initial hypothesis, and very close to zero for those who died at an age close to y. As a first approximation, we may take $n_x/2$, the arithmetical average of n_x and 0, as the proportion to be applied to the total number of deaths of single people, D_x, since these deaths are distributed between x and y; so we may write

$$e_x = D_x \frac{n_x}{2}$$

and this becomes

$$n_x = \frac{M_x}{C_x - D_x/2}.$$

This solves our problem, at the price of an hypothesis and an approximation. We have already discussed the hypothesis; let us now discuss the approximation. In order for it to be acceptable, the interval (x, y) must be small, so that $D_x/2$ becomes negligible in comparison with C_x (see example 1 below). This suggests that it might even be possible to work with intervals short enough to compute the whole series of n_x's without accounting at all for the single deaths D_x.

But there is an obvious objection: if I divide an interval in two, I reduce D_x and therefore, each correction factor for the probabilities of marrying (approximately by half). But two computations will be necessary to bridge the interval from x to y, and each will be done using a measure, the probability, which departs only half as much from the correct value as that used for the single computation. One might fear a priori that the two computations together will result in a total error just as large as the single computation which they are to replace, and that nothing has been gained by the subdivision. But, if we gain nothing by subdividing, perhaps the approximation allowing us to replace e_x by $D_x n_x/2$ may not suffice since this approximation can be justified only for small intervals; the solution offered would then be an illusion. Fortunately, it can be shown that the combination of the two indices does not indeed lose the precision gained for each by dividing the intervals in two.

As we shall see, an interval of one year is small enough in most cases. With

[5]That is to say, at their xth birthday, if x is a round number of years.

such an interval, n_x is the probability of marrying between the xth and the x + 1st birthday, and we have approximately

$$n_x = \frac{M_x}{C_x}$$

where C_x is the number of persons in the generation who are single at the time of their xth birthday and M_x is the number of marriages of single people in the same generation between the xth and the x + 1st birthday.

Example 1:
The following diagram relating to French women gives the number of first marriages and deaths of single persons for the generation of 1930 at age 20 (the deaths are in parentheses).

The number of single people in that generation as of the 1st of January, 1951 is equal to 234 694; we assume that migrations are negligible.

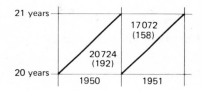

We have:

$$M_{20} = 20\,724 + 17\,072 = 37\,796$$
$$D_{20} = 192 + 158 = 350$$
$$C_{20} = 234\,694 + 20\,724 + 192 = 255\,610$$

$$n_{20} = \frac{M_{20}}{C_{20}} = 148 \text{ per thousand}$$

The influence of the correction $D_x/2$ will be on the order of 7 per ten thousand.

Example 2:
Here is a second example, imaginary in this case, but of approximately the same order of magnitude as the figures for present-day French women.

In one generation, 255 000 women are single at their 20th birthday: 149 000 marry and 1160 die single before their 25th birthday. The probability of marrying between 20 and 25 years is equal to 584·3 per thousand if we divide 149 000 by 255 000 and to 585·6 per thousand if we divide it by 254 420 (255 000 − 1160/2); the relative discrepancy is on the order of 2 per thousand. Here again we can afford to ignore the correction. Don't conclude, however, that the correction can always be ignored. It is possible here because mortality is very low, but if mortality were at the 'primitive' level, that is to say 15 or 20 times higher, the term $D_x/2$ would already represent more than 1 % of C_x for an interval of one year and between 3 and 4 % for an interval of 5 years.

C

b) The probability of remaining single at age x

To be specific, let's consider a female generation and let's take 15 years as the lowest age at marriage for girls and start with that age.

Of 1000 girls at age 15 in the generation, $1000\,n_{15}$ would get married before reaching 16 years (in the absence of mortality) and $1000\,(1-n_{15})$ would still be single on their 16th birthday.

According to the hypothesis we have accepted, the probability n_{16} computed on the basis of survivors at their 16th birthday is also applicable to the girls who would have reached that birthday in the absence of mortality; the number of those who would marry at age 16 would thus be $1000\,(1-n_{15})\,n_{16}$. The number of single girls at their 17th birthday would therefore be $1000\,(1-n_{15})(1-n_{16})$, and it can be seen that we can go from the number single at any birthday x to the following birthday by multiplying the first number by $(1-n_x)$. This number is equal to the product of the initial number, 1000, and the probability of remaining single at age x, γ_x. Thus, we have $\gamma_x = (1-n_{15})\ldots(1-n_{x-1})$.

c) The definitive probability of remaining single

If ω is the age after which there are no more first marriages, the definitive probability of remaining single, γ_ω is given by

$$\gamma_\omega = (1-n_{15})\ldots(1-n_{\omega-})$$

As mentioned before, ω is often taken to be 50, particularly for the feminine sex. This is equivalent to writing

$$\gamma_\omega \simeq \gamma_{50} = (1-n_{15})\ldots(1-n_{49}).$$

Table 5.1 gives an example.

Table 5.1 Computation of the probability of remaining single at age x

Age (x)	n_x per 1000	$1-n_x$ per 1000	γ_x per 1000	μ_x per 1000
15	5	995	1000	5
16	18	982	995	18
17	41	959	977	40
18	77	923	937	72
19	107	893	865	93
20	137	853	772	106
21	160	840	666	107
22			559	

We see that

$$0\cdot977 = 0\cdot995 \times 0\cdot982$$
$$0\cdot937 = 0\cdot977 \times 0\cdot959 = 0\cdot995 \times 0\cdot982 \times 0\cdot959.$$

d) The first marriage column of the nuptiality table

In the absence of mortality and migration, the number of single people can decrease only by first marriage. The difference between the number single at exact age x and the number at exact age $x+1$ is thus equal to the number of first marriages between those ages. But since there is neither mortality nor migration, the size of the generation does not change; the number single is therefore proportional to the probability of remaining single, γ_x. In setting μ_x as the ratio of first marriages at age x to the size of the generation, we write

$$\mu_x = \gamma_x - \gamma_{x+1}.$$

First marriages μ_x are called first marriages of the nuptiality table. We also have

$$\mu_x = \gamma_x n_x$$

since, by our definition of n_x,

$$n_x = \frac{\gamma_x - \gamma_{x+1}}{\gamma_x} = \frac{\mu_x}{\gamma_x}.$$

e) Distribution of the age at first marriage

The series of μ_x gives the age distribution of the $(1 - \gamma_{50})$ marriages that would be observed in the absence of mortality and migration before age 50 in a generation with an initial size made equal to one.

$\mu_x/(1 - \gamma_{50})$ is then the relative frequency of marriages at age x, in complete years, and the series of frequencies $\mu_x/(1 - \gamma_{50})$ constitutes the distribution of ages at first marriage in the generation. This distribution may be described like any other statistical distribution, that is to say by measures of central tendency—mean, median, maximum point or mode, and by measures of dispersion—variance, standard deviation, interquartile interval.[6] The use of a small number of parameters arises from the concern for summarizing a whole table of numerical data in a few figures. The fitting of a simple function to these data derives from the same concern. Graphical portrayal, giving a simple and complete summary of the distribution in question, plays a similar role.

f) Mean age at first marriage

Table 5.2 gives a series of values of γ_x and μ_x.

For each year of age, the mean age at marriage is approximately equal to $x + 0.5$; for all first marriages between 15 and 49 years, the mean age at first marriage, $\bar{x}$, is such that:

$$\bar{x} \times \text{sum of } \mu_x = \text{Sum of } [(x + 0.5) \times \mu_x]$$

which becomes:

$$\bar{x} = 0.5 + \frac{\text{Sum of } (x \times \mu_x)}{\text{Sum of } \mu_x}.$$

[6]Up to now, demography has paid little attention to the dispersion of distributions; a change of attitude may be foreseen, if only because of the interest offered by the dispersion of family sizes in population genetics.

Table 5.2 Computation of the mean age at first marriage

Age (x)	γ_x per 1000	μ_x per 1000	$u=x-20$	$u \times \mu_x$ per 1000	Age	γ_x per 1000	μ_x per 1000	$u=x-20$	$u \times \mu_x$ per 1000
15	1000	6	− 5	− 30	35	138	5	15	75
16	994	17	− 4	− 68	36	133	5	16	80
17	977	40	− 3	−120	37	128	4	17	68
18	937	72	− 2	−144	38	124	4	18	72
19	865	93	− 1	− 93	39	120	3	19	57
20	772	106	0	−	40	117	3	20	60
21	666	106	1	106	41	114	3	21	63
22	560	94	2	188	42	111	2	22	44
23	466	75	3	225	43	109	2	23	46
24	391	60	4	240	44	107	2	24	48
25	331	46	5	230	45	105	1	25	25
26	285	35	6	210	46	104	1	26	26
27	250	28	7	196	47	103	1	27	27
28	222	21	8	168	48	102	1	28	28
29	201	17	9	153	49	101	1	29	29
30	184	13	10	130	50	100			
31	171	11	11	121					
32	160	9	12	108	Total		900		2543
33	151	7	13	91					
34	144	6	14	84					

It is helpful to convert the latter formula in such a way as to eliminate multiplication by the higher values of x; in order to do so we write

$$\bar{x} = a + 0 \cdot 5 + \frac{\text{Sum of } [\mu_x \times (x-a)]}{\text{Sum of } \mu_x}$$

and we take for a an age close to the mode. In this case, we have taken 20 years. The mean age at marriage is thus $20 \cdot 0 + 0 \cdot 5 + 2543/900 = 20 \cdot 5 + 2 \cdot 8 = 23 \cdot 3$ years.

g) Median age

The median age is such that half of the first marriages under consideration happen before it and half after it. In the present case, therefore, it is an age such that 450 marriages occurred before it. The sum of μ_x from age 15 through age 21 is equal to 440; from age 15 through age 22 it comes to 534. Age twenty-one extends from the 21st to the 22nd birthday, so 440 is the number of first marriages before the 22nd birthday, and 534 is the number of first marriages before the 23rd birthday. The median age is therefore located between exact ages 22 and 23. Since it can be accepted that within one year of age marriages are approximately equally distributed over time and it takes one year to go from 440 to 534 first marriages, the time required to get from 440 to 450 can be computed by interpolation; it is equal to:

$$\frac{10 \times 1}{94} = 0 \cdot 1.$$

The median age is therefore equal to $22 \cdot 1$ years.

h) Modal age

This is the age at which the maximum number of marriages occur. This age may not be unique if the maximum is spread out; in this example 20 and 21 years are modal ages. If there had been 110 marriages at age 20 and 105 at age 21, it would have been tempting to give 20 years as the modal age, but it would certainly have been better even to say that the mode covered both 20 and 21 years. In other words, it is preferable not to give one single age when the frequency of marriages at this age does not clearly exceed the frequency at the proximate ages.

Approximations

The method just studied is long; moreover, it can only be used if the observations provide the requisite data—marriages classified according to previous marital status and year of birth, or age, of the spouses; population classified according to marital status and year of birth, or age. Outside Europe, it is rare to have all these data, because marriages are frequently not registered; even in Europe, vital registration data may be missing or may not correspond to the census categories when one is dealing with nuptiality by region, social class, etc. Moreover, one is not assured of reaching acceptable results just by having the necessary data; the data must be of sufficient quality, and this may not always be the case for young single people, who often live alone and are enumerated less completely than the married.

a) The probability of remaining single and the proportion single

It follows from the basic hypothesis that the nuptiality and mortality of single people are independent. In the absence of migration, the number of single people reaching age x out of an initial number N is

$$N\gamma_x \, {_cS_x}$$

where ${_cS_x}$ is the probability of surviving for single people between birth and age x. Since the total number of people reaching age x is equal to

$$NS_x$$

where S_x is the overall probability of surviving to age x, the proportion c_x of single people at age x can be given by

$$c_x = \gamma_x \frac{{_cS_x}}{S_x}. \tag{a}$$

${_cS}/S$ has rarely been measured. In France, we know that it lies between 0·960 and 0·975 at age 50 for the female generations born between 1881 and 1910, and there is reason to think that it is always over 0·95 for the feminine sex. For males the difference is likely to be more marked, and at 50 years ${_cS}/S$ could well fall around 0·90 or even as low as 0·85. But since the probability of remaining single varies a great deal between cultures, and even between countries, an error of 10% or even 15% carries little weight in certain problems.

Thus, the proportion single at 50 years provides an acceptable value for the definitive probability of remaining single, particularly for the feminine sex, *if mortality is the only disturbing factor at work.*[7] This is the case for closed populations, that is to say when migratory movements can be neglected for all practical purposes. It is often the case for a country taken as a whole, but it is not generally so for a region, province, or city.

Relation (a) is still true when migration exists. But if $_cS$ represents the ratio of single people present at age x to the initial number (computed on the basis of the probabilities of mortality and migration for single people) and if S is the equivalent value for the whole population, it is likely that the ratio $_cS/S$ will diverge from unity far more than when there is no migration. Therefore, in the present state of our knowledge, the proportion single at 50 may not be close enough to the probability of remaining single at that age to constitute a good approximation when the population is subject to a significant amount of migration. Consequently, it is necessary to interpret information on the proportions single in open populations with care.

Table 5.3 Proportion single at age 50: selected countries

	Males %	Females %		Males %	Females %
Bulgaria	2·6	2·0	Egypt	2·0	0·9
France	10·3	10·4	United States	8·5	7·8
Hungary	6·0	8·2	Venezuela	22·2	33·9
Ireland	31·0	25·7	India	3·9	1·2
Italy	8·7	14·7	Israel	4·8	4·1
Portugal	11·4	17·0	(Jewish pop.)		
Sweden	15·7	19·1	Japan	1·5	1·4

Source: United Nations Demographic Yearbook, 1958. Because of the age classification used in this yearbook, c_x has been calculated by taking the ratio of single people to the total population in the age group 45–54 years.

Table 5.3 gives an approximate value of c_x at age 50 in generations born around 1900 for a certain number of countries. In the absence of a census, the proportion single at age 50 may be replaced by the proportion single among people dying at age 50 and over in the generation considered. This method is used in historical demography; the problems of interpretation with open populations are, of course, the same as above.

When single people are enumerated sufficiently accurately at all ages and $_cS$ and S are not very different at age 50 (they are then even closer to one another at ages under 50 years) one may replace γ_x by c_x, for any value of x. In this way one derives values of γ_x at various ages from a series of censuses and, by subtraction, the marriage column of the nuptiality table between those ages.[8] But since nuptiality varies very sharply with age both before and after its maximum value, we would like to tabulate the marriage column by single years of age between about 15 and 30 years. Censuses are spaced at least five years apart, so we must estimate γ_x between the two values γ_{x1} and γ_{x2} provided by

[7] The census actually gives the proportion single by age at last birthday and not by exact age. It is possible to take the proportion at age 49 or 50 years (the equivalent, approximately, of exact ages 49·5 or 50·5 respectively) as that for exact age 50 or, better yet, to take the average of the two.
[8] Do not forget that in a census, x is an age at last birthday and not an exact age and that there is a lag of approximately half a year between the two.

two successive censuses,[9] except when the statistical agencies publish annual estimates of the population by age and marital status.[10]

Use of a single census
If we can assume that the nuptiality of the population under consideration has remained unchanged up to the time of the census in question, we may use that single census as if it represented a series of censuses done from year to year. When nuptiality does not change, all generations have, in fact, a similar series of γ_x; if the conditions for equality between c_x and γ_x are fulfilled, the series of proportions c_x given by the census represents approximately the series of γ_x common to every generation. As an example, we present the series of c_x for the Moslem population of Algeria, female sex, from the census of 1948 (see table 5.4).

It will be apparent that the crude c_x values (that is to say those obtained directly from the data) present marked fluctuations. Before they can be used,

Table 5.4 Proportions single and first marriages per thousand women: computed from the census of Algeria, Moslem population, 1948

Age	c_x per 1000		μ_x per 1000	Age	c_x per 1000		μ_x per 1000
	Crude	Adjusted			Crude	Adjusted	
11	1000	1000	2	31	63	58	7
12	998	998	3	32	50	51	6
13	996	995	5	33	45	45	5
14	992	990	90	34	46	40	4
15	902	900	100	35	34	36	3
16	785	800	130	36	39	33	3
17	679	670	135	37	38	30	2
18	495	535	120	38	31	28	1
19	443	415	95	39	29	27	1
20	274	320	60	40	23	26	—
21	283	260	45	41	28	26	1
22	213	215	35	42	28	25	—
23	185	180	28	43	29	25	1
24	161	152	22	44	30	24	—
25	117	130	18	45	21	24	—
26	119	112	14	46	26	24	1
27	106	98	12	47	26	23	—
28	79	86	11	48	21	23	—
29	79	75	9	49	38	23	—
30	53	66	8	50	19	23	—
				Total			977

Note: Since the ages are, in theory, given in completed years, the μ_x figures represent marriages taking place between exact ages $x+0\cdot5$ and $x+1\cdot5$. The median age is $18\cdot5 + 0\cdot2 = 18\cdot7$.

[9]The estimation may be done taking the curve of c_x at each of the censuses as a guide.

[10]Such estimates are made taking into account the surrounding censuses, as well as marriages and deaths, and are therefore more accurate than those made on the basis of data from censuses only.

they must be adjusted, and this adjustment is certainly not very precise, so that the series of μ_x can only be an approximation.[11]

b) Marriage frequencies

The number of marriages M_x at age x conforms to the equation

$$M_x = n_x \times \left(C_x - \frac{D_x}{2} \right)$$

according to the approximate formula for n_x. If we designate by $_cq_x$,[12] the probability of dying for single people at age x, the preceding relationship can be also written

$$M_x = n_x C_x \left(1 - \frac{_cq_x}{2} \right),$$

Besides, the average population at age x is equal to $P_x(1 - q_x/2)$, where q_x is the risk of dying at age x for the whole population. We relate marriages at age x to the average population at age x. This gives m_x, the marriage rate at age x and we have:

$$m_x = \frac{n_x C_x}{P_x} \left(\frac{1 - \dfrac{_cq_x}{2}}{1 - \dfrac{q_x}{2}} \right)$$

or in other words according to equation (a) from the preceding section:

$$m_x = n_x \gamma_x \frac{_cS_x}{S_x} \left(\frac{1 - \dfrac{_cq_x}{2}}{1 - \dfrac{q_x}{2}} \right).$$

But, $n_x \gamma_x$ is equal to μ_x. Moreover, $1 - q_x/2$ is very close to the probability of surviving between age x and $x + 0.5$; the product $S_x(1 - q_x/2)$ is therefore equal to $S(x + 0.5)$ and the product in the numerator is equal to $_cS(x + 0.5)$. Hence

$$m_x = \mu_x \frac{_cS(x + 0.5)}{S(x + 0.5)}.$$

As before, let's first take the case where there is no migration. Because of the excess mortality of single people, $_cS/S$ is smaller than 1. The sum of m_x is therefore smaller than the sum of μ_x and the complement of the sum of m_x is therefore greater than the complement of the sum of μ_x which is equal to the

---

[11] The crude c_x values at 18, 20, 22, 25, 30, 35, 40, 45, and 50 years were replaced by the ratios of the single to the total including all marital statuses in the three-year age groups 17–19, 19–21, 21–3, 24–6, 29–31, 34–6, 44–6, 49–51 respectively. Other values were obtained by graphical interpolation.

[12] The probabilities of dying are defined in chapter 9. Here $_cq_x = \dfrac{D_x}{C_x}$.

probability of remaining single. The complement of the sum of m_x from age 15 to age 49 therefore gives us too high a value for the probability of remaining single whereas, under the same conditions, the proportion single at age 50 yields a value that is too low. This assumes, of course, that there are no errors.

If the difference in mortality between the single and the whole population is small enough, m_x may be taken as the equivalent of μ_x, that is to say the age-specific marriage rates can be taken as equivalent to the marriage column of the table.[13] This condition is fulfilled in a fairly satisfactory way for the feminine sex, but less satisfactorily for the male sex. Table 5.5 shows an example of the computation of m_x for France, female sex, generation of 1944.

It is likely that this approximation will not be applicable when migration is fairly important; the reasons are the same as for the approximation based on proportions single which was described above.

Table 5.5 Computation of first marriage frequencies: France, generation of 1944

Year	Age one 1 Jan.	Size on 1 Jan. thousands	Size on 31 Dec. thousands	Average size thousands	First marriages	m_x per 1000
1959	14	286·9	288·6	287·75	421	1·5
1960	15	288·6	289·1	288·85	2 224	7·7
1961	16	289·1	293·2	291·15	7 087	24·4
1962	17	293·2	300·3	296·75	16 462	55·5

c) Mean age at first marriage and proportion single

Let's imagine first that we know the series of probabilities of remaining single at age x, γ_x, for a given generation from the minimum age up to about 50 years, γ_{50} being taken as the definitive probability of remaining single.

We must compute the mean age $\bar{x}$ at first marriage; it can be taken as the mean age of first marriage celebrated before age 50. Thus, we write for the minimum age of 15 years:

$$\bar{x} = 0.5 + \frac{15\mu_{15} + 16\mu_{16} + \cdots + x\mu_x + \cdots + 49\mu_{49}}{1 - \gamma_{50}}.$$

But $\mu_x = \gamma_x - \gamma_{x+1}$ so that the numerator can be written:

$$15(\gamma_{15} - \gamma_{16}) + 16(\gamma_{16} - \gamma_{17}) + \cdots + 48(\gamma_{48} - \gamma_{49}) + 49(\gamma_{49} - \gamma_{50}).$$

That is to say

$$15\gamma_{15} + (16 - 15)\gamma_{16} + \cdots + (49 - 48)\gamma_{49} - 49\gamma_{50}$$

[13] First marriage frequencies are computed by relating the first marriages of age x to the average population of that age *without regard for marital status*. We shall see that an analogous method is used to compute age-specific fertility rates by age, indices referring to renewable events, i.e. births not distinguished by order. Therefore—and we shall come back to the point—the distinction between renewable and non-renewable events, which is a priori so natural, would have no practical implication if there were no differences in mortality and migration between single people and the whole population. The important distinction is the one between events which are accompanied by discontinuities in mortality and migration, and events which are not accompanied by discontinuities of this sort, if indeed there are any.

C*

or also, since $\gamma_{15} = 1$

$$15(1 - \gamma_{50}) + \gamma_{16} + \cdots + \gamma_x + \cdots + \gamma_{49} - 34\gamma_{50}.$$

Dividing by $1 - \gamma_{50}$, we reach the result:

$$\bar{x} = 0\cdot5 + \frac{15(1 - \gamma_{50}) + \gamma_{16} + \cdots + \gamma_x + \cdots + \gamma_{49} - 34\gamma_{50}}{1 - \gamma_{50}}$$

$$= 15 + \frac{0\cdot5 + \gamma_{16} + \cdots + \gamma_x + \cdots + \gamma_{49} - 34\cdot5\gamma_{50}}{1 - \gamma_{50}}.$$

Let us now suppose that we have a series of proportions single $C_{x+0.5}$ from 15 years on, thanks to censuses and intercensal estimates, and that we can equate c_x and γ_x.

Under these conditions, we have approximately:

$$c_{x+0.5} = \frac{\gamma_x + \gamma_{x+1}}{2}$$

and therefore:

$$0\cdot5 + \gamma_{16} + \cdots + \gamma_{49} - 34\cdot5\gamma_{50} =$$

$$= \frac{1 + \gamma_{16}}{2} + \frac{\gamma_{16} + \gamma_{17}}{2} + \cdots + \frac{\gamma_{49} + \gamma_{50}}{2} - 35\gamma_{50}$$

$$= c_{15.5} + c_{16.5} + \cdots + c_{49.5} - 35\gamma_{50}.$$

Hence:

$$\bar{x} = 15 + \frac{c_{15.5} + c_{16.5} + \cdots + c_{49.5} - 35\gamma_{50}}{1 - \gamma_{50}}.$$

In practice, the completed series of $c(x)$ for the same generation is often not available because censuses are only taken every 5 or 10 years, and there are no estimates for the periods in between. The problem can be solved by replacing the $c(x)$ values with those of the proximate generations; the closer the censuses the more acceptable this is. This actually occurs automatically when the results are given by groups of ages or groups of generations, as was the case in France up to 1936.

Indeed, when the sizes P_x, P_{x+1}, P_{x+2}, P_{x+3}, P_{x+4} of generations constituting an age group are close to one another, we may write

$$\frac{C_{x, x+}}{P^{x, x+4}} = \frac{P_x c_{x+0'5} + P_{x+1} c_{x+1'5} + \cdots + P_{x+4} C_{4+4'5}}{P_x + P_{x+1} + \cdots + P_{x+4}} =$$

$$= \frac{c_{x+0.5} + c_{x+1.5} + \cdots + c_{x+4.5}}{5}$$

(where $C_{x, x+4}$ is the number of single people and $P_{x, x+4}$ is the total population in the age group between x and $x+4$).

In other words, by designating $c_{x, x+4}$ as the proportion single in the age group x, $x+4$ we are saying:

$$c_{x+0.5} + c_{x+1.5} + \cdots + c_{x+4.5} = 5\, c_{x, x+4}.$$

As an example relating to France, table 5.6 gives the proportion single among women for the group of generations born approximately between 1857 and 1861.

Table 5.6 Female proportions single: France, generations of 1857–61

Year of census	Age group	Proportion single $c_{x, x+4}$
1876	15–19 years	0·937
1881	20–24 years	0·602
1886	25–29 years	0·327
1891	30–34 years	0·215
1896	35–39 years	0·164
1901	40–44 years	0·127
1906	45–49 years	0·115
Total		2·487

Note: For 1906, $c_{x, x+4}$ is estimated by interpolation between 1901 and 1911.

Since the size of the generations varies little between 1857 and 1861, the product by 5 of the total 2·487, or 12·435, is approximately equal to $C_{15.5} + C_{16.5} + \cdots + C_{49.5}$ in the group of generations considered.

c_{50}, the equivalent of γ_{50}, is equal to 11·2%, so we can write:

$$\bar{x} = 15 + \frac{12 \cdot 435 - 35 \times 0 \cdot 112}{0 \cdot 888} = 15 + 9 \cdot 59 = 24 \cdot 59.$$

This then yields 24·6 as an approximate value for the average age at first marriage of females for the generations 1857–61 in the absence of mortality and migration.

Errors

If there were no differences in mortality and migration between single people and the whole population, and if the numerical data (i.e. the numbers of marriages and of persons) contained no errors at all, then the approximate findings would be as rigorous as the exactly calculated probabilities of marrying. In other words, under ideal conditions, we could select any one of the three series from the nuptiality table, that of probabilities of marrying n_x, that of probabilities of remaining single γ_x, or that of the marriage column μ_x. The existence of differences in mortality and, perhaps even more serious, in migration between single people and the whole population means that, as we have seen, this interchangeability is impaired and the only rigorous results are the probabilities of marrying. Let us now turn to the influence of census errors (other errors are negligible in developed countries).

Omissions are more common and more difficult to avoid for isolated persons than for the rest of the population, especially when such people are quite mobile. So it can be anticipated that the number of single persons will be underestimated from the age when it is typical for young men and women to leave their family homes, and that this underreporting bias will increase, pass a maximum, and then diminish as progressive stabilization of employment and residence takes place.

These omissions are compounded by errors in the recording of marital status. These are probably more frequent for single people than for the whole population but, in contrast to omissions, their frequency probably increases continuously with age. Such errors concerning single people may combine with various errors concerning the ever married population, and a number of examples come to mind. When there are omissions both among single people and among the total population—the case that is encountered when there is no overcount of the ever married sufficient to compensate for the omission of single people—the proportion single at age 50 is closer to the probability of remaining single at that age than the estimates that can be obtained from the probabilities of marrying or from the age specific marriage frequencies. But in practice, the differences between the approximations and the true value include measurement errors. In the present state of our knowledge, it is usually not known whether one approach is generally preferable to the others. In each case, one will have to keep in mind the comparative precision of the various methods available.

3 Marital dissolution, remarriage

A marriage may be dissolved by the death of a spouse or by divorce. (Let's leave aside judicial separation, an intermediate state which does not permit remarriage.) Dissolution is usually studied on the basis of marriage cohorts. For a study in any depth, the marriage cohorts must be subdivided according to the combined age of both spouses, for instance men aged 25–29 and women aged 20–24, since age is such an important factor in mortality.

A study of this sort may have several goals.
1 It may be a study of the dissolution of marriage as a whole, without paying special attention to any one cause. This is equivalent to studying the mortality of a generation from all causes combined. The results of such a study often include the distribution of marital dissolutions by cause (divorce, death of husband, death of wife); the distribution is the one observed from the real history of a marriage cohort.
2 On the other hand, it may be a study specifically of one of the two types of marital dissolution, divorce or widowhood. The other type is then treated as an extraneous influence and eliminated. Let us examine these two cases without going into detail.

Divorce

The analysis must provide answers to the following questions: 'What proportion of the marriages concluded at a certain time would have ended in divorce if premature widowhood had not reduced the risk of this eventuality?' 'How would the divorces have been distributed with respect to duration of marriage?' The analysis may be carried out for all marriages together or for a certain category, e.g. by age at marriage of the man, of the woman, or both, or by social class, and so on.

Widowhood

In this case, the first question is not of interest since, in the absence of divorce, all marriages would end by the death of the husband or of the wife. Instead, the following question is raised: 'What proportion of the marriages would have been dissolved by the death of the husband, and what proportion by the death of the wife, in the absence of divorce?' The second question is the same as for divorce. Subdivision of the marriage cohort according to age at marriage of both the husband and the wife is indispensable.

Remarriage

The same approach can be applied to remarriage; it is essential to take age into account at the time of the dissolution of marriage. The analysis must provide answers to the following questions: 'What proportion of men widowed (divorced) at a certain age would remarry if mortality and migration did not interfere?' 'Without the influence of mortality and migration, what would be the distribution of remarriages according to their duration of widowhood or divorce?' Analogous questions can be asked for women.

In practice, the disturbing effect of mortality and migration is small since remarriage is most often rapid, so one can operate as if mortality and migration did not exist. The proportion we want is then equal to the number of remarriages in the cohort in question divided by the initial size of the cohort. The distribution of remarriages that we want is the one actually observed.

6

Fertility

1 Some characteristics of the items under study

Characteristics of childbirth

A birth may be:
1 single or multiple. There is approximately one twin birth for every 100 deliveries. The proportion varies with the age of the mother; it reaches a maximum of about 1·5 % for women aged 35–9 years. The proportion of triple births is on the order of 1 per 10 000.
2 at term or premature.

Characteristics of the newly born

A newly born child may be:
1 dead or alive. The stillbirth rate is the proportion stillborn among all births.

Example:
In 1956 there were 821 000 births of which 17 900 were stillborn or died before registration and were distributed as follows: 13 500 true stillborn, 3800 false stillborn and 600 undetermined. The stillbirth rate was then between 16·4 and 17·2 per thousand.

2 boy or girl. The index of masculinity is the proportion male among all births.

Example:
Again in 1956 there were 803 000 live births including 411 000 boys and 392 000 girls. The index of masculinity was then 0 512.
   The sex ratio is actually used more frequently; it is equal to 100 boys/girls. In France in 1956, this ratio was 105 for live births. It is higher for stillborn (whether true or false); in 1951, for example, it was 126 as opposed to 105 for live births.

3 legitimate or illegitimate. The illegitimacy ratio is the proportion illegitimate.

Example:
In 1956 there were 803 000 live births including 51 000 which were illegitimate. The illegitimacy ratio was then 6·35 per thousand.

Characteristics of the mother

a) **Marital status**

See above.

b) **Age**

The proportional distribution of births of a *period* according to the age of the mother has scarcely any analytical interest; it is a function of the population structure among other things.

The distribution of births according to the age of the mother within a *cohort* is also a result of several factors. It is of interest, however, because of its role in various theoretical and practical problems.

Characteristics of the family

Number of children already born or order

The *birth order* of a child is defined by the number of children already born either to the mother or to both the father and the mother or during the present marriage. The number of stillbirths may or may not be counted in the number of children already born, depending on the approach.

If we want to ensure consistency between census and vital registration data, the number and the birth order of children in the family must be defined:

for all the children, legitimate or illegitimate, according to the number of children born alive to the mother;

for the legitimate children, according to the number of children born alive in the present marriage.

2 Fertility without regard to birth order

The study of fertility without distinction by birth order may serve as a prototype. It could be adapted, as the occasion arises, to the study of related phenomena such as artistic, literary or scientific fecundity.

Statement of the problem

As before, we are trying to get at the pure phenomenon, free from the influence of mortality and, if need be, of migration. The first question to ask is similar to those that we have encountered in dealing with nuptiality and, more generally, in dealing with events that are not inevitable and not renewable; it can be stated as follows:

In the absence of disturbances from death or migration, what would be the proportion of members of a cohort who would have at least one child or the complementary proportion, those who would remain childless? When we study the first birth alone, a non-renewable event, the question is posed in identical terms. In principle, then, the study of phenomena relating to renewable events should go hand in hand with the study of phenomena involving the first, in terms of order, of such renewable events. The proportion of persons who have at least one child is equal to the average number of first births per person. The analogous figure for all births becomes the object of the second question.

In the absence of disturbing influences what would be the average number of births per women or per couple? To these two questions, we can add a third, concerning the distribution of births in time.

What would be the distribution by age, or by duration of marriage, at the birth of the children?

Logically, then, three questions rather than two should be asked when dealing with renewable events. In practice, the first of these questions is often left out, undoubtedly for lack of data on birth order; it does come up, in fact, when the observations provide the number of children per woman or per couple (as in retrospective surveys, for instance).[1]

a) Definition of the events being studied

Concerning fertility, it would be possible to take as events deliveries, births including stillbirths, or live births only. In most cases, the units are live births or events that are almost equivalent (e.g. baptisms in historical demography). Attempts have been made to use conceptions instead of births,[2] but research making use of models has shown that it is preferable to limit oneself to births.

b) Definition of the group beng studied

As in the previous chapter, by choice, we are considering only longitudinal analysis. We will follow well defined cohorts throughout their existence, measuring time from entry into the cohort. These cohorts may be:

1) Generations or birth cohorts
Here all births are considered, both legitimate and illegitimate, and we talk about *overall* (as opposed to legitimate) fertility. Time is that which has elapsed since birth, in other words, age. With rare exceptions, we study overall fertility for women only.

2) Marriage cohorts
In this case, we limit ourselves to legitimate births, and fertility is qualified as

---

[1] Furthermore, the first question may be considered of secondary importance if the cohort being investigated is defined by the first of the events to be considered. Such an instance occurs with literary fecundity; we study only that of authors, that is to say of persons who have produced at least one work.

At first sight, this way of presenting things makes short shift of a concern which is frequently encountered when dealing with the repeated production of identical objects: the measurement of production per person or per unit of time, or the productivity of individuals or groups, and the variation of this productivity in time, for instance with age. In fact, raising the question of variation in the productivity or fertility of a cohort through its life is equivalent to asking the third question in a different way since size remains constant (in the absence of mortality and migration) and productivity is proportional to what is produced (births) at that age or for that duration.

[2] It is not necessary to know about every conception to do so. The essential difference between births and conceptions is a difference of date.

legitimate or *marital*. Here the time elapsed since entry into the cohort is the duration of marriage; since physiological factors and behaviour depend a great deal on the age of the women, however, it is normal to introduce age, but not at the expense of marriage duration. This leads to the explicit introduction of age at marriage and to the study of fertility by duration of marriage or by age of cohorts that are defined in terms of the time of marriage (in years or group of years) and age (or group of ages) at marriage.[3]

3) Maternal cohorts
In populations where marital unions frequently take a stable character only after a birth, or can only be identified after a birth (unregistered marriages), one may be led to study fertility in terms of women who have had at least one child. In that case the first child plays the same role as marriage in (2) above.

Fertility rates

In order to answer the questions we have posed, we resort to the same basic hypothesis as in the case of nuptiality: those who died or departed would have had, if they had lived or had stayed, the same fertility as the rest.

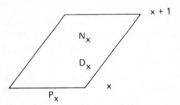

Let us designate as P_x the number of members of the cohort who reach the xth anniversary of their entry (xth birthday, xth anniversary of marriage or the xth birthday of their first child); as N_x the number of births between the xth and the $(x+1)^{st}$ anniversary; as D_x the number of deaths to members of the cohort in the same interval. (We assume that migration can be ignored; this simplifies the formulae without diminishing the generality of the result.)

A reasoning process identical to that used for nuptiality yields f_x, the fertility index we need:

$$f_x = \frac{N_x}{P_x - D_x/2}.$$

But since fertility is a renewable event, the size of the denominator can only be altered by death, so P_{x+1} is equal to $P_x - D_x$. The denominator is therefore

[3]Under conditions of primitive fertility, the age of the woman plays a dominant role so that the above rules may be waived. When birth control is very widespread, however, marriage duration becomes dominant, so that age may be left aside at least for the first stages of analysis. For studies that involve the two kinds of situations, it is necessary to include at the same time both the woman's age and the duration of marriage; since one must also take into account age at marriage, one must choose between two combinations, age at marriage-woman's age or age at marriage-duration of marriage. The two are identical when dealing with continuous intervals and are almost identical with single years of age or duration; they are not identical when dealing with cohorts of age or duration. The choice then is difficult and varies from one author to another.

equal to $(P_x + P_{x+1})/2$, i.e., the average number $\bar{P}_x$ for age or duration x, and we write:

$$f_x = \frac{N_x}{\bar{P}_x}$$

The index f_x is a fertility *rate*, the term rate being reserved for cases where events are related to an average number of people.

We have seen previously that the correction factor $D_x/2$ is often omitted when probabilities are computed. This would also be legitimate here, but is not done, no doubt because the computation of the average size of the population is particularly easy.

a) Discussion of the hypothesis

Strictly speaking, the basic hypothesis does not hold for overall fertility. Since mortality is higher for single persons, the proportion single among the women who die between x and $x+1$ is higher than among those who survive. They would therefore have had lower fertility than the others if they had lived. Theoretically then, one should study overall fertility by individual birth order, or at least distinguish first births from others. This would mean abandoning to some extent the treatment of births as renewable events. Thus, renewable events can only be treated as such if mortality and mobility are the same in the successive stages of life delimited by these events. When this condition is fulfilled, non-renewable events can be treated in the same way as renewable ones, as we have already seen. The approach to different phenomena therefore depends primarily on the importance of the discontinuities in mortality and mobility which accompany the event being observed.

In practice, it is likely that the results will differ little from those that would be obtained if the basic hypothesis were rigorously fulfilled. In historical populations, we observe only a trivial difference between completed fertility (see p. 78) and the average number of children per completed family, as shown in the following example:

Table 6.1 Comparison of completed fertility with the avarage number of children per completed family in a historical population

Woman's age at marriage	Completed fertility	Average number of children per completed family
15–19 years	8·31	8·84
20–24 years	7·01	6·52
25–29 years	5·22	5·07
30–34 years	3·37	3·25
35–39 years	1·64	1·75

There is no systematic difference between the two series. Sometimes one is higher and sometimes the other; a single series could replace them both.

b) Computation of the rates

The computation procedures depend on which rate is being considered—overall or legitimate fertility—and on what data are available. When the appropriate data are missing, less exact procedures must suffice. These are discussed separately, under the heading 'Substitutes'.

1) Overall fertility rates

Such rates are usually computed from vital statistics, and this is the only case we will consider.

Generation rates:

Double classification. Strictly speaking, the computation of fertility rates at age x, i.e. between exact age x and exact age $x + 1$, requires that the births be cross-classified by the mother's year of birth and her age. This double classification exists for France from 1946 on. The computation of the overall fertility rate for the cohort of 1928 at 23 years of age is as follows:

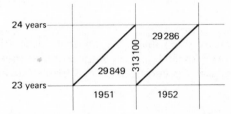

The women born in 1928 have had, between their 23rd and 24th birthdays, 28 849 births in 1951 and 29 286 births in 1952. The size of the generation of 1928 on 1 January 1952, 313 100 women, can be taken as the average of the number of women reaching their 23rd and their 24th birthdays. The rate we want is equal to:

$$\frac{29\,849 + 29\,286}{313\,100} = \frac{59\,135}{313\,100} = 189 \text{ per thousand}$$

Tabulation by the mother's year of birth. If births are classified only by the mother's year of birth, the fertility rates are computed by approximate age on the basis of the births issuing from that cohort during successive calendar years. For example, the fertility rate for the generation of 1938 (i.e. age 23 at last birthday as of 1 January 1962), would be as follows in 1962.

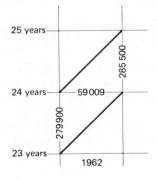

The average size is:

$$\frac{279\,900 + 286\,500}{2} = 283\,200$$

and the rate is equal to:

$$\frac{59\,009}{283\,200} = 209 \text{ per thousand}$$

Rates by age group:
The rates don't have to be computed by single years of age, but as far as cohort rates are concerned, the direct computation of an average yearly overall fertility rate from vital statistics for, say, age 20–24 scarcely simplifies the operation. So the overall fertility rate for the cohort born in 1927 at age 20–24 years will normally be obtained by averaging the 5 rates for 20, 21, 22, 23 and 24 years of age.

Rates by group of generations:
Longitudinal studies are often made by groups of generations. If a double classification of births is available, the computation of overall fertility at 23 years of age for the group of generations 1926–30 from data for 1949–54 would be done as follows:

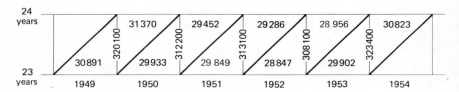

The rate we want is equal to the ratio of the total births:

$$30\,891 + 31\,370 + \cdots + 29\,902 + 30\,823 = 298\,809$$

to the number of women:

$$320\,100 + 312\,200 + 313\,100 + 308\,100 + 323\,400 = 1\,576\,900$$

or:

$$\frac{298\,809}{1\,576\,900} = 189 \cdot 5 \text{ per thousand.}$$

If the double classification had not been available, we would have used the births to the generations 1926–30 from 1949 to 1953 respectively. The rate obtained would be valid for the calendar year in which the members of the group reached age 23. That would be the approximate equivalent of the rate for age 22·5 years. If we want to obtain rates by groups of generations and by groups of ages, we must average the five rates for the ages making up the age group, as above.

Substitutes

Tabulation by age

It sometimes happens that births are classified only by the age of the mother (instead of by date of birth). In this case, the rate obtained by dividing births by the average population can be attributed to an average generation, i.e. the average of the two generations contributing to the births. In 1967, for example, 39 178 children were born alive to mothers aged 19 years in England and Wales; the number of these women was estimated at 393 800 on 30 June 1967.

The rate obtained by dividing 39 178 by the average size of 393 800 is 99·5 per thousand. It is valid for an average generation 1947–8.

Rates by groups of ages:
As above, the rates by age group for a given period are attributed to an average group of generations.

Example:
The average annual number of children born alive in France to mothers aged 20–24 years between 1896 and 1900 inclusively was 221 323. The number of women of 20–24 years at the censuses of 1896 and 1901 was as follows

	1896	1901	*Mean*
	1 604 000	1 617 000	1 610 500

The average rate is:
  221 323 : 1 610 500 = 137 per thousand.

At that time, the births were theoretically classified by the age of the mother. The following diagram would thus be valid.

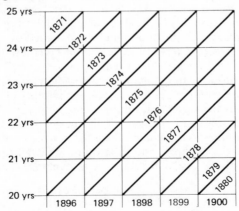

The rate obtained is attributed to a fictitious average generation 1875–6.

After 1907, the births were classified by the mother's year of birth, so from then on the diagram is a little different. This is how it would look for 1921–5:

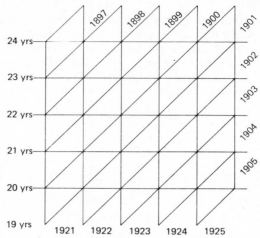

In this instance, the average rate generally corresponds to the interval from exact ages 19·5 to 24·5;[4] it is attributed to the central generation, that of 1901.

2) Legitimate fertility rates

These rates can be computed either from vital statistics or from survey data. Vital statistics, however, do not permit the computation of exactly the rate that meets the analytical requirements. For this reason, we shall start with the second case.

Data collected in surveys:

Surveys taken with a view to investigating fertility normally include questions on the date of birth of the woman, her date of marriage, and at least the dates of birth of children born alive.[5] Age at marriage and also the age of the mother and marriage duration at each birth can then be computed for each woman.

Rates by duration of marriage. At least for contemporary populations, these rates are used more frequently in the study of marital fertility than rates by age. In principle, the marriage cohorts should be subdivided by age at marriage of the women, and legitimate fertility rates should be computed separately for women married at 15–19 years, 20–24 years . . . 45–9 years. The point is to find the correct solution to the fundamental problem of analysis: 'What would be the mean number of children per marriage in the absence of perturbing events such as deaths, divorces and migrations; and how would these births be distributed within the span of married life under these conditions?' The relevant average number is the sum of births for marriages of each duration, in the absence of deaths, divorces and migration. Since all the unions are still extant, the proportional distribution by age at marriage does not change but

---

[4]In France, generations are grouped according to age reached in the course of the year; the group 20–24 thus is made up of women aged 19–23 at the beginning of the year considered.

[5]We are not considering populations where this information cannot be collected because it is neither registered nor known by the respondents.

rather remains at any given time the same as it was at the beginning of the marriage cohort.

Things are different in real life; marriages where the wife is older are sooner broken by death; after say, ten years, they will be proportionately less numerous than the others unless there has been fortuitous compensation through divorce and migration. But these unions are also less fertile, so that the actual fertility of surviving unions of 10-year duration is higher than the fertility of all unions of the cohort would have been without death, divorce or migration.

In order to reconstitute the aggregate fertility, one would have to know the fertilities by duration of marriage for various ages or groups of ages at marriage, and to combine them in the same way that they would have been combined if the proportions by age at marriage had been left unchanged. One would thus have to compute fertility rates by marriage duration for each group of ages at marriage. However, the error that results from treating all ages at marriage together is tolerable providing marriages of women older than 50 years of age are eliminated. But in practice, one does not take advantage of this freedom, because there is a great deal to be learned from the study of the influence of age at marriage on fertility.

Take, as an example of the computation of this rate, the instance of Jeanne Seillé (chapter 4); her first marriage lasted 14 completed years, if we take the date of her husband's death as the close of observation, and 15 completed years if we take 14 March 1941 as the close of observation by virtue of the fact that a woman may still bear a child to her husband nine months after he dies. If we use the latter convention, we must take into account all children born, including posthumous offspring; otherwise, we omit any children born after the husband's death. Here we are using the first convention which is simpler. Let us suppose we want to compute fertility rates by single years of duration from 0 to 4, and by five-year intervals from duration 5–9 on:

In the general formula, the denominator $P - D_x/2$ represents the number of years lived by the women between x and $x + 1$ (or x and $x + 5$). In a survey, the equivalent is the sum of the durations lived in the interval considered. For Jeanne Seillé, the time lived in the interval 10–14 years, for example, is 4·5. Proceeding by hand tabulation, one would operate as follows:

	Duration of marriage (years)														
Case no:	0	1	2	3	4	5–9		10–14		15–19		20–24		25–29	
	B	B	B	B	B	W–Y	B	W–Y	B	W–Y	B	W–Y	B	W–Y	B
1	1	0	1	0	0	5	0	5	1	3·5	0				
2	0	1	0	0	1	5	0	4·5	0						
etc.															
...	...	...	...	...	...	...		...		...		...		...	
Total	203	...	...	...	...	2517·5	441	...		...		...		...	
Number of marriages	542	541	...	...	...	...		...		...		...		...	

One line is devoted to each union. For each of the five first years, one systematically omits those very few marriages dissolved during that year. Thus, there is no point in writing out the number of years lived, since it is always equal to 1. Over 5 years, the number of years lived is given in the column W–Y (woman–years) and the number of births in column B. (The data relative to Jeanne Seillé are written on line no. 2.) For the columns headed 0, 5–9 W–Y, and 5–9 B, the unabridged table would show totals of, respectively, 203, 2517·5, and 441. For the first five years, it is necessary to indicate the number of women observed, which is 542 for duration 0, 541 for duration 1, ... etc. 542 is the number of marriages which have lasted at least one year, 541 the number of marriages which have lasted at least 2 years. After adding up each column, we find, for instance, a legitimate fertility rate of

$$0{\cdot}375 = \frac{203}{542}$$

for duration 0 and of

$$0{\cdot}175 = \frac{441}{2517{\cdot}5}$$

for duration 5–9.

In fact, the fundamental hypothesis does not apply very well to a group of marriage durations when fertility changes rapidly within that duration; consequently it is best to take into account only those unions that have reached the upper limits of each duration group,[6] the fifteenth anniversary of marriage for duration 10–14, for example. In that case, Jeanne Seillé will not be included in observations relative to the group 10–14. We can then eliminate the W–Y column, and the preceding table reads as follows:

Case no.	Duration of marriage (years)									
	0	1	2	3	4	5–9	10–14	15–19	20–24	25–29
1	1	0	1	0	0	0	1			
2	0	1	0	1	0					
etc.	...	...	...	...	...	...	...	...	...	...
Total	203	...	...	...	...	424	...	...	...	...
Number of marriages	542	...	...	...	...	487	...	...	...	...

The rate in the 5–9 group is then:

$$0{\cdot}174 = \frac{424}{5 \times 487}.$$

[6]This possibility does not exist for vital statistics, because births and deaths are collected independently.

Table 6.2 gives legitimate fertility rates for marriage durations 0 to 19 years for women in Great Britain who married in 1919. They are grouped by 2-1/2 years of age at marriage.

Rates by age. For practical purposes, such rates are only computed by age groups. In the preceding instance, unions entered into observation at duration 0. Here entry into observation can occur at any age, so there is no uniform observation period for the age group where marriage takes place. For the other age groups, it is possible either to keep all the observations or, preferably, to use only those where married life has lasted for 5 years. Here is how the computations would be done in the former case, for women married between age 20–24 years.

Case no.	Observed age										
	20–24		25–29		30–34		35–39		40–44		45–49	
	W–Y	B	W–Y	B	W–Y	B	W–Y	B	W–Y	B	W–Y	B
1	1·5	1	5	4	5	3	5	3	0·5	1		
2	2·5	2	5	3	5	2	5	4	4·5	1		
3	0·5	0	5	3	5	3	5	3	5	1	3·5	0
etc.	...	...	...	...	...	...	...	...	...	...	...	...
Total	114	45	221	99	174	63	118	43	86·5	12	51	0
Rate	0·395		0·448		0·362		0·364		0·139		0·000	

The rates are obtained by dividing the total B by the total W–Y.

Tables 6.3 and 6.4 give age-specific fertility rates for the age groups 15–19 to 45–9 by age at marriage, in two historical populations.

Data from vital statistics:
Births are classified in this source either by year of marriage and marriage duration (a double classification which exists for France since 1946), by year of marriage only, or by duration only. Age at marriage is given in some countries. but not in others.

The computation of fertility rates by duration of marriage requires the classification of existing marriages by duration of marriage or year of marriage, combined if possible with age at marriage, or at least including only the marriages of women less than 50 years old. There are few statistics of this type, and almost never for consecutive years, so it is impossible to estimate for each year the unions remaining by year of marriage. But longitudinal analysis of fertility is better and more easily achieved from surveys than from vital statistics. This explains the fact that there have been few attempts to derive statistical series on current unions from census data in order to combine them with statistics on legitimate births. Therefore one would normally use these sources only for the computation of substitute measures as below.

Table 6.2 Legitimate fertility rates by duration of marriage and age at marriage: Great Britain, women married in 1919

Duration of marriage (years)	Woman's age at marriage					
	20–	22·5–	25–	27·5–	30–	32·5–
0	0·43	0·37	0·31	0·28	0·25	0·24
1	0·38	0·36	0·33	0·31	0·30	0·25
2	0·31	0·27	0·25	0·24	0·24	0·22
3	0·25	0·24	0·21	0·21	0·20	0·17
4	0·25	0·21	0·18	0·19	0·17	0·16
5	0·21	0·20	0·16	0·15	0·15	0·09
6	0·20	0·15	0·16	0·13	0·12	0·08
7	0·17	0·15	0·12	0·11	0·10	0·06
8	0·16	0·13	0·11	0·10	0·06	0·05
9	0·14	0·12	0·10	0·06	0·05	0·04
10	0·12	0·11	0·08	0·07	0·04	0·04
11	0·12	0·08	0·06	0·05	0·03	0·01
12	0·10	0·09	0·06	0·04	0·02	0·01
13	0·10	0·06	0·04	0·02	0·01	0·01
14	0·07	0·06	0·04	0·02	0·01	
15	0·07	0·05	0·02	0·01	0·01	
16	0·06	0·04	0·02	0·01		
17	0·06	0·03	0·01			
18	0·05	0·02	0·01			
19	0·04	0·02	0·01			
Total	3·29	2·76	2·28	2·00	1·76	1·43

Source: D. V. Glass and E. Grebenik, *The Trend and Pattern of Fertility in Great Britain* part II, tables, p. 87.

Table 6.3 Legitimate fertility rates by observed age and age at marriage: Crulai, marriages of 1674–1742, women with known date of birth

Woman's age at marriage	Woman's observed age							Cumulated fertility
	15–19 years	20–24 years	25–29 years	30–34 years	35–39 years	40–44 years	44–59 years	
15–19 years	0·324	0·446	0·405	0·378	0·209	0·140	0·000	8·44
20–24 years		0·395	0·448	0·362	0·364	0·139	0·000	7·55
25–29 years			0·415	0·325	0·333	0·090	0·024	4·90
30—34 years				0·473	0·262	0·066	0·000	2·82
35–39 years					0·320	0·188	0·000	1·74
All ages	0·324	0·428	0·431	0·359	0·319	0·119	0·010	

Source: E. Gautier and L. Henry, *La population de Crulai paroisse normande, étude historique, Travaux et documents de l'INED* cahier n° 33, 1958.

Substitutes

These substitutes would be indices obtained by relating the births of year *y* produced by marriage cohort *x*, to the original size of that cohort, i.e. to the number of marriages of the year *x*; the only inputs are births on the one hand,

Table 6.4 Legitimate fertility rates by woman's observed age and age at marriage (adjusted values): Bourgeoisie of Geneva, marriages of men born 1700–1899

Woman's age at marriage	Woman's observed age							Cumulated fertility
	15–19 years	20–24 years	25–29 years	30–34 years	35–39 years	40–44 years	45–49 years	
15–19 years	0·326	0·338	0·186	0·096	0·040	0·000	0·000	3·73
20–24 years		0·392	0·243	0·130	0·050	0·010	0·000	3·17
25–29 years			0·400	0·235	0·130	0·040	0·000	3·32
All ages	0·326	0·368	0·249	0·149	0·078	0·029	0·000	

Source: L. Henry, *Anciennes familles genevoises étude démographique: XVIᵉ-XXᵉ, Travaux et Documents de l'INED* cahier n° 26, 1956.

and marriages on the other, both extracted from vital registration. These indices have no accepted names. We shall call them net rates, because they combine the influence of fertility with that of mortality and migration, like the net reproduction rate. In summary, these rates fail to remove the influence of disturbing phenomena. This can only be justified to the extent that such influences are weak.

Computation of net rates
Here are various situations that might be encountered. The numerical data are for France with missing data distributed proportionately (in thousands).

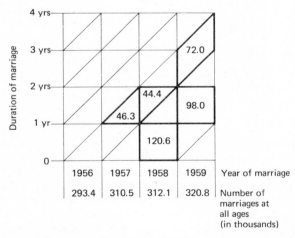

The net fertility rate of the marriage cohort of 1956 at duration 1 (i.e. between first and secondary anniversary of marriage) is equal to:

$$\frac{46\cdot3+44\cdot4}{293\cdot4} = \frac{90\cdot7}{293\cdot4} = 309 \text{ per thousand.}$$

The above rate requires double classification by year of marriage and marriage duration. Even if the tabulation by year of marriage is all there is, a net rate by calendar year can still be computed. The rate for 1959 for the cohort of the 1956 is equal to:

$$\frac{72\cdot0}{293\cdot4} = 245 \text{ per thousand}$$

which corresponds approximately to the duration interval 2·5–3·5.

When births are classified by marriage duration but not by year of marriage, a net rate is obtained by relating births to the average number of marriages for the two relevant cohorts. The latter average is an arithmetic mean for durations of marriage 1 and more. The rate obtained is for duration 1 of a fictitious cohort 1957–8.

$$\frac{98\cdot0}{(310\cdot5+312\cdot1)/2} = \frac{98\cdot0}{311\cdot3} = 315 \text{ per thousand}$$

For the first year of marriage, duration 0, the arithmetic mean is not suitable since the two marriage cohorts involved do not contribute equally to the births. The births, 120·6 in this instance, must be related to a weighted average of the marriages, 310·5 and 312·1. The weights are derived from the proportions, among the births at duration 0 occurring to two equal marriage cohorts, which fall into each year, i.e. the year of observation and the preceding year.[7] In France, that proportion is 1/3 in the year of observation and 2/3 in the preceding year. The desired rate is thus:

$$\frac{120\cdot6}{\dfrac{312\cdot1}{3}+2\times\dfrac{310\cdot5}{3}} = \frac{120\cdot6}{311\cdot0} = 388 \text{ per thousand.}$$

These weights are based on the observations of preceding years for which the double classification is available, or on surveys, or on estimates using first births classified by marriage duration in months.

c) Combined rates

The rates must be combined in order to provide an answer to our second question: in the absence of disturbing factors, what would be the average number of births per women in a given generation, or per marriage in a given marriage cohort? Let us call that number *completed fertility* to eliminate confusion with the average number of children actually observed. The adjective 'completed' indicates both that there is no extraneous influence, and that no further births are to be expected, i.e. the woman has reached the ultimate age of procreation, 50 years for practical purposes. The term cumulative fertility at age x, or by duration x, will be used to designate the number of children born per woman aged less than 50 years—or per marriage of duration such that the woman (or a portion of the women) has not reached 50 years—in the absence of disturbing factors. Under these conditions, the number of women or couples remains the same as at the beginning of the cohort; let us call them respectively F_0

---

[7] This procedure is justified at a later point, in connection with infant mortality.

and M_0. And in addition let $N_0, N_1, \ldots, N_{x-1}$ be the births at each age (starting at 15 years) or at each duration: $0, 1 \ldots x-1$, under the same conditions, i.e. without either mortality or migration.

The total number of children born before exact age x, or before the xth anniversary of marriage, is equal to:

$$N_0 + N_1 + \cdots + N_{x-1}.$$

Cumulative fertility at age x is therefore equal to:

$$\frac{N_0 + N_1 + \cdots + N_{x-1}}{F_0} = \frac{N_0}{F_0} + \frac{N_1}{F_0} + \cdots \frac{N_{x-1}}{F_0}.$$

Under our basic assumption, each term to the right of the equal sign is equal to the overall fertility rates that we have learned to compute. Cumulative fertility at age x for a cohort of women is therefore equal to the sum of the fertility rates for this cohort up to, and including, age $x-1$. Completed fertility is equal to cumulative fertility at 50 years of age.

Similarly, cumulative fertility for a marriage cohort after x years of marriage is equal to the sum of the marital fertility rates for this cohort up to, and including, duration $x-1$. To obtain completed fertility, the summation is continued up to the shortest duration such that all women will have reached 50 years of age.

The following are some examples:

1) Overall fertility
Overall fertility rates are usually obtained from vital registration data, and are normally classified by periods. The first step in longitudinal analysis then consists of shifting from the period classification to a classification by generations or groups of generations. In table 6.5, the numbers read diagonally from upper left to lower right belong to the same group of generations.[8] Our first task is to rearrange them more conveniently, with one line per group of generations. (see table 6.6)

Table 6.5 Period overall fertility rates per thousand women: France, 1891–1935

Period	15–19 years	20–24 years	25–29 years	30–34 years	35–39 years	40–44 years	45–49 years
1891–1895	26	132	169	134	88	38	6
1896–1900	25	137	162	128	86	35	6
1901–1905	27	135	161	119	78	33	5
1906–1910	27	135	147	111	69	27	3
1911–1915	24	119	129	92	61	23	2
1916–1920	14	72	93	75	52	22	2
1921–1925	26	131	142	102	59	22	2
1926–1930	28	130	132	93	54	20	2
1931–1935	30	126	123	85	48	17	2

[8]Strictly speaking, the generations are not absolutely the same across any one diagonal because tabulation by age of the mother was abandoned in 1907 in favour of tabulation by year of birth.

Table 6.6 Cohort overall fertility rates per thousand women: France, generation 1876–1901

Central generation	15–19 years	20–24 years	25–29 years	30–34 years	35–39 years	40–44 years	45–49 years
1876	26	137	161	111	61	22	2
1881	25	135	147	92	52	22	2
1886	27	135.	129	75	59	20	2
1891	27	119	93	102	54	17	
1896	24	72	142	93	48		
1901	14	131	132	85			

Each of these rates represents the *mean yearly number of children* born to women belonging to a certain group of generations at the corresponding ages in the absence of the influence of death and migration.

If we multiply these rates by 5, we therefore obtain the number of children born in 5 years, between the 15th and the 20th birthdays, between the 20th and 25th, and so on, to a cohort of women free from migration and mortality. Cumulative fertility at age 20 is therefore equal to the rate at age 15–19 multiplied by 5; cumulative fertility at 25 is equal to 5 times the rate at age 15–19 plus 5 times the rate at age 20–24 for the same generation, and so on. Cumulative fertility at 5-year intervals for the cohorts represented in the preceding table would be as in table 6.7.

Table 6.7 Cumulative fertility per thousand women: France, generation 1876–1901

Central generation	Cumulative fertility						
	20 yrs	25 yrs	30 yrs	35 yrs	40 yrs	45 yrs	50 yrs
1876	130	815	1620	2175	2480	2590	2600
1881	125	800	1535	1995	2255	2365	2375
1886	135	810	1455	1830	2125	2225	2235
1891	135	730	1195	1705	1975	2060	
1896	120	480	1190	1655	1895		
1901	70	725	1385	1810			

Overall fertility depends on nuptiality, on marital fertility, and to complete the picture, on illegitimate fertility. The first two factors are the most important. Their fluctuations during the war of 1914–18 account for the abrupt decline in fertility and in cumulative fertility, which is most evident for the generations of 1891 and 1896.

Gross reproduction rate:
The female gross reproduction rate is, by definition, equal to completed fertility in daughters. It is obtained by multiplying completed fertility by the proportion of births that are female for the generation in question. For the group centered on the 1876 generation, the gross reproduction rate is:

$$\frac{2600}{1000} \times 0 \cdot 49 \simeq 1 \cdot 27.$$

If we had an estimate of the distribution by age (and hence by generation) of the fathers of illegitimate children, it would be possible to compute a male gross reproduction rate for generations. It would be wrong to assume that this should be equal to the female gross reproduction rate. Suppose that both rates were constant, that all births were legitimate, and that all women had married men who were 5 years older than themselves; then the same number of births would hold for the computation of the reproduction rate for a female generation and for that for the male generation born 5 years earlier. But the size of these generations would not necessarily be the same.

2) Legitimate fertility

Rates by duration:
Here in table 6.8 are the unadjusted data on cumulative fertility at various durations of marriage corresponding to the fertility rates given in table 6.2 (Great Britain, women married between ages 20 and 22·5 in 1919).

Table 6.8 Cumulative fertility by duration of marriage: Great Britain, women married at age 20–22·5 in 1919

Exact duration of marriage	Cumulative fertility
1	0·43
2	0·1
3	1·12
4	1·37
5	1·62
10	2·50
15	3·01
20	3·29

Rates by age:
The legitimate fertility rate at age 15–19 years involves only women married before age 20 years; that observed at age 20–24 years for all ages at marriage combines the fertility of women from two age at marriage groups, 15–19 and 20–24 years. It makes sense to merge these rates only if the women married between ages 20–24 years have the same fertility at those ages as the women married at ages 15–19 years . . . and so on. This condition is certainly not met whenever birth control is fairly widespread.

In that case, cumulation of legitimate age-specific fertilty rates is meaningful only if each age at marriage, or at least each group of ages at marriage, is treated separately. If groups are used, the average number of children ever born should be computed directly for the age group in which marriage takes place. When fertility rates are not related to age at marriage to any significant extent, the fertility rate for all ages at marriage together (times 5 if we are dealing with age groups) cumulated starting from the right, is equal to the mean number of children in the completed family per marriage concluded at age 45, 40 ... 20 years. We can go no further. Between the ages of 15 and 19 years, fertility varies very rapidly with age. The average number of children born within this age span to a woman married at age 15 is not equal to 5 times the average yearly fertility rate between ages 15 and 19. The latter is generally higher because there are very few observations at age 15, 16 or even 17 years. We must be content with an estimate of the completed fertility of women married at age 15–19 years. We add the average number of children born to women married at age 15–19 years before they are 20 years old, to the completed fertility of women married at 20 years. For Crulai, for example, this comes to 0·45. (See table 6.9)

Table 6.9 Fertility rates by age: Crulai

	20–24 years	25–29 years	30–34 years	35–39 years	40–44 years	45–49 years
Rate	0·428	0·431	0·359	0·319	0·119	0·010
Rate × 5	2·140	2·155	1·795	1·595	0·595	0·050
Rate × 5 cumulated	8·330	6·190	4·035	2·240	0·645	0·050

8·330 represents the completed legitimate fertility of a woman married at exactly age 20 years; 6·190 is that of women married exactly at age 25, and so on.

The completed fertility of women married at age 15–19 years is obtained by adding to 8·33 the average number of children born between ages 15 and 20 years to women married at 15–19; that number is 0·45; the completed fertility is therefore:

$$8·33 + 0·45 = 8·78$$

If we wanted to go further and obtain completed fertility of women married at exactly age 15 years, we would have to add to 8·33 the number of births between ages 15 and 20 for women married around their 15th birthday. None were found in the example chosen.

In the second example, in table 6.4, fertility varies with age at marriage. Completed fertility has to be computed separately for each age at marriage group. For women married at age 15–19 years, one adds the rates from ages 20–24 to 45–49 years.

$$0·338 + 0·186 + 0·096 + 0·040 = 0·660$$

The result is multiplied by 5. We add 0·43, the average number of children born between age 15 and 19 years to women married in that age group; the total is 3·73.

Substitutes

When net fertility rates by duration of marriage are all that is available, we compute net cumulative fertility. At marriage duration x, it is equal to the average number of children per marriage born locally between marriage and the xth anniversary of marriage. Let us call the observed births at durations of marriage 0, 1 . . . $x-1$ in years elapsed, N_0', N_1', . . .,N_{x-1}'. If M_0 is the initial marriage cohort size, net cumulative fertility is equal to:

$$\frac{N_0'+N_1'+ \cdots +N_{x-1}'}{M_0} = \frac{N_0'}{M_0}+ \cdots +\frac{N_{x-1}'}{M_0}$$

or, following the above equation, to the sum of the net fertility rates.

The only difference between this result, and the one obtained for cumulative fertility is in the qualification 'net'. Nevertheless, this has some implications which are worth considering. In the ratios N_i'/M_0 above, the births N_i' are births actually observed at duration i in the relevant marriage cohort. In the ratio N_i/M_0, on the contrary, N_i is a hypothetical number of births. N_i'/M_0, in consequence, always equals the net rate, and there is no need to be concerned about the composition of the cohort by age at marriage. But N_i/M_0 is only equal to the gross rate if the fundamental hypothesis is verified; and this logically supposed that age at marriage is the same for all the women. In other words, the sum of the net rates always represents the net cumulative fertility of a marriage cohort, whereas the sum of the rates irrespective of age at marriage represents cumulative fertility only approximately.

Since the births N_1^i . . . are the result of direct observation, it would be possible to compute the net cumulative fertility bypassing the net age-specific rates. It would suffice to add up the observed births from N_0' to N_{x-1}' and divide the sum by M_0 (there is no equivalent for gross cumulative fertility since one has to have the gross rates to obtain the births N_i). In practice, we always do use the net age-specific rates because the vital statistics are published yearly; as each new issue comes out, one computes the net rates and adds them to those of previous years.

Example:
Here in table 6.10 is net cumulative fertility for the marriage cohort of 1949 in France.

Table 6.10 Net cumulative fertility per thousand women: France, marriage cohort of 1949

Duration	Net rate	Anniversary	Net cumulative fertility
0	395	1	395
1	304	2	699
2	244	3	943
3	209	4	1152
4	181	5	1333
5	158	6	1491
6	134	7	1625
7	117	8	1742
8	101	9	1843
9	88	10	1931

If there were no migratory movements, this net cumulative fertility would be equal to the actual cumulative fertility of the marriage cohort of 1949.

D

d) Distribution of births in time: all birth orders

In this instance, a fertility rate by age or duration is equal to the number of births in a horizontal (i.e. not subject to mortality or migration) distribution of ages or durations. The series of fertility rates is therefore a frequency distribution. It would be possible to convert the total to 1000 in order to obtain the relative frequency for the various ages or durations. Usually this is not done, and the distribution is characterized simply by its mean or median value.

In the absence of conventional rates, the series of net rates gives an approximate picture of the frequency distribution when there are no disturbing influences.

Approximations

There were two kinds of approximate solutions for nuptiality:
a) those that gave direct answers to the problems raised by means of retrospective observation
b) those in which age-specific marriage rates were identified with the marriage column of the nuptiality table.

For fertility without distinction by birth order, solution b is identical to the exact solution since the gross rates use the total women of age x or the total remaining marriages of duration x in the denominator. So the only available approximate solutions are provided by retrospective observations in censuses or surveys. The questions asked relate to the number of children (total number, number per couple or number per present marriage), the year or date of marriage and the dates of birth of the children; the number of children and year of marriage are asked in censuses as well as in surveys,[9] but the dates of birth of the children are only asked in surveys (provided the population is sophisticated enough to provide these dates).

An example will show how the situation actually presents itself. In Norway, at the censuses of 1920, 1930, 1940, 1950 and 1960, married women were asked about their number of children in their present marriage, and also about the year of their marriage. The published results include the distribution of women according to year of marriage, age at marriage, by groups of two years of age, and the number of children issuing from the marriage. The absolute figures in table 2.10 reproduce a part of that information relating to women married at age 20–21 years. Let us now consider women married in 1888–90; table 6.11 gives the number of women with a certain number of children ranging from 0 to 18—column (2), the corresponding number of children—column (3), and the distribution given in column (2) converted to a basis of 1000—column (4); dividing the number of children (16 916) by the number of women (2324) gives 7·28. Since the women in question were more than 50 years old in 1950, this

---

[9]Since we have mentioned surveys as sources of the data necessary for the computation of rates, it is important to realize the difference between those surveys that provide the elements of an 'accurate' solution and those that would yield an 'approximate' solution directly. The former kind provides information on all marriages, irrespective of what becomes of them. Family reconstitution from written records belongs in this category. The other kind refers only to some of the marriages, i.e. to those that last to the wife's 50th or at least her 45th birthday, or those that last until the survey. At the least the unions where both spouses have disappeared by the time of the survey will always be missing.

mean can be taken as the completed fertility of the 1888–90 marriage cohorts for ages at marriage 20–21 years.

Table 6.11 Fertility of women married at age 20–21 in 1888–90: Norway

Number of children	Absolute Number of women	Corresponding Number of children	Proportional Number of women
(1)	(2)	(3)	(4)
0	63	0	27
1	64	64	28
2	97	194	42
3	159	477	68
4	163	652	70
5	168	840	72
6	206	1236	89
7	218	1526	94
8	251	2008	108
9	255	2295	110
10	227	2770	119
11	186	2046	80
12	108	1296	46
13	64	832	28
14	22	308	9
15 and over	23	372	10
Total	2324	16916	1000

In contrast to what happens with nuptiality,[10] there is no approximate solution unless the survey or census is addressed to women aged over 50 years. The basic hypothesis actually applies only to the reproductive period; it remains true, or more simply acceptable, for instance, even if after age 50 death hits the very fertile couples selectively to a greater or lesser extent than the others. In fact, mortality after 50 years appears to have little relationship to fertility before that age, so that the approximate solution is certainly acceptable as long as very old women are not interviewed.

The proportion of infertile unions, 27 per thousand, provides an answer to the first question, concerning the probability of avoiding the event in question entirely. It is an exact answer if there is no noticeable difference in mortality, mobility and the frequency of divorce between childless couples and the whole population. This condition is included in the basic hypothesis concerning the number of births undistinguished by order. But if first order births were studied in the same way as first marriages, this condition would no longer be included in the basic hypothesis concerning first order births, and the above solution would be called approximate. In other words, a solution is considered exact if it follows directly from the basic hypothesis, and approximate if another hypothesis is required.

Finally, let us say a few words about a very interesting piece of information, which is easily derived from a survey, but is very difficult to infer from the

[10]In the case of nuptiality, the proportion single at 50 years—the approximate solution—is equal to the probability or remaining single at 50 only if there is no difference in mortality and mobility between single people and the rest. But that condition is not a part of the basic hypothesis.

combination of vital registration and census—the age of the mother at the last birth in completed families. It is interesting because of the insight it offers into the way couples actually utilize the fecund period of marriage, the time during which the woman is still able to bear children. Birth control has been accompanied by a very marked decline in the age at birth of the last child, and it may be considered that this decline and the decrease in the number of children are two of its fundamental characteristics.[11]

Note: Retrospective observation of the marriages remaining in a cohort after the women are well beyond 50 years gives an approximate value of completed fertility only if the age at marriage of the women varies little. This no longer holds if we consider the whole marriage cohort or even the marriages contracted before age 50 in that cohort. Retrospective observation can only be made 35 years later; the youngest women are then 50 years old, and the oldest are 85. Under current mortality conditions, the former represents 93 % of their initial number, the latter 22 % only. It follows that the average number of children computed from answers to a survey is markedly higher than the completed fertility, since the women who married early (and thus have more offspring) will be proportionately much better represented in the survey than at the time of marriage. Completed fertility for a marriage cohort can be obtained from retrospective observation only if we compute a weighted average of the mean number of children per completed family corresponding to each age or group of ages at marriage, taking as weights the proportions married at each age or group of ages at the time of the cohort's origin, i.e. in the year or period when the marriages were contracted (see p. 108).

3 Fertility taking birth order into account

Preliminary remarks

We may conceive of the study of fertility taking birth order into account in two ways:
1 the births of each order *n* are treated as non-renewable events, and each order is subjected to the exact procedures presented in chapter 5 for the study of first marriages
2 fertility without distinction by birth order is studied under the assumption that mortality and fertility are independent. For this to be true, mortality must be identical for the successive stages in the lives of a group of women, whether it be before marriage, between marriage and first birth, or between the first and the second birth and so on, provided age is the same. Otherwise, the women who die during the year would not have the same fertility, if they lived, as those who do live.

If this condition is met, we can study the births of each order in the same way as we studied first marriages in the approximate procedures. The approach to the study of fertility without distinction by order itself assumes that the above condition is met, so it would be illogical to study births taking order into account as if that condition were not met, i.e. as in method (1). Hence, we settle on method (2). This is all the more justified since in practice the study of births

[11]See next chapter, pp. 111–12.

by order concerns only legitimate births and, as a result, mortality differences between single and married women are irrelevant.

Nevertheless there are questions that are specific to each order, as follows: in the absence of mortality and migration, what would be the proportion of women with at least n children who would have a $(n+1)$st birth? Under the same conditions, what would be the distribution of intervals between the nth order birth and later births of order $n+1$? Two analogous questions are raised by the transition from marriage to the first birth; we have already stated the first of these in connection with fertility without distinction by birth order.

There remain differences, however, with the general scheme of study of an event B following from an event A. The questions asked here refer to one or more marriage cohorts and not to cohorts of women giving birth to their nth child during a given year or period. Otherwise we would be in the situation of considering sets of families that would change between one family building stage and the next, as for example the marriage cohort of 1947 and the cohort of women who had their first child in 1948, but do not belong entirely to the 1947 marriage cohort. Besides, birth spacing can hardly be studied independently of the number of children in the family, and we shall in fact take it up in the chapter devoted to the family. In the present chapter, we can leave the second question aside and focus on the first one.

Parity progression ratios

We give the name *parity progression ratio* to the proportion of all families with n children that go on to have at least one more, becoming families of $n+1$ or more children. The conventional symbol is a_n; n may take the value 0, and a_0 refers to the probability of a union not being sterile. Unless otherwise specified, this probability refers to the ideal situation where the marriage will not be broken before the wife reaches age 50. Thus, parity progression ratio is the name given to that proportion yielded by our first question concerning the fertility specific for each birth order. It is usually computed without resorting to rates; as things stand now the rates are not very interesting in themselves, in contrast to age-at-marriage-specific or duration-specific rates computed from births without distinction by order.

Imagine that we have data on marriages for a cohort, classified according to the number of children between marriage and the wife's 50th birthday—in the absence of mortality and migration. It would then be possible to derive the number of marriages that produced 5 births and more and 6 births and more respectively, and the ratio of the latter of these figures to the former would be the parity progression ratio for families with 5 children in that particular marriage cohort, Under our basic hypothesis, an equivalent is to have the above tabulation for the completed families of the cohort, i.e. for marriages that have not been broken by death or divorce before the 50th birthday of the wife.[12] Such a tabulation exists for Norway (table 6.11); the cumulative frequencies in table 6.12 are obtained by adding the proportional numbers, or relative frequencies, in column (4) of table 6.11 from the bottom up.

[12]Since very few women bear children after age 45 years, the limit may be lowered from 50 to 45 years if necessary.

Some interrelationships

Let us call m_n the relative frequency of completed families with n children, and e the average number of children per completed family. a_0 stands for the proportion of families with at least one child and also, if the total number of families is taken as the base, for the number of children of order 1.

The product $a_0 a_1$ represents the proportion of families that have at least 2 children, and under the same conditions as for a_0, the number of children of order 2.

There follows that:

$$e = a_0 + a_0 a_1 + a_0 a_1 a_2 + \cdots + a_0 a_1 a_2 + \cdots a_n + \cdots$$

and that

$$m_n = a_0 a_1 \cdots a_n - a_0 a_1 \cdots a_n a_{n+1}$$
$$= a_0 a_1 \cdots a_n (1 - a_{n+1}).$$

Note 1:
It is necessary to realize that such relationships exist, if only to avoid the all too frequent mistake which comes from treating the various series of indices pertaining to the same phenomenon as independent.

It is also worth remembering that the average number of children can be computed as rapidly by the above formula as by the conventional method. The ratios a_0, a_1 . . . , a_n actually represent the births of order $n+1$, i.e. the frequencies cumulated from the bottom of the table up to row $n+1$. The average number of children is thus equal to the sum of cumulated frequencies, starting with the second; or, for table 6.12:[13]

$$973 + 945 + \cdots + 10 + 12 = 7 \cdot 278 \text{ per thousand}$$

or, after rounding, 7·28 as in table 6.11.

Note 2:
If renewable events of a kind such that the basic hypothesis could not be applied are involved, it would be necessary to study the successive stages leading from entry into the cohort to the first of the renewable events considered, then from that point to the next event, and so on. A probability for the completion of each stage would be determined. This would lead to a series similar to a_0, a_1 . . . a_n.

From that series, one could determine the value corresponding to e, i.e. the mean number of events in the absence of mortality and migration. This mean would be different from the number obtained by adding the rates computed without accounting for order, and also from the mean number of events experienced by people who have reached a great age or the age after which the event in question does not occur any more, if it exists.

Note 3:
The distribution of children born alive for completed families is a classical statistical distribution. The characteristic on which the classification is based is the position at a given time of each component unit making up the whole; it

[13] 12 corresponds to children of order 16 or more.

Table 6.12 Computation of parity progression ratios: Norway, women married at age 20–21 in 1888–90

Number of children	Cumulative frequency	Parity progression ratios
0	1000	973
1	973	971
2	945	955
3	903	925
4	835	916
5	765	906
6	693	872
7	604	844
8	510	788
9	402	726
10	292	592
11	173	
12	93	
13	47	
14	19	
15 and over	10	

Note: Ratios beyond a_{10} have not been calculated owing to the small numbers involved.

has the peculiarity that no component (family) can be found in position n (number of children) unless he was in position $n-1$ before, and that one cannot go back to position $n-1$ after position n has been reached. In all cases like this, the position can be ranked in increasing sequence, by chronological order. The frequency distribution of the final position reached can be analysed by means of probabilities of moving from one stage to the next. These are analogous to parity progression ratios. It is not necessary that the classification criterion be quantitative. Thus, if one neglects retrogression which occurs very seldom, the ranking of civil servants according to hierarchal status at retirement can be studied in this way.

Substitutes

In the annual vital statistics for France, legitimate births are classified according to the year of marriage and according to birth order. Net fertility rates can thus be computed for order n by relating the births of order n to the corresponding marriages. For example, in 1967, 9328 first order births and 23 428 second order births were recorded as issuing from marriages contracted in 1962. Since the latter were 316 900 in number, the net fertility rate for first births in 1967 for the marriage cohort of 1962 is 29·4 per thousand; the second order fertility rate is 73·9 per thousand. The sum of the fertility rates for order 1 gives the average number of children of order 1 per marriage. Likewise, the sum of the fertility rates for order 2 gives the average number of births of order 2.

Similarly, for the cohort of 1947, after 20 years of marriage, i.e. after such a duration that almost all families are completed, we find 763 first order births and 553 second order births per thousand marriages. The net parity progression ratio for childless families would be 0·763 and for families with one child the net parity progression ratio would be 0·725 (553 divided by 763).

7

Other aspects of fertility, the family

1 Other aspects of fertility

The whole of chapter 6 was devoted to the computation and the combination of fertility rates, with and without distinction by birth order. A few figures were mentioned but only as examples without comment. It is time now to present some findings and interpret them. Both physiological factors and behavioural factors enter into the interpretation, the latter acting basically to reduce fertility, principally by means of contraception. We shall therefore have to deal with those factors, but only to the extent that they have a bearing on the analytical problem.

A few results: natural fertility and controlled fertility

Natural fertility refers to the fertility of populations where it is known or presumed that no effective form of birth control is practised. *Controlled fertility* is the fertility of populations which practice birth control effectively. To begin with natural fertility, here are the arithmetic means of 13 series of fertility rates based on all ages at marriage, starting with age group 20–24.[1] (In former times, legitimate or marital fertility at a given age depended little on duration of marriage and therefore on age at marriage.)

Age of woman

	20–24 years	25–29 years	30–34 years	35–39 years	40–44 years	45–49 years
Fertility rate per thousand women	435	407	371	298	152	22
Index	100	93·5	85·3	68·7	34·9	5

The 13 basic series present an undeniable similarity in form, but the levels are very different. At 20–24 years, the extremes are as follows:

Hutterite marriages of 1920–31[2]	0·550
Hindu villages of Bengal 1945–6	0·323

[1] The rate for age 15–19 years is influenced by the age distribution of the marriages in that age group.

[2] An Anabaptist sect of the United States and Canada, which does not practise birth control.

These are in a ratio of 1·7 to 1. A similar ratio (1·76 to 1) is found for the completed fertility of women married at exactly 20 years.

Hutterites	10·9 children
Hindu villages of Bengal	6·2 children

When considering controlled fertility, age at marriage must be taken into account, since fertility at a given age is very different according to whether women have been married for a long or short time. The following series, adapted from data given in a different form, refers to women in Great Britain, married around age 20 years in about 1920.

Age of woman

	20–24 years	25–29 years	30–34 years	35–39 years	40–44 years	45–49 years
Fertility rate per thousand women	320	165	90	50	20	0
Index	100	51·6	28·1	15·6	6·2	0

The corresponding completed fertility is 3·2. Comparison of this series with the preceding one clearly shows the magnitude of the change due to birth control. At the same time as the number of children decreases, the curve of fertility is greatly modified, shifting from a convex to a concave shape (figure 7.1).

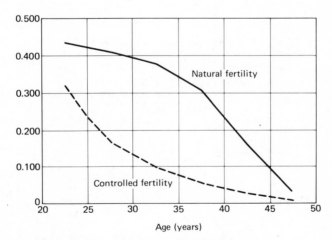

Figure 7.1 Examples of natural and controlled fertility rates

a) The influence of age at marriage

Figures 7.2 and 7.3 below illustrate the data from tables 6.2 and 6.3 concerning, in one case, a Norman village at the end of the seventeenth and in the first half of the eighteenth centuries and, in the other case, Great Britain in the twentieth century. In the historical population, the three curves are, if not overlapping, at

D*

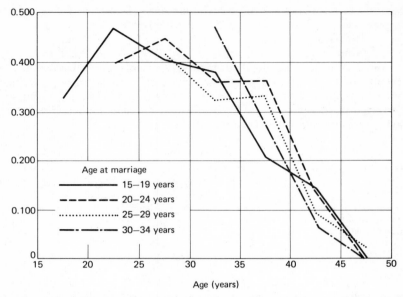

Figure 7.2   Fertility rates by age at marriage in a historical population (natural fertility)

Figure 7.3   Fertility rates by age at marriage in a contemporary population (controlled fertility)

least very little differentiated from one another. This is often the case, and we conclude from it that the influence of age at marriage on fertility is relatively minor under conditions of natural fertility. For the modern population illustrated here, on the contrary, the lag from one curve to the next is very marked. At the same age, fertility is distinctly higher among recently married women than among women who married earlier, and therefore at a younger age.

b) Interpretation

The observed differences, that is changes in the shape of the curve and staggering of the lines, can be explained as consequences of birth control. Let us consider a population under a regime of natural marital fertility that is independent of age at marriage and constant from age 20 to age 40, but nil after that. This fertility is represented by a solid line in figure 7.4. Let us imagine that from a certain time on couples do not want more than a limited number of children, 2 for some and 3 for the rest. As long as the couples don't have the 2 or 3 children that they want, their fertility will be roughly the same as that in the natural regime. From the second or third birth on, depending on the couple, their fertility will be nil, (if the efficiency of contraception is perfect), or at least far lower than that in the natural regime. All the couples will have this very low fertility after sufficient time has passed for them to have had the 2 or 3 children they desire. We shall therefore have fertility curves analogous to those which are pictured by dotted lines in figure 7.4. For two ages at marriage separated by 5 years, we shall have 2 curves, set apart from one another by 5 years, and they represent very different levels of fertility at the same age. Thus, a highly simplified model brings out the essential elements of the changes observed when the shift from natural fertility to controlled fertility occurs, i.e. the change in the form of the curve and the appearance of a marked influence of age at marriage.

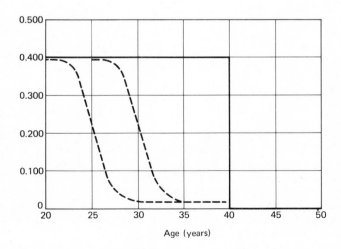

Figure 7.4 Influence of age at marriage on controlled fertility

c) **Completed fertility**

The completed fertility by age at marriage of the wife corresponding to the 13 series is as follows:

Age at marriage	Completed fertility
20 years	8·42
25 years	6·25
30 years	4·21
35 years	2·36

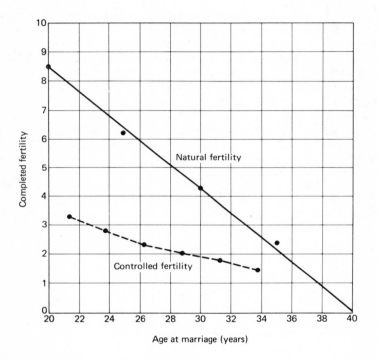

Figure 7.5   Completed fertility and age at marriage

Figure 7.5 shows the points to be in a very nearly linear pattern, and the line fitted to them intersects the horizontal axis at age 40 years. For ages at marriage from 20 to 35 years, it looks as though fertility were constant from marriage to age 40 years and nil after that. The level of fertility from age 20 to 40 years is equal to the fertility rate at age 25 years, i.e. the average of the rates at 20–24 and 25–9 years. This rule does not apply to marriages before age 20 years because of the lower fertility of very young women and sometimes because of the incidence of prenuptial conception.

In Great Britain, the completed fertility of women married in 1919 was as follows:

Age at marriage	Completed fertility
20–22·5 years	3·29
22·5–25 years	2·76
25–27·5 years	2·28
27·5–30 years	2·00
30–32·5 years	1·76
32·5–35 years	1·43

As in the preceding case, we have a decline in completed fertility with the woman's age at marriage, but it does not follow a straight line; if we fit a line to the straight part of the curve, the intersection with the horizontal axis will be far beyond age 40 years. The decline is often interpreted without taking into account the influence of psychological and social factors on the age at marriage and on the desired number of children. It is then attributed to:

1) increasing sterility with age: a woman married at age 25 years has a higher probability of not achieving the number of children she wants to have than a woman married at age 20 years

2) contraceptive failures: a woman married at age 25 years who desires, say, 2 children is exposed for a shorter time to the risk of having one or several more children than she desires than a woman married at age 20 who also wants 2 children.

These two factors do not seem to be sufficient to account for the decline in completed fertility that is actually observed as age at marriage increases. It is likely that the desired number of children is correlated with age at marriage through the influence of psychological and social factors; women who marry earlier also desire or accept more children. There are other reasons as well to believe that the factors enumerated in (1) and (2) are not a sufficient explanation. An overall change in nuptiality in the direction of earlier marriage, such as that which has been occurring in northern Europe over the last thirty years, does not result in increases in the number of children as it should if factors 1 and 2 were the only ones operating. When marriage is delayed due to a war, the fertility of women marrying late, at age 25–9 years, for instance, increases temporarily after the war. Among women marrying at age 25–9 years right after a war there are many who, in normal circumstances, would have married earlier; although held back by events, they have not changed their attitudes as a result. This explains why the fertility of the group aged 25–9 years matched for a few years what it would have been for a group composed of a mixture of women married at 25–9 years and at 20–24 years under normal circumstances.

d) Parity progression ratios

Table 7.1 gives two series for Norwegian women married at age 20–21 years, in 1888–90 on the one hand, and in 1928–30 on the other:

Figure 7.6 illustrates the difference. The complement of a parity progression ratio is the proportion of couples wo do not go on to have another child, either because they become sterile or because they do not want more children. Since it is not likely that sterility has increased, the decrease in the parity progression ratio is essentially the result of the increasing use of birth control in marriage.

Table 7.1 Parity progression ratios:
Norway, selected cohorts of women
married at age 20–21

	Women married in:	
	1888–1890	1928–1930
a_0	0·973	0·966
a_1	0·971	0·841
a_2	0·955	0·702
a_3	0·925	0·653
a_4	0·916	0·597
a_5	0·906	0·625
a_6	0·872	0·597
a_7	0·844	0·623
a_8	0·788	0·616

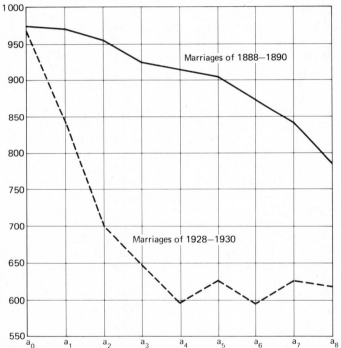

Figure 7.6   Parity progression ratios for women married at 20-21 years: Norway,
selected marriage cohorts

Factors influencing marital fertility

We have now presented a few findings, and we have used them to illustrate
natural fertility and controlled fertility. In the former, there is no conscious
effort to limit the number of children; the number depends only on sexual
intercourse and on physiological factors. In the latter, there is the additional
effect of a particular behaviour pattern, the use of contraception or the resort
to induced abortion.

The distinction between physiological factors and behavioural factors is a necessary one, but it must be further qualified to take into account the fact that physiological factors themselves operate in terms of behaviour; think, for instance, of sexual intercourse, breastfeeding and so on. When we talk about those factors, we do not think of physiological phenomena or behaviour in themselves, but rather of their quantitative and statistical aspects: this is the demographic point of view.

a) Physiological factors

1) A general overview

Since we usually consider only live births when we are evaluating fertility, it is necessary to include intra-uterine mortality among the physiological factors. It is convenient to keep the following factors in mind. We shall come back to this topic in part II, in the course of chapters 14 to 16.

Fecundability:
This is the probability that a married woman will conceive during one menstrual cycle. Fecundability depends, among other things, on a behavioural factor, the frequency of sexual relations. The notion of fecundability was first reserved for those cases where contraception was not practised, but it can be expanded to apply to all cases. For reasons of convenience, the month is often used in place of the menstrual cycle (justification is given in chapter 14).

The probability that a conception will result in a live birth:
This depends on intra-uterine mortality.

The delay in the resumption of ovulation after delivery:
This delay depends statistically on the frequency and duration of breastfeeding, a behavioural factor; it overlaps with another postponement, the delay in resumption of sexual intercourse after delivery, which is also a behavioural factor, and it is the longer of these two delays that should be taken into account. The whole period between conception and the end of the longer of the above delays is called the 'non-susceptible period'.

Total or partial sterility:
A couple is considered sterile when it is henceforth unable to have children. Sterility is total if it exists from the beginning of the marriage, and it is partial if it begins later on, after the birth of one or several children. The proportion of couples which is sterile is clearly an important factor in fertility. In certain models, however, it is not introduced explicitly because it can be accounted for under fecundability. A sterile woman is a woman for whom fecundability is definitively zero. There is also such a thing as temporary sterility; it may prolong the non-susceptible period or it may arise at other times. There is very little information available on this, and it has not been explicitly taken into account up to now, because the non-susceptible period is considered to include the effect of temporary sterility resulting from delivery, and fecundability to account for the other kinds.

If, as is likely, the probability of being temporarily sterile during a cycle depends on the condition during the preceding month, the frequency and duration of temporary sterility should be explicitly introduced. The same is true for the frequency and duration of anovulatory cycles which are merely a special case of temporary sterility. Before doing this however, it is important to be sure that temporary sterility unrelated to delivery plays a sufficient role to merit separate treatment.

Note:

The factors enumerated above are all, more or less, characteristics of the couple. One is often led, however, for the sake of brevity, to talk as if they depended only on the woman.

2) Measurement and numerical values

Fecundability:

When not specified otherwise, this usually means the probability of conceiving in the absence of contraception. Because it varies from one woman to another, it is hard to measure. Its mean value is in the neighbourhood of 0·3 for women aged between 20 and 29 years. The following distribution gives a very approximate idea of the variation in fecundability.

Fecundability	Frequency
0·05	1
0·15	2
0·25	2
0·35	2
0·45	1
0·55	1
0·65	1

The mean of this distribution is 0·32, its standard deviation is 0·179, its coefficient of variation is 0·559. We don't really know how fecundability varies with age of the woman; it is believed that fecundability increases between puberty and some age between 20 and 25 years, maintains a plateau up to 30 years and decreases after that.

Table 7.2 Post partum amenorrhea: Punjab (India)

	Woman's age at end of amenorrhea					
	15–19 years	20–24 years	25–29 years	30–34 years	35–39 years	40 years & over
Mean duration (months)	7·4	9·4	10·7	12·3	12·9	13·5
Standard deviation (months)	5·5	7·6	6·4	6·9	8·8	10·0

Intra-uterine mortality:

Up to now, this has only once been measured absolutely correctly, for a population on one of the Hawaiian Islands (see below, p. 153), but there is reason to believe that the results obtained have fairly general validity. Intra-uterine mortality probabilities were determined for each duration of pregnancy. The probabilities are as follows:

Length of pregnancy* (weeks)	Probability per thousand
4–7	108
8–11	70
12–15	45
16–19	13
20–23	8·5
24–27	3·1
28–31	3
32–35	3
36–39	3·4
40 and over	6·8
Total	237·3

*Counted from last menstrual period

On the basis of other observations, we have established the following evolution by age of woman (20–24 = 100).

Less than 20 years	128
20–24 years	100
25–29 years	119
30–34 years	161
35 years and over	226

The delay in the resumption of ovulation:

This also is not well known, and it is often impossible to distinguish it from the delay in the resumption of sexual relations. A recent study in eleven villages of the Punjab (India) has reported the values in table 7.2 for post partum amenorrhea (absence of menstruation after delivery).

The variation is probably due to the variability of the duration of amenorrhea among women who breastfeed for the same length of time rather than variability in the duration of breastfeeding. The delay in the resumption of ovulation is shorter by about 2 months on the average when the child is not breastfed. After a spontaneous abortion, it is on the order of one month.

Sterility:

Here again there is a paucity of data and, moreover, what there is relates only to historical populations. The average of five series based on European populations is as follows:

20 years	3%
25 years	6%
39 years	10%
35 years	16%
40 years	31%

Definitive sterility compounds the effect of sterility already acquired and that which occurred before the woman had time to conceive. Although it is theoretically easier to measure, it has rarely been observed. The following gives some idea of the orders of magnitude for this series:

20 years	4%
25 years	8%
30 years	12%
35 years	20%
40 years	50%
45 years	95%

b) Behavioural factors

These factors are the following:
1 the frequency of sexual intercourse under normal circumstances
2 sexual taboos at certain times
3 frequency and duration of maternal breastfeeding
4 voluntary efforts to control births by preventing conception or by abortion.

1) Coital frequency

A survey was made in 1957 in the United States among 1165 married couples living in an urban environment, shortly after the birth of their second child.[3] A follow-up study in 1960 succeeded in tracing only 905 of the 1165 couples. The following tabulation gives the distribution of these 905 couples by frequency of sexual intercourse per week:

Times per week	Number of couples
Less than one	48
1	140
1 to 2	142
2	223
2 to 3	81
3	117
3 to 4	60
4	37
More than 4	26
Undetermined	31
Total	905

The delay required for a first conception in months has been shown to vary as follows with weekly coital frequency:

	No contraception	After interruption of contraception
Less than 2 times	11·0	7·1
2 to 3 times	7·1	4·5
3 times and over	6·6	4·4

These observations indicate that fecundability increases with coital frequency as one goes from a low frequency to an average frequency; after that

[3]C. F. Westoff, R. G. Potter Jr, P. C. Sagi and E. G. Mishler, *Family Growth in Metropolitan America* (Princeton University Press, 1961).

the increase is much smaller. Previous observations had offered rather variable results, but none contradictory to these.

2) Sexual taboos

Sexual intercourse while nursing is prohibited among certain populations, particularly in Africa, but it is not always clear whether the rule is observed up to the time when the child is completely weaned or whether it is abandoned earlier. This point should be kept in mind when studies in greater depth are undertaken.

Such taboos have not existed in Europe, but there could have been customs with the same effect; one finds occasional mention of this. It is plausible a priori that they would carry less weight than the taboos referred to above because these populations were monogamous; moreover such customs were not approved by the Church, at least in modern times.

3) The duration of breastfeeding

This is often poorly known, and it is even difficult to define it when weaning takes place over a period of time. One would most like to know the duration of amenorrhea as a function of the duration of nursing but, of course, there is even less information on this point than the preceding one. The duration of breastfeeding is usually lengthy in a primitive population, often more than one year; nevertheless, there are exceptions. Breastfeeding is usually very brief in contemporary developed populations.

4) Birth control

For obvious reasons, there are a good many problems of observation in this area. They are particularly severe as far as illegal abortion is concerned. It is certainly important not to underestimate the extent of the latter practice, but it would also be wrong to exaggerate its importance. In the case of France, very high figures of 800 000 to more than 2 million abortions per year have been quoted. The most serious estimate made by INED[4] in 1966 came to a total of 250 000. In countries where abortion is legal, the number of legal abortions is usually known, but the number of criminal abortions over and above this is always difficult to estimate. It is not easy to make the distinction between induced abortion and spontaneous abortion; one must avoid treating all abortions as induced under the pretext that induced abortion is very common or is believed to be so.

5) Contraception

Efficacy:

Among the various problems that are raised with regard to contraception, efficacy is the only one that has a bearing on demographic analysis. It is tempting to define efficacy by the proportion of those couples using contraception who have no more children than they want. A measurement of this kind actually has no meaning because effectiveness defined in those terms also depends on the length of exposure to the risk of an additional conception.

For instance, with a residual fecundability—that is to say during the period of contraception—of 0·0005 the proportion of successes and failures varies as follows according to the duration of exposure to risk:

[4]Institut National d'Études Démographiques, Paris (translator's note).
[5]When the residual fecundability per month is 0·005, we have:

$$0·74 = 0·996^{60} \qquad 0·55 = 0·995^{120} \qquad 0·40 = 0·995^{180}.$$

Duration (years)	Success %	Failure %
5	74	26
10	55	45
15	40	60

Theoretically efficacy is defined as follows: a contraceptive method is $e\%$ effective if it reduces fecundability to $(1-e)\%$ of its natural value. The figure 0·0005 above has been obtained by assuming a fecundability of 0·25 and an efficacy of 90%. One should remember that efficacy of 90% reduces fecundability to 1/10 of its natural value; efficacy of 98%, to 1/50, efficacy of 99%, to 1/100.

Up to now, however, there has been no attempt to measure the efficacy defined in these terms directly. The usual practice is to give the number of conceptions per 100 years of exposure to risk as an index of efficacy. This index was introduced by R. Pearl in the 1930s. If we designate it by R,

$$R = \frac{\text{Number of conceptions} \times 1200}{\text{Number of months of exposure to risk}}.$$

The result actually depends on the length of the period of observation. For example, table 7.3 shows the values of R at the beginning of marriage as found in the survey quoted above.

Table 7.3 Contraceptive efficacy (R) by length of period of observation

Duration of period of observation	R
One month	42·4
Less than 6 months	37·1
Less than 12 months	35·7
Less than 18 months	30·8
Less than 24 months	29·4
Less than 36 months	27·3
Less than 48 months	26·2

Note: Except for the first figure (one month), the indicated length of time refers to the duration of observation of women who have not yet conceived at the end of 6 months, 12 months . . . 48 months of exposure to risk. For those who do become pregnant, the length of observation goes from the beginning of observation to the end of the month where conception occurs.

R decreases as the duration of exposure to risk increases because the groups obvserved are heterogeneous with respect to residual fecundability. Let us take, for example, an aggregate composed of one group of 1000 couples practising contraception with 100% effectiveness and a second group of 1000 couples with 0·30 fecundability practising 80% effective contraception. Residual fecundability r is nil among the former and is equal to 0·06 among the latter. For this case, the computation of R is shown in table 7.4.

Table 7.4 Number of conceptions for two groups with different fecundability and contraceptive efficacy

Month	Number of couples under observation at beginning of month			Cumulated number	Corresponding conceptions
	1st group	2nd group	Total		
0	1000	1000	2000	2000	60
1	1000	940	1940	3940	116
2	1000	884	1884	5824	169
3	1000	831	1831	7655	219
4	1000	781	1781	9436	266
5	1000	734	1734	11 170	310
6	1000	690	1690	12 860	251
7	1000	649	1649	14 509	390
8	1000	610	1610	16 119	427
9	1000	573	1573	17 692	461
10	1000	539	1539	19 231	493
11	1000	507	1507	20 738	524
12	1000	476	1476	22 214	

The values of R, (R_1, R_6 and R_{12}, for 1, 6 and 12 months of observation, respectively) are as follows:

$$R_1 = \frac{60 \times 1200}{2000} = 36$$

$$R_6 = \frac{310 \times 1200}{11\,170} = 33\cdot3$$

$$R_{12} = \frac{524 \times 1200}{20\,738} = 30\cdot3.$$

By definition, $R_1 = 1200r$, where r is residual fecundability. But it is usually impossible to derive r from the other values of R, in particular for those corresponding to fairly long durations. On the other hand, much information is lost if we limit ourselves to values of R for short durations. A partial solution consists of using a well defined R corresponding to a duration which is neither too short nor too long, namely R_{12}. We should not forget that this convention has been in use for less than 10 years and, therefore, that quoted values of R may well not be comparable among themselves. An approximate relationship between values of R_{12} below a value of 30 and contraceptive efficacy has been established:

R_{12}	Efficacy %
1·5 to 2	99·5
3 to 4	99
6 to 8	98
12 to 21	95
About 30	90

Variation in contraceptive efficacy during marriage:
The same survey cited above gives the value of R_{12} for all contraceptive methods taken together according to the stage of married life and the desired number of children.

Stage of married life	Number of children desired		
	2	3	4 and over
Before the 1st birth	30	37	60
Between the 1st and 2nd births	13	23	32
After the 2nd birth	4	15	22

We see that effectiveness increases as the number of children already born approaches the number wanted, and it becomes very high when that number is reached. The improvement in efficacy is the result of increased vigilance and not of change of method. This is demonstrated by table 7.5 which refers to couples who had used one of the three most effective methods current at the time (condom, diaphragm or withdrawal) from marriage to the time of the survey.

Table 7.5 Contraceptive efficacy of couples at various stages of married life

Stage of married life	Number of children desired			Number of children desired		
	2	3	4 & more	2	3	4 & more
	R_{12} index			Efficacy in %		
Before first birth	21	27	46	90 to 95	90	less than 90
Between the 1st and 2nd birth	8	14	16	98	95	95
After the 2nd birth	3	16	13	99	95	95

The finding is very significant because it provides insight into what is going on or might be going on. In the light of this, it seems less surprising that contraception was effective in the past, even though it was practised without mechanical or chemical aids. (In France, contraceptive practice was widespread in rural areas as early as the Revolution and perhaps even before.) This result also explains why the proportion of couples having more children than they want is rather small, even though the *average* effectiveness of contraception is too low to be responsible for such results.

2 The family

Introduction

In this second part of chapter 7 we turn to family formation. As is customary, we follow the reverse of the chronological order. We start with the final result, the number of children, and then proceed to examine how this was achieved.

a) Family statistics

In France, a whole collection of census data falls under the term *family statistics*. Coming as they do from this source, we realize that these are statistics on population structure related to a particular topic, the family.

The family can be defined in several ways. Statisticians are only concerned with those definitions where the *family* designates a group of people consisting of parents and children, including cases where there are no children and cases where the parental couple has been reduced to only one person by disruption of the union, either through death or divorce. Even so, several definitions must be considered. In a statistical sense, the family may consist of:

1 the parents and all their live-born children, including those who have died as well as those who are still alive at the time of the census
2 the parents and their surviving children at all ages or under a certain age
3 the parents and their dependent children
4 the parents and their children living at home.

The first definition is closely related to fertility. In some English-speaking countries, such statistics are even put under the heading of 'fertility of marriages'. The second definition depends on fertility, on the distribution of births in time within the family, and on mortality among the children. The third definition depends either on the de facto economic emancipation of the children, or on their legal status, the latter being a more or less accurate translation of the former. The fourth definition is closely related to the statistical treatment of households and dwellings.

In what follows, we shall be concerned exclusively with the two first definitions, and more with the first one than with the second. In other words, we shall look at the family as the result of a process; it is this very process which the study of fertility investigates in its various aspects.

b) Vital registration, census and survey

In a closed population, it is possible to reconstitute families on the basis of vital registration alone.[6] We know from these data the history of all the families from their formation at the marriage of the parents, to a certain date such as that of a survey of a census, to the end of the union, or to the disappearance of the parental couple at the death of both spouses. Theoretically, a survey could provide the same total of information for surviving couples (if the survey relates only to married women), or for those couples where at least the wife is still alive, or for all the couples where at least one spouse is alive. A survey therefore always leaves out some of the unions, at the least those where the death of both the husband and the wife has removed the couple from observation. The survey is biased, therefore, to the extent that there is a connection between fertility and the disturbing phenomena of mortality and divorce. This connection could exist if, for instance, the couples most exposed to divorce were also those that desired fewer children. The bias is not necessarily very important, and we know that it can be ignored in the case of natural fertility. We are less well informed concerning present times because we do not have adequate observations. The respondents' lapses of recall, their carelessness or negative attitude and errors

[6]This possibility has been realized only for small populations. For very large populations, it remains a theoretical possibility because the financial resources are not available to carry it out.

of observation add to the biases already present. A survey must be planned to take such factors into account.

c) Family composition

This is described at any given moment in terms of the number of children and their age. In the case of our first definition, the one closely identified with fertility, it is preferable to talk about number of children or family size, about intervals between marriage and births, and about intervals between births. These essential data may refer to families which are:

in formation: a surviving union where the wife is less than 50 years of age

terminated: 1) a union broken before the wife was 50 years old
2) a union broken after the wife reached 50 years of age
3) a surviving union where the wife is older than 50 years of age.

The families under categories (2) and (3) are called completed families. The number of children in terminated families is considered the *final number* or the *final size*.

Number of children

From census reports we obtain only a classification of families according to the number of children they had up to the census date. They constitute completed

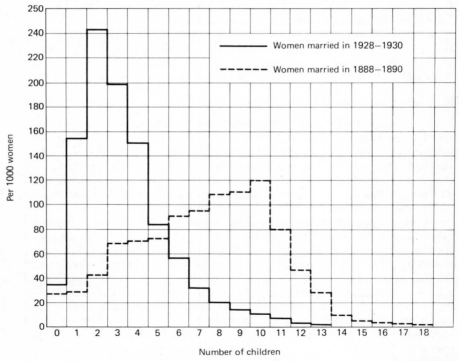

Figure 7.7   Completed families by number of children born for women married at 20-21 years: Norway, selected marriage cohorts

families when the wife is married and more than 50 years of age. The classification is most valuable when it is cross-tabulated by the wife's age at marriage.

Table 2.10 gave the distribution of women married at age 20 and 21 years according to the year of their marriage and the number of live births resulting from that marriage, in absolute numbers and per thousand marriages of the same year (Norway, census of 1920). These data, and a similar set extracted from the 1960 census are illustrated in figure 7.7.

A survey may include a question on the date of birth of the children, and on the basis of this information the number of children born by various durations of marriage can be determined for each family. This was done in Great Britain for the 1946 survey. Table 7.6 presents the proportional distribution according to the number of live births for various marriage durations for women married between exact ages 25 and 27·5 years in 1920–24. These families may be considered completed in 1946, since the youngest women were then 46 years old.

On the basis of this table, the average number of childern per family can be computed to begin with. This is shown in table 7.7. It is interesting to see what proportion of the average final number had already been reached by each duration. This proportion is given in the column to the right. It illustrates the fact

Table 7.6 Distribution of women by marriage duration and number of children ever born: Great Britain, 1946, women married between age 25 and 27·5 in 1920–24

Duration of marriage	Number of children									
	0	1	2	3	4	5	6	7	8	All
1 year	716	270	12	2						1000
2 years	451	500	44	5						1000
3 years	340	506	140	13						1000
4 years	278	467	216	35	3	1				1000
5 years	237	430	253	69	10	1				1000
10 years	164	315	288	138	58	26	8	2	1	1000
15 years	151	285	277	149	69	34	19	9	7	1000
Final	150	282	273	148	70	35	20	11	11	1000

Table 7.7 Average number of children per family: Great Britain, 1946

Duration of marriage	Average number	% of final average number
1 year	0·30	15
2 years	0·60	30
3 years	0·83	41
4 years	1·02	50·5
5 years	1·19	59
10 years	1·74	86
15 years	1·97	97·5
Final	2·02	100

that wanted births are concentrated at the beginning of marriage in contemporary populations. Half the total number of children are born during the first four years of marriage; in the absence of birth control, the corresponding proportion would have been on the order of 30%.

a) Average number of children per family

We are interested above all in the average number of children per completed family. This number generally varies with age at marriage, so it is necessary to be careful when analysing the differences in the average number of children per marriage based on all ages at marriage together for marriage cohorts with marked differences in age at marriage. Along the same lines, one must be careful to take into account selection due to the ageing of a marriage cohort when analysing data collected by retrospective observation. This bias is studied in more detail in the next section.

Because of the insignificant difference between the average number of children per family and *completed fertility* when age at marriage is held constant, what has been said before about *completed fertility* and its variation with age at marriage applies just as well to the average number of children per completed family. Hence it is unnecessary to repeat the point.

b) An error to be avoided

Let's go back to the 1946 survey in Great Britain. The average number of children per completed family for women married in 1890–99 under 45 years of age who were interviewed in the survey is 4·34. But the proportion of women who had married young was much higher by 1946 than during the period of their marriage, since the ones marrying older would almost all have been dead before 1946. The extraneous influence of mortality must be eliminated if we want to make comparisons. One way of doing so is to compute the average number of children per completed family that would hold without mortality. This can be done by calculating the weighted mean of the average number of children per completed family for each category of age at marriage; the weights are the relative frequencies of the various ages at marriage *at the time of marriage itself*. The computations are given in table 7.8. The average corrected number is 4·0 instead of 4·34.

c) Number of brothers and sisters

The number of children in a family is closely connected with the number of brothers and sisters of each of the children, in that it exceeds the latter by a constant number equal to one. Because of this relationship, it is tempting to conclude that the two notions are equivalent except for the difference of one. This can be either true or false depending on how one envisages the equivalence. We need to be more precise.

The family is a (primary) statistical unit characterized, among other things, by the number of children. Those among the children who survive to the time of a survey are different (secondary) statistical units, and they can be interviewed concerning the number of their brothers and sisters, or even

Table 7.8 Weighted average number of children per completed family: Great Britain, 1946

Age at marriage	Average number of children	Frequency of ages at marriage in 1890–1899	Corresponding number of children
Less than 20 years	5·86	100	586
20–24 years	4·43	530	2348
25–29 years	3·24	250	810
30–34 years	2·51	80	201
35–39 years	1·59	30	48
40–44 years	0·89	10	9
Total	4·34	1000	4002

concerning the number of children born to their parents. This would be done in order to answer the type of questions which asks whether successful men, or college students, or members of religious orders, are more or less likely than others to come from large families.

To answer such a question, it would normally be necessary to interview the members of the group being studied as well as others; at least a representative sample from each source should be considered.

In practice we would like to save the expense of a survey among the 'others'. They are more or less indistinguishable from the population at large, and it does not seem far fetched to use the published family statistics for them. But if care is not taken, this can lead to a serious error, that of comparing the average value obtained for a characteristic with a certain distribution of interviewed units, to the average value for this characteristic in an aggregated unit with a completely different distribution. On the one hand, we have the average number of children per family obtained from a sample of families and, on the other hand, the same average number obtained from a sample of children. Would one think of making such a comparison between the distribution of French cities according to the number of their inhabitants and the distribution of inhabitants of France according to the size of cities where they live?

Example:
The following example will help to explain the risks involved. Let us imagine we have interviewed 850 heads of family on the one hand and the children of these families on the other hand, and that they are distributed as follows:

Size of the family	Heads of family	Children
1	282	282
2	273	546
3	148	444
4	70	280
5	35	175
6	42	252
Total	850	1979

The average number of children per family is equal to 2·33 (1979/850) whereas the average number of children in the families into which the children were born is higher (3.14). The difference is simply due to the fact that a family is represented by as many children as it contributed to the population of 1979 children. A way of avoiding confusion between the two averages is to give them different names. 2·33 is the average number of children per family having at least one child. 3·14 is the average number of children in the family of origin of the respondents.

How can this problem be resolved? One way of by-passing the issue is to convert the sample of children into a sample of families by keeping only those children which have a certain characteristic; thus, there can be one, and only one child per family having this characteristic, and each family has the same probability of having a child with this characteristic. This is the case for the first and the last child. A question of birth order should therefore always be included. But this solution has the drawback of mixing effects which pertain to family size with those which are due to birth order. When the effect of order is approximately linear, we avoid this drawback by including both the first and the last child (counting single children twice in the process). If the effect is not linear, it might be better to accept the situation as one of those cases where a mistake in the observation technique cannot be corrected by clever analysis.

Important note:
The double condition mentioned at the beginning of the preceding paragraph is essential. Age alone could not satisfy it. If we exclude twins, who are rare enough to be ignored, a family can have no more than one child who is 10 years old. But the probability of one family having a child of 10 years old is not the same for families of all sizes: it increases with the number of children.

This can be illustrated in a simplified example. In a certain stationary situation, families are distributed as follows according to the final number of children:

1 child	20
2 children	30
3 children	30
4 children	10
5 children	10

The birth intervals, expressed as the difference between the birth dates (in calendar years) and assumed to be unvarying, are as follows:

Interval 1–2	2 years
Interval 2–3	3 years
Interval 3–4	3 years
Interval 4–5	3 years

The children born in 1950 are surveyed in 1960. They are distributed as shown in table 7.9 according to birth order and number of children in the family in 1960. The average number of children achieved per family is 2·6. But the average size of the family of origin of the children is 3·12, despite the fact that future families of 5 whose eldest child is 10 years old in 1960 have not yet terminated childbearing.

Table 7.9 Number of children born in 1950, by birth order and number of children in the family in 1960: hypothetical survey

Number of children in 1960	Birth order					Total
	1	2	3	4	5	
1	20					20
2	30	30				60
3	30	30	30			90
4	20	10	10	10		50
5		10	10	10	10	40
Total	100	80	50	20	10	260

The family building period

The family building period is of interest only for completed families. It is defined as the lapse of time between marriage and the last birth, and it should therefore be studied by looking at duration of marriage at the time of the last birth. Up to now this kind of study has not been done. In existing research only the age of the wife at the birth of the last child has been considered, and even that has been done only a few times since the data can be assembled only in a survey.

Age at birth of last child

Age at marriage must be taken into account without fail in a study of this subject because a woman who marries at a given age, 25 years for example, cannot have had her last child before that age, whereas this is possible for women who married earlier. For practical purposes, we consider only women married before 30 years of age and classify them in two or three groups according to their age at marriage.

Table 7.10 presents some observations made in Sainghin-en-Mélantois, a village in the north of France.

Although there are no observations on age at the birth of the last child for contemporary populations in developed countries, there is reason to believe that on average it is fairly low, of the order of 30 years, for instance, and that birth control has led both to a decrease in the number of births and to a very serious reduction in the period of time required for family building, and hence in age at the birth of the last child. This is the result that would be expected with the use of very effective contraception if the number of births decreases without much change in spacing. The surveys on attitudes show that the intervals between wanted pregnancies scarcely exceed those observed in the absence of family limitation when breastfeeding was the rule

The series below which refers to the upper classes in Geneva, gives an idea of the evolution of the average age at the birth of the last child when marital fertility is voluntarily reduced. This series is for women married at 20–24 years.

Husband's date of birth	Mean age at birth of last child
Before 1600	38·7
1600–1649	38·2
1650–1699	34·4
1700–1799	31·9
1800–1899	31·7

The average number of children per completed family, which was nearly 8 for women with a husband born between 1600 and 1649, dropped to a little more than 3 for those whose husbands were born between 1700 and 1899.

Table 7.10 Mother's age at birth of the last child for completed families: Sainghin-en-Mélantois

	Number of last births at indicated age			
Mother's age	Women married before 1770		Women married in 1770–1829	
	At 20–24 years	At 25–29 years	At 20–24 years	At 25–29 years
25 years	—	—	1	—
26 years	—	—	—	—
27 years	—	—	3	1
28 years	—	—	—	1
29 years	—	—	—	1
30 years	—	—	—	—
31 years	—	—	1	1
32 years	—	—	1	2
33 years	—	—	1	1
34 years	—	—	3	1
35 years	—	1	2	3
36 years	1	3	4	6
37 years	1	1	—	3
38 years	—	3	5	3
39 years	1	1	2	2
40 years	2	1	4	9
41 years	4	5	6	4
42 years	2	5	5	10
43 years	4	2	6	5
44 years	4	4	2	8
45 years	1	2	2	2
46 years	—	—	—	3
47 years	1	—	—	1
Total	21	28	48	67
Mean age	42·4	41·2	38·8	40·1
	41·7		39·6	

4 Birth spacing

A family is characterized by a number of births and the distribution of these births in time. So it is not sufficient to study family size; we must also look at the intervals. Several aspects of this topic deserve attention, such as intervals from marriage to each successive birth and intervals between births including the interval between marriage and the first birth. This last aspect is the one most often investigated.

a) The interval between marriage and the first birth

This must be studied for unions of fairly long duration, the more so when dealing with populations which practise birth control extensively. Five years is acceptable as a minimum duration for historical populations, 10 years for modern populations. The age at marriage of the woman must be taken into account as far as possible.

1) Premarital conceptions

Their frequency is a cultural characteristic that should not be neglected. Because the duration of pregnancy is variable, premarital conceptions can only be distinguished from others in an approximate way. Since the compensating errors are about equal, the best solution is to consider as premarital those conceptions resulting in a birth after less than 8 months of marriage, that is to say within marriage duration of 0 to 7 completed months.

Example:

The first births of women married at 20–29 years in 1790–1829 in Sainghin-en-Mélantois (Nord) are distributed by marriage duration as follows:

Duration of marriage (completed months)	First births	
0	17	
1	11	
2	9	
3	13	
4	19	}89
5	10	
6	6	
7	4	
8	11	
9	13	
10	18	
11	11	
12 and over	39	
Total	181	

The percentage of premarital conceptions is 49·2 (89:181).

2) Other first births

A separate study of births occurring after 8 months or more of marriage is always interesting: under primitive conditions, this sheds light on the relationship between the distribution of these births, fecundability, and intra-uterine mortality; and in a Malthusian situation, the distribution depends as well on the proportion of couples using contraception and on the efficiency of contraceptive practice. The following is an example, for women married at 20—29 years in 1740—99 from three villages in Ile-de-France:[7]

[7]J. Ganiage, 'Trois Villages d'Ile-de-France au XVIIIe Siècle', *Travaux et documents de l'INED* (1963), **40**, 147 pp.

Duration of marriage (completed months)	First births	Duration of marriage (completed months)	First births
8	10	21	1
9	22	22	—
10	19	23	3
11	13	24	4
12	16	25	2
13	8	26	—
14	8	27	1
15	9	28	1
16	4	29	—
17	2	30	—
18	6	31 and over	3
19	2		
20	—	Total	134

Detail of 31 and over: 32, 33, 38

When the average interval is computed, the result is

$$\frac{1792}{134} + 0\cdot5 = 13\cdot4 + 0\cdot5 = 13\cdot9.$$

For historical populations, it is also common to compute the proportion of these births occurring before the first anniversary of marriage. In this case, it is equal to 64/134, or 48%.

3) All first births
The average interval between marriage and the first birth is computed in the same way.

b) Intervals between births
The computation of such intervals must be based on completed families as much as possible or, at least, on families of duration 8 to 10 years beyond the first of two successive births in order to avoid the bias introduced by truncation of the distribution owing to disruption of marriage. It is possible to determine the distribution of an interval, between the second and third birth for instance, for all families having births of the considered order—in the present case, for families with three or more children. But this procedure leads to the following relationship between the interval and the final size of the family:

Interval	Final size
1–2	2 and over
2–3	3 and over
3–4	4 and over
4–5	5 and over
5–6	6 and over

As the final family size is correlated with the intervals, the difference between intervals 1–2 and 2–3, for instance, will be influenced both by birth order and by the final family size. Since it is the task of analysis to separate the influence of the various factors as much as possible, we must isolate the effect of order from that of the final family size. Otherwise, we would be exposed to serious errors of interpretation.

1) Final size and intervals

The families to be investigated are first differentiated by the final number of children. It might be tempting to attribute such differences simply to differences in the duration of exposure to the risk of conception, differences in the ability to conceive, and differences in behaviour. This would be forgetting that family building may be seen as a random process; in this kind of process, chance produces differentiation which has no cause or has causes unrelated to the phenomena being investigated. If we don't take the effect of chance into account, we are in the same position as those who conclude that the winners of a lottery had a better chance of winning than the others from the start.

Example:

This effect of chance can only be isolated in a mathematical model. In the following, families of equal capacity are subjected during approximately 18 years to constant conditions (constant fecundability, constant non-susceptible period, zero intra-uterine mortality, zero sterility during 73 calendar quarters, but total sterility thereafter).[8] The distribution of 10 000 families according to the final number of children would be as follows:

7 children	15
8 children	523
9 children	4463
10 children	4887
11 children	112
Total	10 000

The average interbirth intervals are constant in each size-class of family, so there must be an interval characterizing each class; its value is as follows:

Number of children	Characteristic interval (months)
7 children	29·25
8 children	27
9 children	24·8
10 children	23·0
11 children	21·5
Mean	24·0

The data included in the model ensure that the average interbirth interval does not vary with birth order; none of the fundamental functions vary over the duration of 73 quarters.

Nevertheless, different results are obtained if we compute the average interbirth intervals for all families:

[8]See *Population* (1960), **2**, pp. 261–82.

E

Intervals	Mean length (months)
1–2 to 6—7	24·0
7·8	24·0
8–9	23·8
9–10	22·9
10–11	21·5

The average interval decreases as order increases from the point when the births of the relevant order pertain only to a portion of the families. This decrease does not stem from the influence of order which has been excluded by our hypothesis. It is the result of a kind of statistical artifact: the average values above are the means for the proper intervals, but with weights which vary from intervals 7–8 on. Thus, interval 8–9 is equal to the average of the relevant intervals, that is to say those of the families with 9, 10, and 11 children; and families with 7 and 8 children are excluded.

$$23 \cdot 8 = \frac{24 \cdot 8 \times 4463 + 23 \cdot 0 \times 4887 + 21 \cdot 5 \times 112}{9462}$$

2) Two findings

To begin with, table 7.11 gives mean intervals, in months, according to the order and the final family size for a group of completed families with at least five children, based on data extracted from various historical monographs. These families originated in marriages celebrated from the last quarter of the 17th century up to about 1780.

Table 7.11 Mean intervals (in months) by birth order and final family size: selected historical populations

Total number of children	Number of families	Intervals between births of order										
		1&2	2&3	3&4	4&5	5&6	6&7	7&8	8&9	9&10	10&11	11&12
5	61	24·6	28·5	32·9	39·8							
6	76	24·9	28·3	31·8	32·6	39·9						
7	60	22·2	26·9	27·1	28·8	33·0	39·2					
8	80	22·8	25·6	25·4	27·3	28·4	30·3	37·2				
9	52	20·9	24·2	23·4	26·1	25·9	26·3	30·6	38·1			
10	41	20·1	22·5	24·6	25·4	22·4	24·6	24·8	29·2	34·9		
11	36	19·5	21·8	21·4	22·8	25·0	24·1	24·7	24·3	29·4	30·4	
12	20	18·5	20·8	20·9	23·9	22·7	19·7	20·7	20·7	26·1	25·0	28·9

Table 7.12 refers to completed families for women aged between 45 and 54 years at the time of a survey taken in France in 1954 in connection with the census.

Although the two examples represent very different populations, there is a certain similarity between the two series of curves (figures 7.8 and 7.9). For the historical population, the increasing length of interval with order was probably only a result of the evolution of the fundamental functions of fecundability, the non-susceptible period, and intra-uterine mortality related to the age of the women rather than to birth order. The physiological factors mentioned above

Table 7.12 Mean intervals (in months) by birth order and final family size: France, 1954

Final number of children	Number of families	Intervals between births of order						
		1 and 2	2 and 3	3 and 4	4 and 5	5 and 6	6 and 7	7 and 8
2	8950	61·2						
3	5200	42·0	64·0					
4	2960	33·6	45·5	60·7				
5	1660	27·9	35·9	44·0	56·7			
6	1000	24·4	30·0	33·4	39·5	51·9		
7	610	23·3	26·4	29·8	32·3	36·6	45·5	
8	360	22·2	24·6	26·4	27·8	30·9	34·1	42·7

still play a certain role in the more recent results, most of all for large families. To these must be added the number of children wanted, the desired spacing, and the efficacy of contraception between wanted pregnancies and after the last wanted birth. In this instance, the behavioural factors are much more closely linked to birth order than to age, but in such a way that the results follow not dissimilar patterns.

3) The instance where there are few observations
When there are too few observations to permit cross-classification by birth order and final size, it is possible to proceed as follows for families of sufficient size (6 children and more, for example). Each mean interval starting with

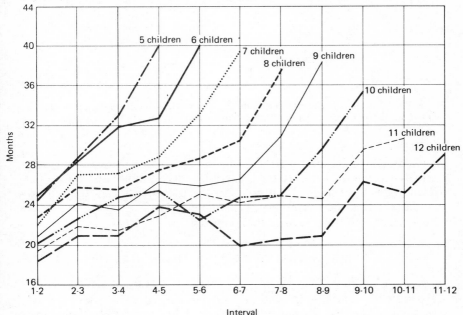

Figure 7.8 Intervals between births according to birth order and number of children in the completed family: historical populations

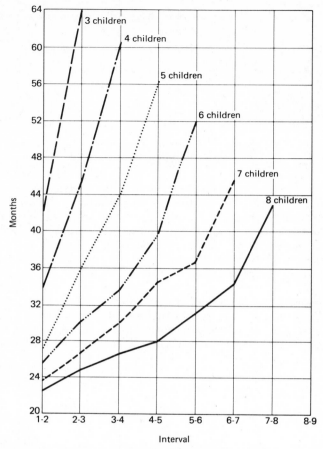

Figure 7.9   Intervals between births according to birth order and number of children in the completed family: contemporary population

interval 1–2 is computed for the entire group of families excepting those intervals which involve the last birth, e.g. 5–6 in the example cited. Subsequent to that, the average intervals are computed in reverse order starting with the last one: the last, the next to last, the second to last.

This leads to a table such as the following:

Interval						
1–2	2–3	3–4	4–5	Second to last	Next to last	Last
24·1	26·9	27·7	31·3	32·0	31·9	39·7

To present this table graphically, the average number of births per family of 6 children and more is computed; here it is equal to 7·6. The three last intervals are located as if they corresponded to intervals 4·6–5·6, 5·6–6·6, 6·6–7·6 (figure 7.10).

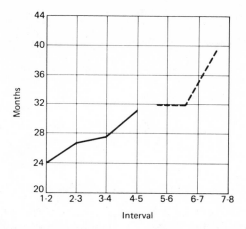

Figure 7.10 Intervals between births when the number of observations is small

4) Interpretation of the result

In the above method, each family receives an equal weight. Therefore, there is no relation between the birth order considered and the final size of the family.

The resulting relationship, showing a very sudden increase between the penultimate and the last interval, certainly has general validity. If this were the only calculation of this sort, there would be no justification for believing that it applies to every size of family, except as a hypothesis to test. But since a number of observations and models have shown that the variation of the mean interval with birth order follows the same trend for all family sizes, it is legitimate to accept this finding for any final size of 6 children or more.

5) Duration of marriage and intervals

In each family, the duration of marriage up to the birth of order n, D_n, is equal to the sum of intervals i_0 (marriage to first birth), i_1 (interval 1–2) ... i_{n-1} (interval n–1–n)

$$D_n = i_0 + i_1 + \cdots + i_{n-1}$$
$$D_n = D_{n-1} + i_{n-1}.$$

This last equality is true for means based on families with n children and also for families with n or more children but only up to the nth order birth. If all the families with $n-1$ or more children are taken together, it is no longer true, since D_{n-1} then relates to all the families whereas i_{n-1} exists only for families with n children and more. As a result, it is not correct to compute the average interval between births by taking the differences between the average durations D_n based on the whole collection of families having children of order n.

For the example using the mathematical model above, the average durations and the differences between the average durations are as follows:

Order	Average duration of marriage (months)	Differences (months)
1	13·5	
2	37·5	24
3	61·5	24
4	85·5	24
5	109·5	24
6	133·5	24
7	157·5	24
8	181·4	23·9
9	203·8	22·4
10	218·9	15·1
11	225·5	6·6

After 9 children, the series of differences declines very fast and terminates with impossible values for birth intervals; the children of order 10 are actually followed by a child of order 11 more often if the duration of marriage at the time of their birth is shorter.

When the intervals i_n between births n and $n+1$ are kown for all families with $n+1$ or more children, together with the parity progression ratios a_{n1}, it is possible however to compute the average duration of marriage to a last birth of order $\bar{D}_{n,0}$.

Since the mean duration of marriage $\bar{D}_{n+1}$ for all births of order $n+1$, and $\bar{D}_{n,+}$ for births or order n which are not the last, it is always true that:

$$\bar{D}_{n+1} = \bar{D}_{n,+} + \bar{i}_n \tag{1}$$

where $\bar{i}_n$ is the mean interval between the nth and $(n+1)^{\text{th}}$ birth in families with more than n children.

On the other hand, we have

$$\bar{D}_n = a_n \bar{D}_{n,+} + (1-a_n) \bar{D}_{n,0}. \tag{2}$$

This relation tells us that $\bar{D}_n$ is a weighted mean of average durations combining two groups of families having at least n children: those families that will go on (proportion a_n) and those that stop at n (proportion $1-a_n$).

Formula (1) allows the computation of the series of $\bar{D}_{n,+}$ if we know the series of $\bar{D}_n$ and that of $\bar{i}_n$. The following example uses the data given for the model used before.

n	$\bar{D}_{n+1}$	$\bar{i}_n$	$\bar{D}_{n,+}$
6	157·5	24·0	133·5
7	181·4	24·0	157·4
8	203·8	23·8	180·0
9	218·9	22·9	196·0
10	225·5	21·5	204·0

Since $\bar{D}_{n,+}$ is known, the following relation (3) results from formula (2);

$$\bar{D}_{n,0} = \frac{\bar{D}_n - a_n \bar{D}_{n,+}}{1-a_n}. \tag{3}$$

Hence the following computation for $D_{n,0}$:

n	$\bar{D}_n$	a_n	$a_n\bar{D}_{n+}$	$D_n - a_n D_{n,+}$	$1 - a_n$	$\bar{D}_{n,0}$
6	133·5	1000	133·5	0	0	indet.
7	157·5	0·998 5	157·2	0·3	0·001 5	200·0
8	181·4	0·948	170·6	10·8	0·052	207·7
9	203·8	0·528	103·5	100·3	0·472	212·5
10	218·9	0·022	4·5	214·4	0·978	219·2
11	225·5	0·000	0	225·5	1·000	225·5

Replacing $\bar{D}_{n,+}$ by its value computed from (1) we can write (3) under the form

$$\bar{D}_{n,0} - \frac{\bar{D}_n - a_n(\bar{D}_{n+1} - i_n)}{1 - a_n} = 0. \tag{4}$$

In this form, the equation shows that the five values, $\bar{D}_n$, $\bar{D}_{n,0}$, $\bar{D}_{n+1}$, i_n and a_n are not independent but are formally related.

This relation is always valid and permits the computation of $\bar{D}_{n,0}$ which is not usually observed directly, from the four other values that are more frequently observed.

8

Comparisons: Cross-sectional analysis and synthesis

Let us consider one kind of observation, such as the annual number of births, for two populations.

The number observed depends on several factors:

1 background factors
2 the local setting (space) or temporal setting (time)
3 the size and composition of the population or, in short, size and structure.

Ordinarily one would take two populations with a common background. Examples might be a common civilization, state of advancement in medicine and hygiene, or an unchanging physiological characteristic. Then any differences observed would be the result of differences in the spatial or temporal setting and differences in size and structure. In chapter 3, we saw how the effect of size could be eliminated by converting to a standard population base of 1000 or 10 000. In doing this, we were replacing an absolute number by a rate, which preserved the simplicity of the unadjusted data. We now need to eliminate the effect of structure, again without losing the obvious simplicity of the comparison between two figures. To accomplish this, the following problem must be solved: to distinguish in the difference between the two rates that which is due to their different settings in space and in time from that which emanates from their different structures. This must be done in such a way that, after elimination of the structural effect, the comparison can be presented in terms of two numbers.

1 The usual procedure

The problem that has just been described cannot be solved if we insist on a solution that is simultaneously both rigorous and simple. If rigor is maintained, then we must accept a comparison between two series of indices with all the ensuing complications. Otherwise, we have to give up rigour, which means being content with a solution that is valid only under certain conditions. The effect of size can be eliminated, as we have seen, by using rates that involve conversion to a standard base size. In a similar way, the effect of structure can be eliminated by converting to a standard population structure. But whereas in conversion to a standard size, the result does not depend on the size chosen, the same cannot be said for a standard structure. The result does vary with the structure chosen, although not much if one stays with common structural types.

Conversion to a standard structure is known mostly under the term population standardization, but many methods of comparison in current use boil down to this.

First example

At the time of selection, future recruits are subjected to a series of tests and receive a score reflecting their 'general level of intelligence'.[1] In France, there is an average score for each *département*, and average scores by occupation are computed for each *département* as well. In the two tables below, five occupations have been selected as an illustrative example. The problem is to analyse the extent to which the score for each *département* depends on the occupational distribution of the recruits coming from that *département*.

The solution is to compute an 'adjusted' average score for each *département*. This is a weighted mean of the average scores for each occupation using weights that are equal to the proportion represented by each occupation in France as a whole. This would be the computation for Ain:

Profession	Scores (Ain) (1)	Weights (all France) (2)	Product (1) × (2)
Farming	7·4	0·482	3·57
Mechanical trade	12·9	0·210	2·71
Building trade	8·9	0·121	1·08
Warehouse labour	6·4	0·099	0·63
White-collar	15·3	0·088	1·35
Total	8·9	1·000	9·34

The standardized mean score of 9·34 is higher than the observed average score. In other words, Ain has an occupational distribution that is 'less favourable' than that of the country as a whole.

Second example

Let us now imagine that we know the distribution of the recruits in each *département* by occupation but not the average scores cross-classified by occupation and *département*. Since the above method cannot be applied, the average score that would obtain on the basis of the scores for each occupation for France as a whole and the occupational distribution of the *département* is computed. This can then be compared with the actual score to find the relative position of the *département*.

Comparing the result with the average score for Ain of 8·9, it is obvious that the *département* is below the national average when structure is kept constant. The conclusion is the same as that obtained using the direct method of standardization in the first example: 9·34 is indeed smaller than 9·64, and moreover the difference is the same as that between 8·90 and 9·20, indicating

[1] Maurice de Montmollin, 'Le niveau intellectuel des recrues du contingent', *Population* (1958), **2**, pp. 259–68.

E *

that the results of the comparison will be similar for a wide variety of weighting systems.

Profession	Scores (all France) (1)	Weights (Ain) (2)	Product (1) × (2)
Farming	7·56	0·629	4·76
Mechanical trade	13·64	0·174	2·37
Building trade	8·88	0·082	0·73
Warehouse labour	6·86	0·052	0·36
White-collar	15·61	0·063	0·98
Total	9·64	1·000	9·20

Third example

Here we anticipate the study of mortality somewhat; when the deaths in an age group over one calendar year are related to the average size of the age group, a death rate is obtained. We can then compute the number of deaths which these rates would produce in a standard population and relate this number to the size of that population. The result is a standardized death rate.

Table 8.1 gives the computation of such a rate for France in the period 1908–13. The standard population taken is the combined population of France, England, Germany, Italy and Sweden around 1910.

Table 8.1 Computation of the standardized death rate: France, 1908–13

Age	Males			Females		
	Rate p. 10 000 (1)	Standard pop. (2)	Deaths (1) × (2) (3)	Rate p. 10 000 (4)	Standard pop. (5)	Deaths (4) × (5) (6)
less than 1 year	1404	116	16·3	1143	113	12·9
1– 4 years	127	445	5·7	123	438	5·4
5–14 years	29	1023	3·0	32	1012	3·2
15–24 years	56	870	4·9	51	895	4·6
25–34 years	74	737	5·5	66	774	5·1
35–44 years	104	611	6·4	78	635	5·0
45–54 years	166	482	8·0	114	512	5·8
55–64 years	305	340	10·4	216	379	8·2
65–74 years	669	205	13·7	534	242	12·9
75–84 years	1647	67	11·0	1409	85	12·0
85 years and over	3924	8	3·1	3292	11	3·6
All sexes and ages					10 000	166·7

The standardized death rate is 166·7 per 10 000, whereas the crude rate is 184. This particular standardized rate is only of historical interest. When age-specific death rates are available by single years of age or by age groups, it is preferable to compute a life table and derive the corresponding expectation of life (see chapter 9). In the case of mortality, another method of comparison, the so-called standard mortality technique, is more useful. It has often been employed to study mortality by occupation. For a group such as coal miners whose age distribution by individual years or by groups at the beginning of each year is known as well as the total number of deaths, not distributed by age, a calculation is made of the number of deaths that would be observed using the age-specific death rates of the total male population. The ratio of the observed number of deaths to the computed number is called the *comparative mortality index*.

Fourth example

We will consider the age-specific fertility rates given in the last line of table 6.5. When they are applied to a standard population, such as that used in the third example, we obtain a standardized birth rate. If we restrict ourselves to a standard population of women between the ages of 15 and 49, the result is a total fertility rate. The simplest standard population is composed of 35 000 women evenly distributed among the 35 years of age from 15 to 49 years. The total fertility rate is obtained by multiplying each 5-year fertility rate by 5000, adding the product obtained and dividing the sum by 35 000. Table 8.2 shows the computation.

Table 8.2 Computation of the total fertility rate: France, 1931–5

Age group	Age specific fertility rate (1)	Product (1)× 5000
15–19 years	0·030	150
20–24 years	0·126	630
25–29 years	0·123	615
30–34 years	0·085	425
35–39 years	0·048	240
40–44 years	0·017	85
45–49 years	0·002	10
Total	0·431	2155:35 000 = 61 per thousand

Fifth example

There were 748 000 legitimate births in France in 1953, and 754 000 in 1954. The difference could stem from differences in behaviour, or it could originate at least partly in structural changes. In particular, the distribution of couples by duration of marriage comes to mind or the distribution in time of the marriages of previous years, which amounts to almost the same thing.

By dividing the births in 1953 issuing from marriages of, say, 1948 by the number of marriages in 1948, we obtain a net marital fertility rate. By multiplying this by 1000, we get the number of births in 1953 per thousand marriages of 1948. If we do the same for each marriage year and add up the results, we obtain the number of legitimate births that would have been observed in 1953 if the number of marriages in 1953 and in each previous year had been constant and equal to 1000. This comes to 2292; it is the number of legitimate births that would be expected if there were a constant number of 1000 marriages per year, that is to say for a uniform standard structure of marriages.

The computation proceeds as shown in table 8.3. The same computation for 1954 yields a total of 2332 births. Thus, the difference between the observations for the two years does not result simply from differences in the distribution of marriages over time.

Table 8.3 Legitimate births standardized by the number of marriages in previous years: France, 1953

Year	Marriages (thousands)	Corresponding births in 1953 (thousands)	Births per 1000 marriages
1953	308·4	39·7	129
1952	313·9	127·4	406
1951	319·7	85·5	268
1950	331·1	75·7	228
1949	333·8	66·6	195
1948	360·7	60·7	163
Total		747·7	2292

Sixth example

We now consider first order births alone, rather than all the legitimate births. The computation is carried out exactly as before. Table 8.4 gives an example relating to Switzerland.

Table 8.4 First order births standardized by the number of marriages in previous years: Switzerland, 1948

Year	Marriages (thousands)	First births (absolute numbers)	Per 1000 marriages
1948	39·27	5823	148
1947	39·40	14 354	364
1946	38·77	4769	123
1945	35·64	1839	52
Total		29 596	768

The result has been called the period parity progression ratio for families without children, but the term is inappropriate. In fact, it is the number of first order births that would be expected if there were a constant number of 1000 marriages per year, that is to say for a uniform standard population of marriages.

It is conceivable that the same computation could be carried out if marriages were replaced by, say, second order births and first births by third order births. The necessary statistics exist for France from 1959 on. When they are missing, a substitute method can be used. It is best described by returning to the example of first births for the year 1948 in Switzerland. Instead of summing up the ratios in the right hand column, it would have been feasible to divide 29 596, the total number of first births, by a weighted average of the marriages. The weights would be the proportions of first births occurring within the calendar year of marriage, in the year following, etc. A superficial survey carried out before 1948 gives the following weights per hundred: 17, 44, 17, 9, 5, 3, 2, 2, 1.

We must thus relate the first births of 1948 to the following average:[2] $0.17 \times$ marriages of $1948 + 0.44 \times$ marriages of $1947 + 0.17 \times$ marriages of $1946 + \ldots$. This average is equal to 38 300. Dividing the number of first births, 25 596, by that average, we get 773, a result which is very close to 768. Thus, the so-called weighted average method is still a way of converting to a standard population.

Another interpretation

Let's go back to the fourth example. Aside from the coefficient of 1000, the first computations, i.e. multiplication by 5000 and summation, are the same as the steps taken to obtain the cumulative fertility for a female generation. The sum obtained thus represents the cumulative fertility of a fictitious cohort of 1000 women having at each age the rates actually observed for the period 1931–5.[3]

The same interpretation applies to the results obtained in the fifth and sixth examples; 2292 would be the number of live births for a fictitious cohort of 1000 marriages having at each duration (in whole years) the net rates observed in 1953 for the same durations in a succession of cohorts. In the sixth example, 768 is the number of first births which a fictitious cohort of 1000 marriages would have if at each duration (again in whole years) they had the net rate observed in 1948 for the same durations in a succession of cohorts.

Thus, in some cases the results obtained by standardization may also be considered as the cumulative fertility (obtained by summation) of a fictitious cohort characterized by the series of rates actually observed for different cohorts in a given year (or a period of several years).

Seventh example and comments

To the preceding examples of standardization we may add the following one which refers to first marriages. In England and Wales in 1951 the average size of the female population, not classified by marital condition, and the number of first marriages by age group were as shown in table 8.6. The total of 1041 represents the number of first marriages which would have been observed in England and Wales in 1951 for women below age 50 if the female age distribution between 15 and 49 years had been constant with 1000 women at each single year of age.

The ratio of first marriages at a certain age, x, to the average population of that age, without distinction by marital status, is closely related to the

[2] In practice, the computations are laid out as shown in table 8.5.
[3] In practice, the gross reproduction rate of the period, i.e. the fictitious total number of female births, is usually substituted for total fertility.

Table 8.5 Computation of the number of first births per 1000 marriages each year, by the weighted mean method: Switzerland, 1932–50

Products $a_i m$ (multiplied by 10 and rounded)

Year of marriage	Marriages m (thousands)	1932	1933	1934	1935	1936	1937	1938	1939	1940	1941	1942	1943	1944	1945	1946	1947	1948	1949	1950
1950	37·11																			63
1949	36·99																		63	163
1948	39·27																	67	173	67
1947	39·40																67	173	67	35
1946	38·77															66	171	66	35	19
1945	35·64														61	157	61	32	18	11
1944	34·77													59	153	59	31	17	10	7
1943	35·69												61	155	61	32	18	11	7	7
1942	36·82											63	162	63	33	18	11	7	7	4
1941	36·13										60	159	60	32	18	11	6	7	4	
1940	32·47									55	143	55	29	16	10	6	6	3		
1939	31·51								54	139	54	28	16	9	6	6	3			
1938	31·03							53	136	53	28	15	9	6	6	3				
1937	30·39						52	124	52	27	15	9	6	6	3					
1936	29·63					50	130	50	27	15	9	6	6	3						
1935	30·50				52	134	52	27	15	9	6	6	3							
1934	32·49			55	143	55	19	16	10	6	6	3								
1933	31·97		54	141	54	29	16	10	6	6	3									
1932	31·96	54	140	54	29	16	10	6	6	3										
1931	32·27	142	55	29	16	10	6	6	3											
1930	32·13	55	29	16	10	6	6	3												
1929	31·24	28	16	9	6	6	3													
1928	30·05	15	9	6	6	3														
1927	28·59	9	6	6	3															
1926	28·08	6	6	3																
1925	28·11	6	3																	
1924	28·51	3																		
sum divided by 10		31·8	31·8	31·9	31·9	30·90	30·4	30·5	30·9	31·3	32·4	34·4	35·2	34·9	35·1	35·8	37·5	38·3	38·4	37·6
First order births (thous.)		22·58	22·34	22·70	22·23	21·62	21·09	21·64	22·51	22·51	25·02	28·22	29·19	28·89	28·92	29·04	29·30	29·60	28·41	27·81
First order births (per 1000 marriages)		710	702	711	697	700	694	710	729	719	772	821	829	828	824	812	781	773	740	740

Weights a_i, %: 17, 44, 17, 9, 5, 3, 2, 2, 1

Table 8.6 Female first marriages, absolute numbers, and per 5000 women in each group: England and Wales, 1951

Age (years)	Female population (thousands)	First marriages	
		Absolute numbers	per 5000 in each age group
15–19	1369	54 138	197
20–24	1500	170 382	568
25–29	1654	55 783	169
30–34	1565	17 478	56
35–39	1691	8795	26
40–44	1707	5074	15
45–49	1616	3179	10
Total			1041

marriage column of the nuptiality table for the generation considered. (The difference originates in differences in mortality and migration between the single and the total populations.) The sum through age 49 years of the ratios based on one generation is therefore close to the sum of the marriage column through that age. This sum is equal to the complement of the definitive probability of remaining single and is by definition less than 1.

But what is true for the longitudinal addition of the marriage column of the nuptiality table is not necessarily true for cross-sectional summation, and there are cases (such as England and Wales in 1951) where the result of such a cross-sectional summation exceeds the common size given to the generations, here 1000. In this case it would be impossible to interpret the result obtained by cross-sectional summation as that which would be obtained if a fictitious cohort had over time the same number of marriages as the various actual cohorts observed in 1951. The primary interpretation, that of considering 1041 as the number of marriages that would hold for a certain standard structure, remains, on the contrary, perfectly legitimate *in all cases*.

We can make yet another cross-sectional synthesis by combining the probabilities of marrying of one period as if they were those of a generation. Let's for instance, take the probabilities of marrying for single women during the period 1930–32 in France.

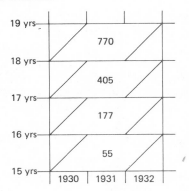

Each probability concerns a group of two generations, 1914–15 in the first case. Let us consider the series of these probabilities from n_{15} to n_{49} as if they were a series for a fictitious cohort, and combine them like cohort probabilities. Starting with 10 000 women at 15 years of age, the total number of women who are still single at age 16 is $10\,000 \times 0.9945$, and the number single at age 17 is 9945×0.9823 and so on until we reach age 50 when the number of women still single, based on the series of probabilities for 1930–32, is 1012. In this kind of cross-sectional synthesis, there is no risk of ending up with a result that would be formally absurd. The complements $(1-n_x)$, of the nuptiality rates range between 0 and 1. Their product therefore ranges between 0 and 1, and the same is true for the complement of that product.

However, it is only a fleeting advantage that this method of cross-sectional synthesis cannot lead to a formal absurdity. The very fact that the result of the synthesis by addition is sometimes absurd is actually a precious piece of information that should not be ignored.

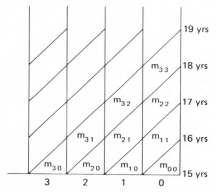

Let us number the calendar years backwards starting with the year of observation, year 0, and let us give the subscript i to the cohort that reaches 15 years of age during calendar year i. We will call m_{ij} the number of nuptiality table marriages for the cohort i during the year j. With this numbering system, the nuptiality table marriages for the observation year are $m_{00}, m_{11}, m_{22}, \ldots,$ m_{ii}. If the age distribution of the marriage column of the table does not change between one cohort and the next, we have:

$$m_{00} = a_0(1-\Gamma_0)$$
$$m_{11} = a_1(1-\Gamma_1)$$
$$\cdots\cdots\cdots\cdots$$
$$m_{ii} = a_i(1-\Gamma_i)$$

where Γ_i is the definitive probability of remaining single in generation i and x_i is the proportion of marriages that take place in the calendar year when the cohort reaches $15+i$.

Hence, we have:

$$\sum m_{ii} = \sum a_i(1-\Gamma_i)$$

with

$$\sum a_i = 1.$$

The sum of the m_{ii} is thus a weighted average of values $1 - \Gamma_i$, which are all less than 1. It is itself smaller than 1. It is therefore impossible to obtain a result greater than 1 by adding the nuptiality table marriages in a cross-sectional way if the age distribution of the marriages is the same in every cohort. Thus, when we obtain a result greater than 1, we can be certain that the distribution by age of the nuptiality table marriages is not the same in all cohorts, and we can rightly assume that the same is true for real marriages, since their age distribution is not very different from that of the nuptiality table marriages. So a finding which may look absurd from one point of view provides very useful information when interpreted correctly.

The changes in age distribution which cause the excess over 1 are not necessarily accompanied by changes in the definitive probability of remaining single. Cross-sectional synthesis by addition transforms a change in timing into a change in the average number of events per person (here, first marriages); this confusing property is not unique to it, however. It can also be found in cross-sectional syntheses based on probabilities (i.e. by multiplication) and here our attention will not be called to the fact that the final product exceeds 1! Consider the following imaginary example.

Let's assume that the probability of remaining single is 10% in all the cohorts at a given time. But circumstances have modified the timing of marriage by age and, hence, marriage probabilities in one group of 5 single year generations. In order to develop a simple pattern, we take a five-year period as time unit and replace the annual marriage probabilities by quinquennial probabilities.

The quinquennial probability of marriage between 30 and 35 years is 0·350 for every group of 5 cohorts except for the one that has been disturbed, where it is 0·440. The cross-sectional synthesis on the basis of quinquennial marriage

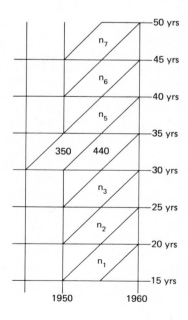

probabilities derived by the observation in, say, 1950–59 will be the result of the product:

$$(1 - n_1) (1 - n_2) (1 - n_3) (1 - 0 \cdot 440) (1 - n_5) (1 - n_6) (1 - n_7).$$

But since the definitive probability of remaining single is the same for each cohort, cross-sectional synthesis gives:

$$(1 - n_1) (1 - n_2) (1 - n_3) (1 - 0 \cdot 350) (1 - n_5) (1 - n_6) (1 - n_7) = 0 \cdot 10.$$

The preceding product is therefore equal to:

$$0 \cdot 10 \times \frac{(1 - 0 \cdot 440)}{(1 - 0 \cdot 350)} = 0 \cdot 086.$$

Thus, the group of 5 fictitious cohorts which have as quinquennial marriage probabilities the series of those that were observed between 1950–59 would have a definitive probability of remaining single of 8·6 instead of 10%.

This is the reason why it is necessary to be very cautious when interpreting chronological series of period indicators obtained by cross-sectional synthesis. Through cross-sectional synthesis, a progressive transformation of the timing of an event may give the illusion of a progressive evolution of the average number of events per head, even though the latter remains the same in every generation. The danger is even greater because the device of the fictitious cohort has introduced into cross-sectional synthesis a terminology which is, strictly speaking, appropriate only for longitudinal synthesis.

2 General overview and criticisms

In commenting on the seventh example, we discussed a combination of period indices, i.e. probabilities of marrying, calculated in a way other than by addition. We shall come back to this in the next chapter with regard to mortality where it plays a leading role. The result obtained is a synthetic index that we can interpret as being the one which would be observed in a fictitious cohort having at each age the probabilities observed for that age in the period studied. A similar interpretation was given for the fourth example. This leads to a generalized procedure: the combination of rates or of probabilities (by age, duration, interval) for one year or one period as if they referred to a single cohort. To sharpen the image and identify the concept, let us call it *the fictitious cohort trick*. We shall see in more detail how it is applied in the instance of mortality. For the time being, let us remember that two kinds of approaches exist to the problem presented at the beginning of this chapter— standardization and the fictitious cohort trick.

These two approaches are identical when the second one is based on the simple addition of rates, but the choice of interpretation exists only if the result obtained is not impossible for a cohort. When this is not the case, the result can be interpreted only in terms of conversion to a standard structure, an interpretation that is not subject to any limitation.

The fictitious cohort trick, whether done by addition of the rates or by multiplication of the complements of the probabilities, has the effect of transforming timing changes between real cohorts into an apparent modification of the number of events per person in the fictitious cohort. Many errors of interpretation have been committed because this effect had gone unrecognized or neglected; the most frequent of these has been to attribute, after a superficial survey of the evidence, a reduction in the number of legitimate births from a standardized distribution of the married population to a decrease in the cumulated fertility of marriage, whereas changes in the timing of childbearing as a reaction to events such as an economic crisis are actually the main cause of the decrease.

This transformation of changes in timing into changes in the number of events per person cannot occur when we are dealing with non-renewable events such as death, and when the trick of the fictitious cohort is used in such a way that the number of survivors approaches zero as age increases. The use of cross-sectional synthesis in the study of mortality therefore avoids the drawbacks mentioned above.

It should be emphasized that the fictitious cohort trick is and, above all, was constantly used in the cross-sectional study of demographic phenomena. It offered a cross-sectional synthesis to cap an analysis that was likewise cross-sectional, since it was confined within the framework of a year or of a period of some years. In the present unsatisfying state of development of the terminology, the indices yielded by such cross-sectional synthesis are often called period indices to distinguish them from the cohort indices of the same name.

Criticisms

Seductive though they are at first sight, the proposed methods are nevertheless subject to criticism. We compare two situations by replacing the existing structures with a standard structure. But the choice of the latter structure is arbitrary. If the direction of the differences between two populations is not the same age for age, for example, the standard population might be chosen in such a way that one or the other of the two populations is given an advantage. But for this to happen the standard population chosen would have to deviate considerably, in general, from the typical age composition. If one stays with a more usual age composition, the advantage usually does not change sides when the standard populations are changed. Even the standard structure used in examples 4, 5 and 6 is arbitrary. Nevertheless it is similar to the usual structure of populations that have evolved slowly and without major disturbances.

Whatever the case may be, one should not forget in the interpretation of the findings which series of computations one has passed through in order to get from the crude observations to the 'adjusted' findings for purposes of comparison with other adjusted findings. Thus the size of the adjusted difference between Ain and France is strictly speaking entirely dependent on the standard structure which was used. With a standard structure that gave much more importance to the occupational classification of construction, the difference would be less marked. It would be more marked, on the contrary, with a standard structure that gave more importance to the mechanical trade. But minor variations of structure, such as those between Ain and France, scarcely modify this difference, as shown in the comparison of examples 1 and 2. By resorting to the fictitious cohort trick, it appears possible to avoid the arbitrary choice of a standard structure. The fact that the two methods coincide in certain cases, however, shows that this is not really true. Besides, this trick sometimes leads to formal absurdities. The methods of example 6, if applied to France in 1946, give a number of first births per thousand marriages which is larger than 1000. This is no problem if we are referring to conversion to a standard structure, but it is if we are referring to a fictitious cohort. On the one hand, the choice of a standard structure is arbitrary; on the other hand, the trick of the fictitious cohort is a convention, and may not fit the facts.

In addition, the choice of the structures to be compared on a common basis is sometimes open to criticism. Let us imagine that the fifth example concerned the comparison of the years 1946 and 1956. Would the most important structural effect be eliminated by converting to a basis of 1000 marriages per year? Certainly not. In 1946, the main differences between couples did not stem from duration of marriage but from their history during the war—some had been separated, others had not. That is not accounted for in any way when we control for duration of marriage without paying attention to the content of this duration, that is to say to the history of the household considered. One should beware therefore, especially following a disturbance, of concluding that a difference does not depend on a structural effect simply because it has been observed that it persisted after converting to a standard structure. Other structural characteristics besides the one considered could be coming into play.

One should not conclude, however, from these criticisms that standardization, or the fictitious cohort trick, are worthless methods. These methods are useful, and they are frequently resorted to. One should simply be cautious of asking more of them than they have to offer. Thus in a period of post war recovery, the number of legitimate births, related to a constant number of marriages, does permit the separation of that which is due to the making up of postponed births from that which is the result of the making up of marriages deferred by the war. But this number certainly cannot be treated as if it represented the final cumulative fertility of a marriage cohort. The postponing-making up complex in fact, introduces a change in the distribution of births by marriage duration. This change shows up in period indices as a change in the number of births, converted to a standard structure even if, after a complete recovery, there is no significant change in the average number of children per marriage. In order for the period index not to transform changes in the timing of events into a change in the number of events per head, it is necessary that there be no such changes of timing. When the timing of events is the same for all cohorts, the number of events in a year converted to a uniform standard structure is equal to a weighted average of the number of events per head in the relevant cohorts. But it is impossible to evaluate changes in timing without preliminary longitudinal analysis.

9

Mortality

It is usually assumed that mortality during a given year depends more on the health conditions of the period—weather, epidemics, famines, wars, medical knowledge, the practice of hygiene—than on the past experience of individuals. This is the equivalent of admitting that the effect of selection is minor compared to changes in period conditions. Now, it is these very period conditions, their variation and their evolution, which are of primary interest to the officials responsible for public health. Since the effect of current conditions is largely independent of experience, we are in a situation where cross-sectional analysis is useful (this is not the case where nuptiality and fertility are concerned; the effect of period conditions may then depend very heavily on the past for the making up of marriages or births presupposes a previous postponement). Moreover, the non-renewable nature of death removes the main drawback from synthetical indices as seen in chapter 8. For these two reasons—the interest in, and the appropriateness of, this kind of approach—cross-sectional analysis has priority in the study of mortality.

Factors:
It has always been known on the basis of every-day observation that the risk of death varies greatly with age. Other demographic factors, marital status, for instance, play a role, but they are secondary compared to that played by age. No study of mortality can be done without taking age into account.

The result is that the *crude death rate* (that is to say, as we saw in chapter 3, the ratio of yearly deaths to total population) cannot be a good index of the health situation of a country. It depends too much on the age distribution of the population.

Thus, in 1967, France had a crude death rate of 10·8 per thousand, Spain of 8·7 per thousand. Nevertheless health conditions in France were better than those in Spain; France simply had proportionately more old people. Still, short-term variations in the crude rate do provide information on short-term changes in health conditions, since the effect of short-term variations in age distribution is essentially trivial.

1 Standardized mortality rates

These are intended for comparison of the mortality of various populations holding structure constant.

Direct standardization

It is possible to compute the death rate that each of these populations would have if their own health conditions (characterized by a series of age-specific death rates) were combined with age distribution of one selected population, called the standard population. The latter might be, for instance, the average of all the populations compared. The standardized rate t_c is linked to the age-specific rate $t(x)$ and to the standard size of the age group x, $P_t(x)$ by the relation:

$$t_c = \frac{\Sigma P_t(x)t(x)}{\Sigma P_t(x)}.$$

The data necessary for the computation of t_c (see chapter 8, section 1) are the same as those that permit the computation, at least in an approximate way, of a life table. In this case, it is better to compute such a table than to calculate t_c.

Indirect standardization of mortality

This method, mentioned in the first section of the previous chapter consists of computing the deaths D_c that would be expected in each of the populations under standard health conditions (characterized by a series $t_t(x)$ of age-specific mortality rates), for instance the average health status of the whole population:

$$D_c = \Sigma P(x)t_t(x).$$

The ratio D/D_c (where D represents the observed deaths) is taken as the mortality index for each population. This method does not require age-specific death rates for each population, and it allows comparisons that would be impossible with a method that did require these rates.

2 Age-specific mortality rates, probabilities of dying

Mortality rates at age x

The mortality rate at age x is the ratio of the annual number of deaths at age x to the average population at age x. The mortality rate of the age group $(x, x+4)$ is the ratio of the annual number of deaths at ages x to $x+4$ to the average population of the age group $(x, x+4)$.

In France, these rates are actually computed by generations or groups of generations. Approximate age x is the age at last birthday as of the 31 December of the year considered.

The probability of dying at age x

Consider a closed population. Let D_x be the number of deaths observed between the xth and the $(x+1)$st birthday of the individuals making up this population during one year; let V_x be the number of individuals reaching age x during that year. The probability q_x is given by:

$$q_x = \frac{D_x}{V_x}.$$

In the case of an open population, migratory movements play the role of the disturbing phenomenon. If we assume that migrants have the same mortality as the whole population and that they are present on the average for only half of the year, we write:

$$q_x V_x = D_x + \frac{q_x}{2} E_x - \frac{q_x}{2} I_x$$

This indicates that in the absence of disturbance by migration, there would be, on the one hand, $q_x E_x / 2$ more deaths (E_x being the number of out-migrants) and, on the other hand, $q_x I_x / 2$ less deaths (I_x being the number of in-migrants). Hence:

$$q_x = \frac{D_x}{V_x - \frac{1}{2}(E_x - I_x)} .$$

This formula is analogous to the one encountered in the study of nuptiality (chapter 5, p. 50). Net migration ($E_x - I_x$) replaces the deaths of single people.[1]

Multi-annual probabilities of dying

The probabilities of dying defined above relate to the period of one year between one birthday and the next. Multi-annual probabilities relating to a period of years between the xth and the $(x + a)$th birthdays can also be used. They are designated by the symbol $_a q_x$.

The most frequently used of these probabilities are $_4 q_1$, covering the deaths between the first and the fifth birthday, and $_5 q_5$, $_5 q_{10}$ . . . covering deaths between two birthdays that are multiples of 5. It is also possible to use $_5 q_0$ for deaths between birth and the fifth birthday.

Relationships between probabilities and rates

a) First case

The rate t_x is equal to the ratio of the number of deaths, D_x, in a generation during the year considered, to the average size P_x of the generation during that year.

We have by definition:

$$t_x = \frac{D_x}{P_x}$$

and

$$P_x = \frac{P_0 + P_1}{2} = P_0 - \frac{D_x}{2} .$$

[1] The formulas including migration apply to mortality by marital status.

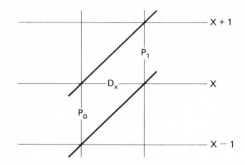

Respectively P_0 and P_1 are the size of the generation on 1 January and on 31 December. Dividing this last relationship by D_x, we get:

$$\frac{1}{t_x} = \frac{1}{k_x} - \frac{1}{2}$$

where k_x designates a special type of probability of dying D_x/P_0 used in population projections that we shall call 'prospective probability'. This relationship is valid for every year of life except the first.

b) Second case

The rate t_x is equal to the ratio of the number of deaths at age x, D_x, to the average population at age x.

In this case, the deaths considered all take place between the xth and the $(x+1)$st birthday, but relate to two different generations. The older one, numbering V_{x+1} at its $(x+1)$st birthday, provides d deaths; the other one, numbering V''_x at its xth birthday, provides d' deaths.

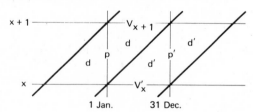

Suppose now that, under the conditions prevailing during the year of observation, there were also d deaths in the older cohort between the xth birthday and 1 January and d' deaths in the younger between 31 December and the $(x+1)$st birthday. Under these conditions, the probabilities corresponding to the conditions of the year are given by:

$$q_x = \frac{2d + 2d'}{V_{x+1} + 2d + V''_x}.$$

The numerator is equal to $2D_x$, since $d + d' = D_x$. The denominator can be written:

$$V_{x+1} + d + V''_x - d' + d + d' = P + P' + D_x = 2P_x + D_x.$$

Dividing the two terms by $2D_x$, we obtain:

$$\frac{1}{q_x} = \frac{1}{t_x} + \frac{1}{2}$$

This formula is similar to the one found in the first case. But it is applicable only to the extent that the hypothesis holds at least approximately. In practice, this is only true after age 2 years, or at most after age 1 year.

From this we derive:

$$q_x = \frac{t_x}{1 + t_x/2} \qquad t_x = \frac{q_x}{1 - q_x/2}$$

and by multiplying the numerator and the denominator by P_x:

$$q_x = \frac{P_x t_x}{P_x + P_x t_x/2} = \frac{D_x}{P_x + D_x/2}$$

This formula enables us to compute a probability on the basis of a classification of deaths by age only.

Relationships between conventional probabilities and prospective probabilities

The size of the population that reaches exact age $x - 1/2$ is equal to $P_0 + d_1'$ $- d_1$. It is not very different from P_0 when d_1 and d_1' are approximately equal.

As for the deaths between exact ages $x - 1/2$ and $x + 1/2$, these are equal to the deaths between 1 January and 31 December when d_2 is also approximately equal to d_2'.

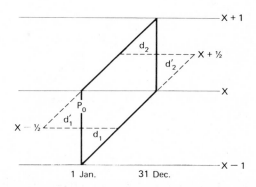

As a result, except for very young ages, the prospective probability is almost equal to the probability of dying at age $x - 1/2$, x being the age reached during the year by the generation in question.

3 Period life table

The set of probabilities of dying at different ages taken together for a given population during a period of one or more years, say 1960–64, is called the life table for the population in question in 1960–64. Life tables actually give, in addition to the probabilities of dying, three other indices derived from the probabilities: the number of survivors, the life table deaths and the expectation of life, all of these being valid for age x.

Survivors at age x

The complement of q_x, p_x, is the probability of surviving between age x and age $x+1$.

The product

$$p_0 p_1 \cdots p_{x-1} = {}_x p_0$$

is the probability of surviving between birth and age x for the members of a fictitious cohort who experience at all ages the probabilities of dying of the period considered. An analogous computation was presented in chapter 8, example 7.

The survivors at age x, S_x, are calculated by multiplying ${}_x p_0$ by S_0, the initial size of the fictitious cohort, or radix of the life table.[2]

The radix of the life table is usually taken as 1000, 10 000, or most frequently of all, 100 000.

Life table deaths at age x

Let us call these deaths d_x. According to the definition of the probability of dying in the absence of migration:

$$q_x = \frac{d_x}{S_x}$$

and hence,

$$d_x = q_x S_x.$$

We also have:

$$S_{x+1} = S_x(1 - q_x) = S_x \left(1 - \frac{d_x}{S_x} \right) = S_x - d_x$$

and hence:

$$d_x = S_x - S_{x+1}.$$

The latter formula is the one that is used to compute d_x. It indicates that the number of survivors at the $(x+1)$st birthday is equal to the number of survivors at the xth birthday diminished by the number of deaths at age x, that is to say between these two birthdays.

From the two preceding formulae, we conclude that:

$$q_x = \frac{S_x - S_{x+1}}{S_x}.$$

[2]The symbol 1_x is often used for survivors at age x; it is derived from the English word *living*.

and

$$_aq_x = \frac{S_x - S_{x+a}}{S_x}.$$

Probable length of life

The probable length of life at age x is the number of years between age x and an age y by which only half the survivors at age x are still alive.

$$S_y = \frac{1}{2} S_x.$$

The *probable length of life at birth* or median length of life is the age z for which S_z is equal to $1/2$. z is the median of the distribution of life table deaths. The probable length of life at age x is not given in life tables.

Expectation of life or mean length of life

a) Definitions

The *expectation of life at age x*, or mean length of life at age x, is the average number of years remaining to be lived starting at the xth birthday. The *expectation of life at birth* is the average number of years to be lived by a cohort subjected from beginning to end to the series of probabilities of dying q_x; it is also the mean age of the distribution of deaths d_x.

b) Computation of the expectation of life

1) Complete computation
We assume that persons dying at age $x + t$ have lived, on the average, $t + 0.5$ year after their xth birthday. e_x being the expectation of life at age x, we write:

$$e_x = \frac{0 \cdot 5 d_x + 1 \cdot 5 d_{x+1} + 2 \cdot 5 d_{x+2} + \cdots + (t + 0 \cdot 5) d_{x+t} + \cdots}{S_x}.$$

$$= \frac{0 \cdot 5 (d_x + d_{x+1} + \cdots + d_{x+t} + \cdots) + d_{x+1} + 2 d_{x+2} + \cdots + t d_{x+t} + \cdots}{S_x}$$

but $d_x + d_{x+t} + \cdots + d_{x+t} + \cdots = S_x$, since the survivors at age x will all die, and therefore we can write:

$$e_x = 0 \cdot 5 + \frac{d_{x+1} + 2 d_{x+2} + \cdots + t d_{x+t} + \cdots}{S_x}.$$

We also know that regardless of the value of $u(u = x+1, x+2, \ldots x +t, \ldots)$ $d_u = S_u - S_{u+1}$.

Hence:

$$e_x = 0\cdot5 + \frac{S_{x+1} - S_{x+2} + 2(S_{x+2} - S_{x+3}) + \cdots}{S_x}$$

$$= 0\cdot5 + \frac{S_{x+1} + S_{x+2} + S_{x+3} + \cdots}{S_x}$$

and for expectation of life at birth, e_0:[3]

$$e_0 = 0\cdot5 + \frac{S_1 + S_2 + S_3 + \cdots}{S_0} .$$

2) Abridged computation

The survival function, that is the whole set of values S_x, is often given in an abridged form that includes only S_0, S_1 and the survivors at 5-year intervals starting with S_5. To compute the expectation of life from abridged tables, we assume that children dying before age 1 year lived a half year, that children dying at age 1–4 years, or between their 1st and 5th birthdays, lived exactly 2 years after their 1st birthday, that people dying between two birthdays that are multiples of 5 lived, on the average, 2-1/2 years between these two birthdays. For $x = 5, 10, 15 \ldots$, we write therefore:

$$e_x = \frac{2\cdot5(S_x - S_{x+5}) + (7\cdot5(S_{x+5} - S_{x+10}) + 12\cdot5(S_{x+10} - S_{x+15}) + \cdots}{S_x}$$

$$= 2\cdot5 + \frac{5(S_{x+5} - S_{x+10}) + 10(S_{x+10} - S_{x+15}) + \cdots}{S_x}$$

$$= 2\cdot5 + \frac{5(S_{x+5} + S_{x+10} + S_{x+15} + \cdots)}{S_x} .$$

For $x = 1$, we write:

$$e_1 = \frac{2(S_1 - S_5) + 6\cdot5(S_5 - S_{10}) + 11\cdot5(S_{10} - S_{15}) + \cdots}{S_1}$$

$$= \frac{2S_1 + 4\cdot5S_5 + 5(S_{10} + S_{15} + \cdots)}{S_1}$$

$$= 2 + \frac{4\cdot5S_5 + 5(S_{10} + S_{15} + \cdots)}{S_1}$$

[3] e_0^0 is often used instead of e_0 as the symbol of the expectation of life at birth.

and, finally for e_0:

$$e_0 = \frac{0{\cdot}5(S_0 - S_1) + 3(S_1 - S_5) + 7{\cdot}5(S_5 - S_{10}) + 12{\cdot}5(S_{10} - S_{15})}{S_0}$$

$$= 0{\cdot}5 + \frac{2{\cdot}5S_1 + 4{\cdot}5S_5 + 5(S_{10} + S_{15} + \cdots)}{S_0}.$$

Modal age at death

The distribution of d_x exhibits a maximum in the first year and another toward the end of the adult years or in old age. The age where this last maximum is reached is called *modal age at death*. In western populations, it occurs at present between 70 and 80 years of age.

How to compute a life table

For probabilities of dying other than those of the first year (infant mortality), we start with observed deaths classified by age or by both age and year of birth (double classification) and with living persons as of a certain date classified by age or by year of birth. A table is constructed for each sex and for both sexes together. Let us first take up the case of a closed population classified by year of birth for which the double classification of deaths is available (as is the case for France).

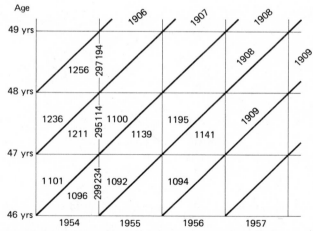

The Lexis diagram above relates to France (male sex). The population is that on 1 January 1955, as estimated from the census of 10 May 1954.

Take as an example the probability of dying at 47 years, q_{47}. It is computed as follows:

$$\frac{(1\,211 + 1\,100) + (1\,139 + 1\,195)}{(295\,114 + 1\,211) + (299\,234 - 1\,092)} = 7{\cdot}81 \text{ per thousand.}$$

The first parenthesis in the numerator represents the deaths at age 47 years observed for the cohort of 1907 during the years 1954 and 1955; the second parenthesis refers to the deaths at age 47 years observed for the cohort of 1908 during the years 1955 and 1956. The first parenthesis in the denominator represents the number of persons in the cohort of 1907 reaching their 47th birthday; the second parenthesis represents the corresponding figure for the cohort of 1908.

This method excludes the deaths at age 47 years observed during 1954 and 1956 for the cohorts of 1906 and 1909. The result is that the years 1954, 1955 and 1956 are not given the same weight; the weight given to the year 1955 is approximately twice as large as that of each of the others. If we wanted to take into account the deaths at 47 years in the cohorts of 1906 and 1909 and thus give the same weight to each of the years 1954, 1955 and 1956, it would be necessary to add 1236 and 1141 to the denominator, and half of the sum of persons surviving to their 47th birthday in the cohorts of 1906 and 1909 to the numerator. This would yield a probability of dying of 7·86 per thousand.

If we wanted to compute a life table for a single year, say 1954, it would be necessary in theory to compute a twofold series of probabilities of dying: one of the q'_x probabilities between the xth birthday and 1 January of the following year, and another of the k'_x probabilities between 1 January and the $(x+1)$th birthday. The denominator of the former would consist of the number of persons reaching their xth birthday, and the denominator of the latter, of the size of the cohort on 1 January.

We would therefore have for 1954:

$$q'_{47} = \frac{1211}{295\,114 + 1211} \qquad k'_{47} = \frac{1236}{297\,194 + 1256 + 1236}.$$

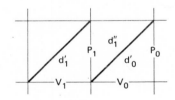

The period probability at age 47 years, q_{47}, would be derived as follows:

$$q_{47} = 1 - (1 - q'_{47})(1 - k'_{47}) = q'_{47} + k'_{47}(1 - q'_{47}).$$

q'_{47} is equal to d'_0/V_0, a ratio which differs little from, if it isn't equal to, d'_1/V_1. $1 - q'_{47}$ is, therefore, almost equal to $(V_1 - d'_1)/V_1$, that is to say equal to P_1/V_1. In addition, k'_{47} is equal to d''_1/P_1; the term $k'_{47}(1 - q'_{47})$ is equal to:

$$\frac{d''_1}{P_1} \times \frac{P_1}{V_1}$$

and can be reduced therefore to d_1''/V_1, the ratio that we shall call q_{47}'' and, in general, q_x''.

Using this convention, we can write:

$$q_{47} = q_{47}' + q_{47}''.$$

4 Computation of probabilities of dying without the double classification of deaths

We use the formula given in section 2 of this chapter:

$$q_x = \frac{D_x}{P_x + D_x/2}$$

in the form:

$$q_x = \frac{\text{Sum of } D_x}{\text{Sum of } (P_x + D_x/2)}$$

D_x designates at age x, P_x the average population at age x.

Example:

With the numerical data of the figure on page 143, the sum of deaths at age 47 years in 1954, 1955 and 1956 is:

$$2447 + 2239 + 2336 = 7022.$$

The average population 47 years old in 1954 is equal to the mean of the numbers at those ages on 1 January 1954 and on 1 January 1955. The latter number is equal to 295 114. The former is obtained by adding to 297 194 the deaths occurring in 1954 for the relevant generation. With a tabulation by age only, these deaths are not known. But they can be replaced by half of the sum of deaths at ages 47 and 48 years.

$$\frac{2447 + 2519}{2} = 2483$$

hence:

$$P_{47}(1954) = \frac{297\,194 + 2483 + 295\,114}{2} = \frac{594\,791}{2}.$$

In a similar way we have:

$$P_{47}(1955) = \qquad\qquad = \frac{592\,158}{2}$$

$$P_{47}(1956) = \qquad\qquad = \frac{591\,767}{2}$$

and therefore:

$$
\begin{aligned}
\text{Sum of } P_{47} &= 889\,358 \\
\text{Sum of } D_{47}/2 &= 3\,511 \\
\text{Total} &\ \ 892\,869
\end{aligned}
$$

hence:

$$
q_{47} = \frac{7022}{892\,869} = 7{\cdot}86
$$

which is comparable to the figures 7·81 and 7·86 obtained by the two methods that were based on the double classification.

In the instance of multi-annual probabilities, there exist tables that enable us to convert the rates into probabilities of dying. They are to be found in *Demographic Analysis* by R. Pressat, the English edition quoted above, on pp. 132–40 and 481–9.

5 Computation of infant mortality

Let us take the same years as in the preceding discussion. Instead of starting with children enumerated in 1954, we start with births during the years 1954 and 1955. In a case like France, the false stillbirths (children born alive who died before their births were registered) must be added to the births and the deaths. Those for whom it is unknown whether they were actually born alive or stillborn are sometimes included and sometimes left out. Accordingly, two essentially identical rates of infant mortality are obtained.

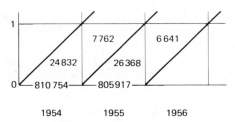

The computation that corresponds to the figure is as follows:

$$
\frac{7762 + 6641 + 24\,832 + 23\,368}{810\,754 + 805\,917} = \frac{62\,863}{1\,616\,671} = 38{\cdot}9 \text{ per thousand} \qquad \text{(a)}
$$

$$
\frac{62\,863 + 591 + 597}{1\,616\,671 + 591 + 597} = \frac{64\,051}{1\,616\,671} = 39{\cdot}6 \text{ per thousand} \qquad \text{(b)}
$$

591 and 597 are the numbers of registered stillbirths for whom it is unknown whether they were actually born alive.

Infant mortality of the year

The so-called *infant mortality rate* is really a probability. As a rule, this is the only probability that is computed every year.

In line with what has been demonstrated above, the infant mortality rate for a year is given by

$$q_0 = q_0' + q_0'' \tag{1}$$

and

$$q_0' = \frac{d_0'}{N_0} \qquad q_0'' = \frac{d_1''}{N_1}$$

where N_0 is the number of births of the year considered, N_1 that of the previous year, d_0' the number of deaths in the year considered among the children born during that same year, and d_1'' the number of deaths in the year considered among children aged less than 1 year born during the preceding year.

Weighted average method

Let us call d the sum of deaths d_0' and d_1''.

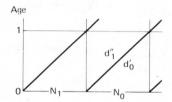

Then:

$$d = d_0' + d_1'' = N_0 \frac{d_0'}{N_0} + N_1 \frac{d_1''}{N_1}. \tag{2}$$

What denominator N can we choose so that $q_0 = d/N$? Obviously it must be d/q_0 and it is obtained by replacing d and q_0 by their values derived from (1) and (2):

$$N = \frac{d}{q_0} = N_0 \frac{d_0'}{N_0} + N_1 \frac{d_1''}{N_1} \bigg/ \frac{d_0'}{N_0} + \frac{d_1''}{N_1}$$

N is a weighted average of N_0 and N_1; the weights are:

$$\frac{d_0'}{N_0} \bigg/ \frac{d_0'}{N_0} + \frac{d_1''}{N_1} \quad \text{and} \quad \frac{d_1''}{N_1} \bigg/ \frac{d_0'}{N_0} + \frac{d_1''}{N_1}.$$

They actually vary little. At present, in France, the first is on the order of 3/4; the second on the order of 1/4. This is equivalent to saying that in a generation subjected to health conditions that vary little between the calendar year of its

F

birth and the next year, 3/4 of the deaths before 1 year of age occur before 1 January of the following year.[4] The preceding computations constitute a vindication of the weighted average method as it applies to cross-sectional analysis. Do not lose sight, however, of the fact that this justification is based on an approximation. This method is used in cases where the double classification of deaths does not exist.

Example:

Let us take as an example the year 1946 in France.
The data are as follows:

Live births $\qquad\qquad\begin{cases}1945\text{---}647\,000 \\ 1946\text{---}843\,900\end{cases}$

Deaths in 1946 of children aged less than 1 year $\quad\begin{cases}\text{born in }1945\text{---}16\,159 \\ \text{born in }1946\text{---}44\,541\end{cases}60\,700$

We have:

$$q_0' = \frac{44\,541}{843\,900} = 52{\cdot}8 \text{ per thousand}$$

$$q_0'' = \frac{16\,159}{647\,000} = 25{\cdot}0 \text{ per thousand}$$

hence:

$$q_0 = 25{\cdot}0 + 52{\cdot}8 = 77{\cdot}8 \text{ per thousand}$$

Using as weights 1/3 and 2/3 respectively, the method of the weighted average gives:

$$q_0 = \frac{60\,700}{\dfrac{647\,000}{3} + \dfrac{2 \times 843\,900}{3}} = 78{\cdot}1 \text{ per thousand}$$

whereas with 1/4 and 3/4 it yields 76·4 per thousand.

Endogenous and exogenous mortality

Two broad groups of deaths to children under 1 year can be distinguished; on the one hand, those that result from causes that precede birth (malformation, debility) or from delivery itself (obstetrical trauma); on the other hand, those that can be attributed to the outside environment and are caused by lack of hygiene, poor nutrition, infection or accident. The first group of deaths is called endogenous, the second exogenous.

Statistics on causes of deaths are often insufficient to permit this distinction.

[4]The computation of infant mortality by month or by quarter follows a similar procedure (see the English edition of R. Pressat, *Demographic Analysis* (London: Edward Arnold, 1972) p. 85.

We are indebted to J. Bourgeois-Pichat for another method for which we need only the distribution by age of deaths at less than one year, e.g. less than one month, 1 month, 2 months . . . 11 months.

The rule is as follows:

a) On a graph, the series of points which are located horizontally by a certain function of exact age, and vertically by the cumulative number of deaths from birth to the exact age, fall in a straight line, at least after 1 month.

b) If this line is extended to the left, it intersects the vertical axis at a point where the ordinate is equal to the number of endogenous deaths. The remainder of the total constitutes the exogenous deaths. The values on the horizontal axis are proportional to the following numbers:

1 month	335	7 months	1265
2 months	574	8 —	1361
3 —	758	9 –	1450
4 —	911	10 —	1533
5 —	1043	11 —	1611
6 —	1160	12 —	1685

There are some exceptions to the rule. In certain instances (particularly in several regions on the border of the Mediterranean) the straight line holds only for the early months; after age 3 or 4 months, the cumulated deaths fall above where the trend based on the first months would fall if extended to the right. This means that there is excess exogenous mortality.

In those populations where the rule holds fairly true, exogenous mortality is equal to 5/4 of mortality from the 2nd through the 11th month. This permits a faster assessment than can be done with a graph. Table 9.1 provides an example based on Tuscany during the period 1951–3. The points that should fall on a straight line would be those located on the horizontal axis by the first number of each of the following pairs and on the vertical axis by the second:

Table 9.1 Infant mortality by months: Tuscany, 1951–3

Age in completed months	Deaths per 1000 live births	
	Per month	Cumulated
0	28·2	28·2
1	2·4	30·6
2	1·8	32·4
3	1·6	34·0
4	1·3	35·3
5	1·1	36·4
6	1·0	37·4
7	1·0	38·4
8	0·7	39·1
9	0·8	39·9
10	0·5	40·4
11	0·6	41·0

335 and 28·2
574 and 30·6
758 and 32·4
. . . .
. . . .
1685 and 41·0

They are indeed on a straight line (see figure 9.1). The trend line intersects the vertical axis at the point where the ordinate equals 25·0, and this then is the endogenous mortality.

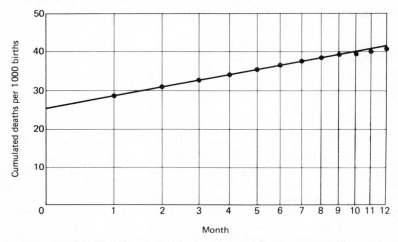

Figure 9.1 Determination of the endogenous component of infant mortality: Tuscany, 1951–3

The exogenous mortality is found by the difference:

$$41·0 - 25·0 = 16·0$$

The number of deaths from the 2nd to the 11th months is equal to 12·8 (41·0 − 28·2); 5/4 times this is equal to 16·0 in agreement with the preceding results.

Another way of subdividing the first year

Today in France, the distribution of deaths at less than one year of age is in days as follows:

Period	Corresponding horizontal axis value
0–27 days	313
28–60 days	576
61–90 days	757
91–120 days	908
121–150 days	1039
151–180 days	1154
181–210 days	1259
211–240 days	1355

241–270 days	1443
271–301 days	1528
302–332 days	1607
333–364 days	1685

In this case, the horizontal scale to use is in the right hand column—313 for deaths less than 28 days, 576 for those of less than 61 days and so on. Where the rule fits the data well, exogenous mortality is equal to the number of deaths between 28 and 364 days, multiplied by 1·228.

Perinatal mortality

This term refers to the sum of the endogenous mortality and stillbirth rates. It lends itself better to comparison since false stillbirths are always included among perinatal deaths whereas they are sometimes included among stillbirths, and sometimes among endogenous deaths.

Example:
France 1962

Births (children *declared* alive)	828 920
Deaths of children declared alive	17 997
False stillbirths	3433

The graphic method indicates that there are 8600 endogenous deaths among the 17 997. Hence, by subtraction, there are 9397 exogenous deaths. If we add 3433 to 8600, we obtain 12 033 endogenous deaths of children *born* alive (the number of those children being 832 353 = 828 920 + 3433).

The rates are as follows:

Endogenous mortality $\dfrac{12\,033}{832\,353} = 14\cdot45$ per thousand

Exogenous mortality $\dfrac{9397}{832\,353} = 11\cdot30$ per thousand

Infant mortality rate	25·75 per thousand
Stillbirth rate	15·1 per thousand
Perinatal mortality (16·1 + 14·45)	30·55 per thousand

Note that infant mortality and stillbirth rate are not, in theory, computed on the basis of the same denominator. Therefore, perinatal mortality is not exactly equal to the ratio of the sum of the stillbirths and endogenous deaths to the live births or to the total births (live born and stillborn). But the difference is trivial.

6 Intra-uterine mortality

In theory, this includes all the deaths in the mother's womb, whatever the cause or the duration of pregnancy. In practice, the name refers specifically to spontaneous abortions together with stillbirths. Suppose that to begin with we have a count of all the pregnancies which have reached a certain duration of gestation, say 4 weeks, and the outcome of these pregnancies (induced abortion, spontaneous abortion, stillbirth or live birth). The relative frequency of uninduced intra-uterine mortality after 4 weeks would be obtained by relating uninduced intra-uterine deaths (spontaneous abortions plus stillbirths) to the number of pregnancies minus the number of induced abortions.

In fact, we never know all the pregnancies that reach the duration of gestation in question. Some of those that terminate in an abortion remain unrecorded. If it is an induced abortion, it does not hinder the measurement of spontaneous intra-uterine mortality; but a significant proportion of those pregnancies that end in spontaneous abortion are also unknown, particularly if the abortion occurred early. Intra-uterine mortality is thus underestimated by relating intra-uterine deaths to known pregnancies that terminated in spontaneous abortion or birth. To avoid this problem, it is necessary to compute an intra-uterine life table. This has been done only once; the unit of time chosen was the period of 4 weeks; the first period, from 4 to 7 completed weeks' duration of gestation, was counted from the last menstruation.

Let us keep this classification and call:

G_t the number of observed pregnancies after t periods of 4 weeks of gestation; or in other words, at the beginning of the period that falls between times t and $t+1$

D_t the intra-uterine deaths
N_t the live births (if relevant)
E_t the other withdrawals from observation (departures or deaths of mothers) $\}$ between t and $t+1$

I_t the entries into observation (arrival between t and $t+1$ or pregnancies that were recognized only between t and $t+1$).

G_t is computed line by line:

$$G_t = G_{t-1} - D_{t-1} - N_{t-1} - E_{t-1} + I_{t-1}.$$

The probability of intra-uterine mortality q_t and the probability of a live birth V_t between t and $t+1$ can be computed by the following formulae:

$$q_t = \frac{D_t}{G_t - \frac{N_t + E_t}{2} + \frac{I_t}{2}}$$

$$v_t = \frac{N_t}{G_t - \frac{D_t + E_t}{2} + \frac{I_t}{2}}.$$

The product $(1 - q_1)(1 - q_2) \ldots (1 - q_{t-1})$ is equal to the probability of survival, S_t, from 4 weeks of gestation to the beginning of period t (in the absence of live births). The product $(1 - v_1)(1 - v_2) \ldots (1 - v_{t-1})$ is equal to the probability of continuing pregnancy, R_t, beyond the period $t-1$ in the absence of intra-uterine mortality. The product $S_t R_t$ is the probability that a pregnancy that entered observation at exactly 4 weeks duration of gestation will still be under observation at the beginning of period t, in the absence of in-

or out-migration. If d_t and n_t are the life table deaths and live births respectively, we have:

$$d_t = q_t \left(S_t R_t - \frac{n_t}{2} \right)$$

$$n_t = v_t \left(S_t R_t - \frac{d_t}{2} \right).$$

The terms of 3rd order can be ignored and we write:

$$d_t = q_t S_t R_t \left(1 - \frac{v_t}{2} \right)$$

$$n_t = v_t S_t R_t \left(1 - \frac{q_t}{2} \right).$$

The sum of the life table deaths gives the probability that a pregnancy that reached 4 weeks duration of gestation according to the convention used (i.e. on the average 2 weeks of real duration) will terminate in a non-induced intra-uterine death.

Example:

The numerical data in table 9.2 are taken from a study made in Kauaii (Hawaii) by the doctors French and Bierman in 1953–6.[5]

Out of a total of 3083 pregnancies observed for at least part of their duration, there were at most 306 (273 + 33) that terminated by an intra-uterine death, or 99 per thousand. The underestimation is thus considerable since the sum of d_t is equal to 237·2 per thousand.

Moreover, distributions of intra-uterine deaths by duration of gestation similar to D_t have often been the basis for the belief that the risk of spontaneous abortion reaches its peak around 2 to 3 months of gestation. In fact, this is not true; d_t is inversely related to t. This example shows how important it is to have a reliable technique of analysis.

Observation: The authors of this study used a slightly different procedure for their computations. They did not include $N_t/2$ in the denominator of q_t, nor did they include $D_t/2$ in that of V_t, and they computed d_t as the product of q_t and $S_t R_t$. The values obtained for d_t are the same, but the two last values of q_t are smaller than those above, 6·8 instead of 13·6, for example, for the last one. Both values are correct, but they do not have the same meaning: 6·8 per thousand is the probability of dying taking births into account, whereas 13·6 per thousand is the probability disregarding births.

[5]F. E. French and J. M. Bierman, *Probabilities of Fetal Mortality*, Public Health Reports (1962), **77**, pp. 835–47.

Table 9.2 Computation of the intra-uterine mortality table: data from Kanaii (Hawaii), 1953–6

t	Periods in weeks after gestation	G_t	I_t	D_t	N_t	E_t	Denominator of q_t	q_t, per thousand	Denominator of v_t	v_t, per thousand	S_t, per thousand	R_t, per thousand	$S_t r_t$, per thousand	$S_t r_t \left(1 - \dfrac{v_t}{2}\right)$	d_t, per thousand
1	4–7	0	592	32	0	0	296	108·1	280·0	0	1000	1000	1000	1000	108·1
2	8–11	560	941	72	0	1	1030	69·9	994	0	892	1000	892	892	62·4
3	12–15	1428	585	77	0	2	1719·5	44·8	1681	0	830	1000	830	830	37·2
4	16–19	1934	337	28	0	2	2101·5	13·3	2087·5	0	792	1000	792	792	10·5
5	20–23	2241	248	20	1	9	2360	8·5	2350·5	0·4	782	1000	782	782	6·6
6	24–27	2459	175	8	4	6	2541·5	3·15	2539·5	1·6	775	1000	775	774	2·4
7	28–31	2616	98	8	25	4	2650·5	3·0	2659	9·4	772	998	770	766	2·3
8	32–35	2677	67	8	72	6	2671·5	2·95	2703·5	26·6	770	989	762	752	2·2
9	36–39	2658	40	9	1074	3	2139·5	4·2	2672	402·1	768	963	739	590	2·5
10	40 and over	1612	0	11	1601	0	811·5	13·6	1606·5	996·6	765	576	441	221	3·0
	Total		3083	273	2777	33									237·2

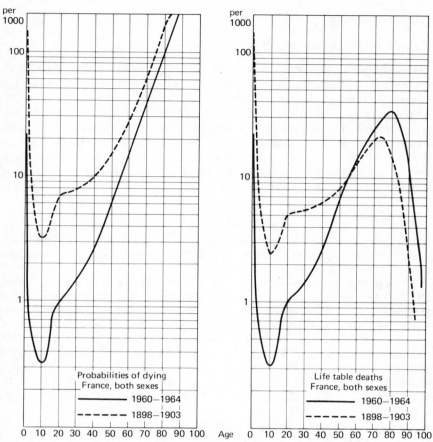

Figure 9.2 Life table functions – probabilities of dying and life table deaths: France, both sexes, 1898–1903 and 1960–64

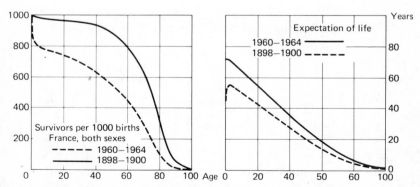

Figure 9.3 Life table functions – number of survivors and expectation of life: France, both sexes, 1898–1903 and 1960–64

F *

7 Some findings

Curves of probabilities of dying

The probabilities of dying, the number of survivors, the number of life table deaths and the expectation of life of the life tables, both sexes together, for France in 1898–1903 and 1960–64 are presented in figures 9.2 and 9.3. Although the two life tables represent very different pictures of mortality, the general shape of the curves and, in particular, that of the probability of dying remains the same—decreasing mortality between birth and 10 years of age, then increasing slowly up to about the middle of the adult years and more rapidly thereafter. This shape of the curve of the probability of dying is common to every known table.

Time trends

The decrease in mortality, first in developed countries, then in other countries, is one of the major phenomena of modern times. Table 9.3 gives the expectations of life at birth for France.

The female expectation of life has always been higher than that for males, but the difference has increased as mortality decreased. Lower mortality for women is considered to be a universal phenomenon. However, it is not certain that there are no exceptions in populations with a very low level of development. Excess mortality of women during their fertile years (for practical purposes between 15 and 40 years) is characteristic of populations of that type. It is due to deaths related to childbirth (so-called maternal mortality) which in those populations are on the order of 2 per 100 deliveries as opposed to 0·03 in France today. In France again, infant mortality has evolved as follows:

Around 1750	200 to 250	per thousand
1850	170	per thousand
1900	165	per thousand
1950	73	per thousand
1960	27·4	per thousand
1965	20·4	per thousand

Table 9.3 Time trends in expectation of life at birth: France

	Male	Female
18th century	About 30 years	
1820–1822	38·0 years	39·2 years
1850–1852	41·8 years	42·7 years
1898–1903	45·3 years	48·7 years
1908–1913	48·5 years	52·4 years
1920–1923	52·2 years	56·1 years
1928–1933	54·3 years	59·0 years
1933–1938	55·9 years	61·6 years
1946–1949	61·9 years	67·4 years
1952–1956	65·0 years	71·2 years
1960–1964	67·5 years	74·4 years

The decrease has not been restricted to exogenous mortality. Endogenous mortality has also decreased from rates on the order of 80 per thousand during the 18th century to 50 per thousand around 1850, 25 per thousand around 1900, and as low as 15 per thousand today. Progress in obstetrics has certainly played a large role in this decline, especially in the early part of the series.

8 Cohort life table

Although mortality is studied primarily on a period basis, there are a few longitudinal studies, in particular one by P. Delaporte.[6]

Open population

In an open population, which is generally the case, one begins with the probabilities of dying for the selected generation (or group of generations). Because life tables have until recently been established only at the time of a census, the whole sequence of probabilities of dying is not usually available. The method used to determine the missing ones depends on the purpose of the table.

a) If the decision is made to restrict the study to the evolution of trends, then deaths resulting from war and exceptional epidemics (such as the 1918 influenza) must be excluded. The missing probabilities can be determined by interpolation between the probabilities given in tables that have been adjusted, if necessary, for deviations from the trend. Take as an example the probability q_{36}; the tables for 1920–23, 1928–33, 1933–38 ... provide several values for this, each relating to a different group of generations. The chronological series of mortality rates for age 35–9 years, year by year, is available as well. From the latter the trend can be determined, and a coefficient can be assigned to each rate indicating the extent to which it deviates from the trend, a coefficient of 1·02, for example, for a rate which exceeds the trend value by 2%. Imagine that the coefficient in question is 1·01 on the average for the years 1928–33. By dividing the q_{36} value in the life table for 1928–33 by 1·01, we obtain the corrected value; it would be centered on 1931. In a similar way, we can find corrected values of q_{36} centered on 1921 and 1936.

b) If, on the other hand, fluctuations of mortality are to be taken into account, it is necessary to multiply each corrected or interpolated probability, obtained as described above, by the coefficient for the corresponding year and the relevant age. In the case of corrected probabilities this computation is actually unnecessary since it merely yields the probability given in the initial table.

It would be possible to use this procedure even for infant mortality. But when the double classification is available, it is preferable to compute from the start the series of infant mortality rates relating to each cohort. For case (a), we replace this series by trend values; in the second case, we use it as given.

Closed population

This may be the situation for historical populations with negligible

[6] P. Delaporte, *Evolution de la mortalité en Europe depuis les origines des statistiques de l'état civil* (Paris: 1941).

international migration, or for restricted groups covered in monographs, genealogies or updated files. If all the deaths are known, a table of deaths by age, or groups of ages, would be available. The example in table 9.4 refers to a group of women observed from age 15 years on.

Table 9.4 Female deaths by age in a cohort of women observed from age 15 on: example from historical data

| Age | Deaths | Survivors | |
		Absolute numbers	Per thousand at 15 years
15–19 years	7	265	1000
20–24 years	9	258	974
25–29 years	10	249	940
30–34 years	5	239	902
35–39 years	15	234	883
40–44 years	11	219	836
45–49 years	12	208	785
50–54 years	10	196	740
55–59 years	18	186	702
60–64 years	22	168	634
65–69 years	26	146	551
70–74 years	41	120	453
75–79 years	29	79	298
80–84 years	25	50	189
85–89 years	15	25	94
90 years and over	10	10	38

By adding the deaths starting from the bottom, we find the survivors at the beginning of each slice of the age distribution: 10 at 90 years, 25 at 85 years, 50 at 80 years of age . . . 265 at 15 years. By dividing each of these numbers by 265 and multiplying by 1000, we find the number of survivors at 5-year intervals of age per thousand 15-year olds.

The probabilities are obtained simply by dividing the deaths in an age group by the number of survivors at the beginning. Thus

$$_5q_{50} = \frac{10}{196} = 51 \text{ per thousand}$$

The English astronomer Halley used a similar method to study the mortality of Breslau in the period 1687–91. But 'Halley's method' is appropriate only for cross-sectional data if the population in question is closed and stationary, conditions which are practically never met.

10

Moves and migrations

1 Introduction

Birth, marriage, and death are indeed common events: the first and the last of these events happen to everyone, and the second to almost all of us. But, for each person taken separately, these are singular or infrequent events, usually marked by festivities or ceremonies.

Moves, in contrast, occur every day, even in populations that are said to be sedentary. They get little attention and, of course, they are not usually registered. There are certain moves, however, that stand out from the others. For the individual, these are the moves that have made a difference in his life, such as the departure from his native village, an important change of residence, or migration out of the country. In popular opinion and for the authorities, the important moves are those that raise problems, such as the 'flight from the countryside', certain international migrations, some seasonal migrations, or the daily commuting of millions of workers. For the demographer there is the additional concern to account for, and to study, an important factor in the evolution of populations.

Indeed, demography is a matter of examining particular populations defined in terms of time and space: the population of a certain country, the population of a certain region, the population of a certain district, township, city, state or urban area. Its subject includes the distribution of the population over a territory and the changes that occur in this respect. The demographer must therefore study the movement of population in space and time. Such movement has a variety of consequences. The daily commuting of workers does not modify the population, whether defined by presence or by usual residence. Other kinds of moves, such as seasonal migration, do not change the population defined by usual residence, and have little influence on the population that would be enumerated as present if the census was taken, as is customary, on a date when mobility is limited. Yet others are characterized by a change of residence. In the abstract one could very well consider that this would result in a change in the distribution of the population; however, if it does not at the same time involve a change of enumeration area, such moves are also of little concern to the demographer, at least in the present situation.

One should not forget that the distribution of the population over a territory is expressed in statistical form; this implies subdivision into classes or categories, into which hundreds or thousands of local units can be assembled.

The move that interests the demographer then is that which implies a change of subdivision, but since the categories are made up differently from one study to another, migratory movements in so far as it is of interest to, and is studied by, the demographer, has a definition which varies from one study to another. Thus, if France is subdivided by communes, a move which takes a farmer from his village to the neighbouring town is counted, whereas the moves of a family within the Paris area are left out, even when the number of miles covered is much greater than in the first case. The changing definition of migratory movement is a question of circumstances and scale.

On a national scale, migration from one country to another is the only kind that is counted, and in some circumstances it monopolizes all attention at the expense of internal movements. Among the latter, the so-called flight from the countryside or the flow of population toward certain parts of the country, have drawn much more attention than movement between cities, for example.

Problems of definition exist also in other fields. Although they do not occur in mortality, they appear in the study of fertility, especially if it is not restricted to live births; they remain minor, however. Nuptiality may raise more severe problems in certain populations, but those are not the ones where demography has been most developed. Thus it is with regard to migration that the difficulties in question are the greatest. They are such that the same words may cover different facts, according to whether we are talking about out-migration from a village or from a large city, for instance. It is important to keep this in mind, because otherwise one could be led to comparisons which are as devoid of meaning as comparisons between the nuptiality of one country and the fertility of another. We shall come back to these matters.

In addition, if one is only concerned with changes in distribution, as is often the case, it is tempting to consider as without interest those movements which tend to compensate each other, however sizable they may be in either direction. In other areas of demography, the analogy would be the balance of births and deaths and all that relates to replacement and reproduction (in a demographic, non-biological sense). But these notions are not relevant until after the fact, when we are looking into the consequences of phenomena that have been examined in and of themselves, because they are clearly distinguishable. The case of migration, a phenomenon where net balance is especially interesting, is of a similar nature, and this peculiarity, together with the difficulty of observation, has placed the focus on the end result, that is on the migratory balance. To persist indefinitely in this approach, however, would be contrary to the evolution of demography toward an ever finer analysis of the phenomena being studied. Even if migratory balances remain of primary importance, it is no longer possible to ignore the component movements.

On the other hand, in a textbook devoted to analysis, there is no need constantly to adapt the definition of migratory movement to changing circumstances. A part of the analysis, at least, is independent of that definition, and this is certainly true when we are dealing with migration proper. Daily commuting between home and work is beyond the usual framework of demography anyway.

In practice, we pay attention only to those changes which involve both residence and administrative unit. These are events that can be observed and are even known in certain countries through compulsory registration. Certain questions asked in the census may refer to mobility as well. Then, the study of migratory movement or, at least, of some of its aspects, can be related to the study of other demographic phenomena. As with these last, one must be concerned with both direct measurement of the phenomenon and with indirect measurement which makes use of the connection between the movement of a population in the past and its present state. Indirect measures are all the more important in cases where direct measures are deficient. They can therefore be expected to play a considerable role in the study of migration.

We must also stress that because of the problem of definition of geographic mobility, its study presents itself as that of a group of related phenomena, which can be examined by analogous, if not exactly the same, methods. But likeness in this respect does not guarantee comparability. The approach is the same as for fertility, whether the latter is defined in terms of live births, of births at term, or of terminations of pregnancies of whatever duration; we could even study artistic fertility in the same way, but that does not mean that we can compare the fertility of a novelist with that of a married women.

The concern for linking the analysis of migration with data extracted from censuses or surveys does not prevent the separate treatment of overall measures from the start; this conforms to the approach whereby we presented at the beginning of this book the elementary indices of natural movement, i.e. the crude death rate, birth rate, and marriage rate, before going into analysis of the corresponding phenomena.

Open and closed phenomena

Among the main phenomena studied up to now—nuptiality, the fertility of couples, and mortality—only the first, nuptiality, connects two populations, those of marriageable men and women. For the two others, there is no relationship at all of this kind. The connection established by nuptiality is also an opportunity for exchanges, so we characterize nuptiality as an open phenomenon, and the two others as closed phenomena.

Migration establishes relationships, and leads to exchanges between populations, so it belongs to the category of open phenomena. We can distinguish a population of origin and a population of destination. The relationship between these two populations is far less close, however, than in the case of nuptiality. In the latter case, a specific man corresponds to a specific women or, at least, to a small number of women. The same is only encountered in migration where an individual is summoned by relations or friends who are already settled elsewhere. Otherwise, the attraction of one population for members of the other is a characteristic of the whole population, or of an extended segment in that population.

The important thing to remember is that in the present state of development of demography, it is impossible to study open phenomena as such. With rare exceptions, one has to be content with studying them as one would closed phenomena. This is equivalent to assuming that changes which the phenomenon brings about in the two related populations do not modify the probability of the event in question in the population being studied; this would be true, for example, for out-migration as far as the population of origin is concerned.

Nevertheless, this does not prevent us from considering the destination of migrants. Tables which cross-tabulate the place of origin, for instance, and the place of destination are important in the study of migration. But it would be an exaggeration to view this as the essence of migration, or even to imagine that it is necessary to develop these tables to the point of cross-tabulating the 40 000 communes of France, each one separately with all the others. Communes, especially small ones, are really population elements and it would make scarcely more sense to give a lot of information on each one than to describe persons enumerated one by one.

One should not forget that the demographer studies migration insofar as it is a factor in the evolution of size and structure of particular subdivisions of populations that interest him, and hence that it is the exchanges between such subdivisions (nations, regions, classes of communes, etc.) that are to be examined. Tables made up for this purpose have a relatively small number of cells. In any case, the problem of comparison stemming from the definition would remain even if each commune were studied separately. Migration in and out of a large city such as Toulouse and that in and out of a remote village of Haute-Garonne do not have the same meaning.

Arrivals or departures[1]

Emigration from region A represents the departure of persons *of that region.* The situation is similar to that of deaths or that of marriages of single people. The event in question concerns members of the population being studied and it removes them from that population.

Immigration into region B represents the arrival of persons *foreign to that region.* Indices which relate the number of arrivals to the receiving population differ from classical demographic indices in the sense that those events which are included in the numerator do not concern particular members of the population represented in the denominator.

Because of this, there is no symmetry, in a movement from A to B, between the emigration from A toward B and the immigration into B coming from A. Under these conditions, the study of migratory movement is, at least in its theoretical aspect, a study of departures, or of emigration. Nevertheless, we shall be led to introduce indices of immigration because of the need to calculate the two components of the balance in the same way.

2 Measures

Indirect measures

a) Natural increase, the balance of migration, errors

Let us imagine that the population of a country was perfectly enumerated on

[1]According to the United Nations demographic dictionary, a distinction is sometimes made in English between migration within a country (for which the terms 'in-migration' and 'out-migration' are used). and migration across national boundaries (for which the terms 'immigration' and 'emigration' are preferred). However, in this chapter, the distinction will not be made, and only the terms 'immigration' and 'emigration' will be used (translator's note).

two successive dates, t_1 and t_2, and that births and deaths between t_1 and t_2 were registered without error as well. Let us designate as P_1 and P_2 the populations present at t_1 and t_2 respectively; N is the births, D is the deaths between t_1 and t_2. Invariably:

$$P_2 = P_1 + N - D + (I - E)$$

where I stands for immigration, E for emigration, between t_1 and t_2. Consequently:

$$(I - E) = (P_2 - P_1) - (N - D)$$

which means that the balance of migration, the excess of immigration over emigration, is equal to the difference between the growth of the population and natural increase (i.e. the excess of births over deaths) during the same period.

Under the assumed condition of total absence of errors, this formula is always exact. But its implication varies considerably according to whether births and deaths given for the population occurred in the territory in question or elsewhere. Let us consider the example of a rural community today. A large number of women go to a city hospital to deliver their babies. Children born outside of the village thus figure as immigrants in the migratory balance. On the other hand, a certain number of inhabitants of the community die in a hospital in a city and their deaths are not registered in the communities. In the balance, they are considered as emigrants. Let us call N_e and D_e the outside births and deaths, N_i and D_i the local births and deaths, and we have:

$$P_2 = P_1 + N_i - D_i + N_e - D_e + (I - E)$$

The difference $(P_2 - P_1) - (N_i - D_i)$ is now equal to the sum of $I - E$ and $N_e - D_e$, and it gives us no information whatsoever about migration.

This problem is generally eliminated when working with large units, such as the province (although it remains for provinces which have a very large city where the births and deaths of residents of other provinces occur). Moreover, this is a recent problem; it can be considered almost negligible before 1914. With historical populations, one must be careful about the deaths among children sent out to wet-nurses for these are equivalent to permanent immigration to the countryside and to permanent emigration from the city. Since 1951, in France, births and deaths have been based on the place of residence. The problem is thus eliminated, but this time populations P_1 and P_2 are populations of usual residence and not the de facto populations.

If errors are introduced, instead of P_1 and P_2, we have $P_1 + \Delta P_1$, $P_2 + \Delta P_2$, and the difference $P_2 + \Delta P_2 - \Delta P_1 - (N - D)$ is equal to $I - E + (\Delta P_2 - \Delta P_1)$. ΔP_2 and ΔP_1, the errors in the censuses, may be of the same magnitude if census methods have been the same, at least when large territorial or administrative units are involved; but one cannot be sure. In general ΔP_2 and ΔP_1, without necessarily being equal, will be in the same direction. The difference between them will thus be equal at most to the larger of the two. The difference between the sums $P_1 + \Delta P_1$ and $P_2 + \Delta P_2$ will thus give an idea of migration only if it is clearly larger than the enumeration error; for example, clearly larger than 2%.

We have not mentioned the error in N and D. In developed countries, this is insignificant; when it is not, there is no way of estimating residual migration by subtraction.

Example:

In 1962, the mountainous district of Vicdessos (Ariège) numbered 2171 inhabitants. In 1968, the population of usual residence was only 1873, which is 298 persons less. In the meantime, 109 births and 228 deaths among persons enumerated in the district were registered, giving a difference of − 119. Residual migration between 1962 and 1968 was thus equal to:

$$-298 - (-119) = -179.$$

This represents a balance in favour of emigration amounting to 8·2% of the initial population size.

This method may be applied to age groups, excluding the first one. Table 10.1 gives an example relating to Aveyron, female sex, censuses of 1926 and 1931. For the cohorts 10 to 25 years old in 1926, a net balance in favour of emigration is observed; for the others, the residual is usually negative (emigration) but small. The fact that there are two positive residuals of approximately similar magnitude suggests that residuals of less than 200 are not very meaningful.

Table 10.1 Residual migration between the censuses of 1926 and 1931: Aveyron, female population

Age in 1926 (1)	Numbers in 1926 (2)	Deaths 1926–1930 by age group (3)	cohort (4)	Numbers in 1931 Expected (5)	Observed (6)	Residual migration (7)
5– 9 years	8812	131	100	8712	8 8992	+ 180
10–14 years	14 523	80	145	14 378	13 256	− 1122
15–19 years	14 800	188	243	14 557	12 233	− 2324
20–24 years	12 356	280	276	12 080	11 178	− 902
25–29 years	10 841	274	281	10 560	10 404	− 156
30–34 years	9915	285	279	9636	9818	+ 182
35–39 years	10 585	276	300	10 285	10 166	− 119
40–44 years	10 908	316	362	10 546	10 557	+ 11
45–49 years	11 218	393	473	10 745	10 574	− 171
50–54 years	10 384	526	599	9 9785	9638	− 147
55–59 years	9681	648	840	8841	8741	− 100
60–64 years	8546	968	1164	7382	7327	− 55

Note: The deaths in column (3) are the sum of deaths observed each year in the age group considered, 131 for ages 5–9, 80 for ages 10–14 etc. We have taken as deaths in the cohort a weighted average, 2/5 for that line and 3/5 for the line below; thus, $243 = \dfrac{2 \times 188}{5} + \dfrac{3 \times 280}{5}$.

b) Another method

The method described above yields the residual migration for the period between two censuses. The following method, used in historical demography when death registration can be presumed complete, gives residual migration by group of generations, either for their whole life, or from birth to the date of a census. The method consists of subtracting the initial size of the group of generations, that is to say the births of a certain period, from the deaths among these persons occurring in the area over the period until the group has completely died out, or from the sum of the deaths and of persons present at the time of the census if the group has not died out by the latter date.

Table 10.2 gives an example for a village in the north of France, Sainghin-en-Mélantois, (already cited in table 7.10).

Table 10.2 Residual migration for the cohorts 1740–59 to 1840–49: Sainghin-en-Mélantois

Cohort	Births in Sainghin (1)	Deaths in Sainghin (2)	Enumerated in 1851 (3)	Deaths plus number enumerated (4)	Residual migration (4)−(1)
1740–1759	611	558	1	559	−52
1760–1769	321	284	11	295	−26
1770–1779	257	194	35	229	−28
1780–1789	340	197	99	296	−44
1790–1799	406	220	173	393	−13
1800–1809	383	159	184	343	−40
1810–1819	449	170	212	382	−67
1820–1829	526	159	301	460	−66
1830–1839	557	156	337	493	−64
1840–1849	530	123	358	481	−49

In interpreting this table, we should not forget that migration is most important before 30 years of age. From the cohorts of 1820–29 on, the balance of migration shows a continually decreasing portion of the ultimate balance which would only have been known if observation had been pursued well beyond 1851.

c) Lifetime migration

Place of birth is usually asked in the census. This information gives us, for example, the proportion of persons living in each province who were not born there. This proportion depends on both arrivals and departures in a rather complex way, so it is of little interest.

The same is not true for the analogous proportion of all nationals born in any given country. They constitute an almost closed population, so that the sum of the people who were not born in the province where they were enumerated represents the amount of lifetime emigration, between birth and the date of the census. This means that the people included neither died nor returned to their province of birth. To obtain an equivalent measure for a particular province, the enumerated persons must be regrouped by province of birth and then classified by province of residence.

A classification of this sort was made in 1901 in France. This time we will take Seine (see table 10.3).

Table 10.3 Place of birth and place of residence, French nationals: Seine, census of 1901

Citizens born in Seine			Citizens born elsewhere, enumerated in Seine	Total enumerated in Seine
Total	Enumerated elsewhere	Enumerated in Seine		
(1)	(2)	(3)	(4)	(5)
1 595 594	426 055	1 169 539	1 759 513	2 929 052

The number in column (2) represents lifetime emigration from Seine, that in column (4) lifetime immigration into Seine.

For France as a whole, columns (1) and (5) on the one hand, and (2) and (4) on the other hand, are each equal, and the result is table 10.4.

Table 10.4 Place of residence, French nationals: France, census of 1901

Citizens enumerated		
In the *département* of birth	In another *département*	Total
(1)	(2)	(3)
29 461 131	7 002 984	36 646 115

The number in column (2) represents both lifetime emigration and lifetime immigration, of internal origin, at the time of the census of 1901. The same data exist by age groups for each sex, but only for France as a whole. Table 10.5 gives the beginning of the tabulation for the male sex, after excluding French people born outside France.

Table 10.5 Place of birth by age, native born males: France, census of 1901

Cohort	Age (years)	Born in the *département* (thousands) (1)	Born in another *département* (thousands) (2)	Total (thousands) (3)
1896–1901	0– 4	1663	110	1743
1891–1895	5– 9	1426	135	1561
1886–1890	10–14	1393	178	1571
1881–1885	15–19	1299	268	1567
1876–1880	20–24	901	587	1488
1871–1875	25–29	1048	370	1418
1866–1870	30–34	955	356	1311

The numbers in column (2) represent once again lifetime emigration, but this time it corresponds to specific periods which increase with age. A similar table exists for 1911. We give it here for the same birth cohorts as above (table 10.6).

Table 10.6 Place of birth by age, native born males: France, census of 1911

Cohort	Age on 1 Jan 1911 (years)	Born in the *département* (thousands) (1)	Born in another *département* (thousands) (2)	Total (thousands) (3)
1896–1900	10–14	1410	194	1604
1891–1895	15–19	1256	263	1519
1886–1890	20–24	854	589	1443
1881–1885	25–29	1027	398	1425
1876–1880	30–34	994	395	1389
1871–1875	35–39	944	371	1315
1886–1870	40–44	869	331	1200

If there were neither migration abroad, nor mortality, the comparison of two figures corresponding to the same cohort, 263 and 135 for example, would give the emigration between 1901 and 1911 for this group, i.e. 128. We should then be able to obtain the same result by subtracting 1256 from 1426, whereas actually a higher figure, 170, is obtained.

Let us call deaths among those born and living in the area D_s, deaths among the emigrants D_e, and departures not followed by a return E, for the period between the two censuses. We have:

$$1256 = 1426 - E - D_s$$

$$263 = 135 + E - D_e$$

or two equations with 3 unknowns. To solve them we need a third equation. Let us give the value a to the ratio D_e/D_s. We then write:

$$D_e + D_s = 1561 - 1519 = 42$$

and

$$\frac{D_e}{D_s} = a$$

which gives:

$$D_s(1 + a) = 42$$

and therefore:

$$E = 170 - \frac{42}{1 + a}$$

If we assume that the mortality of emigrants is the same as that of the native residents, we can say:

$$a = \frac{263 + 135}{1256 + 1426} = \frac{398}{2682} \simeq 0 \cdot 15$$

hence:

$$D_s = 37$$
$$E = 133.$$

Note that if the mortality of migrants is nil, $E = 128$; if it is twice that of the resident born population,

$$E = 138.$$

In other words, when mortality is low, the difference in mortality between the native residents and emigrants is not very important.

Note 1:
If we knew D_s, the problem could be resolved without the additional hypothesis. In particular studies, monographs for instance, we may obtain D_s by an appropriate classification of the observations.

Note 2:
Tables 10.5 and 10.6 associate age with another characteristic which may vary with age. In such a situation, it is customary to replace the absolute numbers in the tables by numbers adding to 1000 for each row. Since we are using only one characteristic and its complement here, we can show simply the proportion having that characteristic. Table 10.7 presents the relative numbers of persons who were enumerated in the *département* where they were born.

Table 10.7 Proportion of persons enumerated in their province of birth per thousand of the same cohort, 1901 and 1911: France

Cohort	Age in 1901 (years)	1901	1911
1896–1900	0– 4	937	879
1891–1895	5– 9	914	827
1886–1890	10–14	887	592
1881–1885	15–19	829	721
1876–1880	20–24	606	716
1871–1875	25–29	739	718
1866–1870	30–34	728	724

Later we shall look into the meaning of these proportions.

Another and more recent method of getting at net migration is to ask in the census or survey, the place of residence at an earlier date, perhaps at the beginning of the preceding year or at the time of the preceding census. This last question was asked in France in the census of 1962. The US census has included a question on the residence at a date 5 years before the census.

As in the case of the place-of-birth question, this gives net migration, but this time between two dates rather than just since birth. Table 10.8 presents the distribution for 1962 of women age 24–31 years who were living in the Paris area in 1954. Those who were enumerated in 1962 in an area other than the Paris area are shown as emigrants.

Table 10.8 Residence status of women in the Paris region in 1954: women aged 24–31, census of 1962

	Non-migrants	Emigrants	Total
Absolute numbers	363 800	38 000	401 800
per thousand	905	95	1000

The emigrants could also be distributed according to their place of destination, either by increasing the number of columns in the above table, or by setting up a separate table like table 10.9

Table 10.9 Places of destination of emigrant women living in the Paris region in 1954: France, 1962

	Region of destination			
	Champagne	Picardie	. . . .	Total
Absolute numbers	1400	2660	. . . .	38000
per thousand	37	70	. . . .	1000

Finally, when working with small units, it is possible to compare nominal lists and determine in this way the net arrivals, and the combination of deaths and net departures. Vital registration gives the deaths occurring locally, and the residual departures can be obtained by subtraction. If deaths occur frequently in hospitals, the method cannot be used unless they are identified

Table 10.10 Micro-study of migration: a village of the Brie region, males, 1856–61

Age in 1856 (years)	Enumerated in 1856	Total departures	Deaths	Residual departures	Residual arrivals	Difference
0– 4	52	11	1	10	2	− 8
5– 9	57	7	1	6	4	− 2
10–14	32	6	—	6	7	+ 1
15–19	37	10	1	9	3	− 6
20–24	33	15	—	15	17	+ 2
25–29	37	13	—	13	12	− 1
30–34	54	7	1	6	5	− 1
35–39	28	5	1	4	3	− 1
40–44	32	4	1	3	1	− 2
45–49	23	4	2	2	3	+ 1
50–54	17	2	2	—	2	+ 2
55–59	37	7	5	2	5	− 1
60 and over	69	20	16	4		
Total	508	111	31	80	64	−16

by place of residence. Table 10.10 gives an example based on the male sex for a village in Brie.[2]

Table 10.11 Male migrants by age and marital status: rural districts of Denmark, 1966

Age (years)	Single	Married	Widowed	Divorced	Total
Less than 5	8422				8422
5– 9	4345				4345
10–14	3281				3281
15–19	15408	111			15519
20–24	16850	4803	1	23	21677
25–29	3343	4717	7	116	8183
30–34	955	3291	15	139	4400
35–39	527	2130	8	124	2789
40–44	406	1614	18	119	2157
45–49	276	1224	27	118	1645
50–54	224	1000	52	102	1378
55–59	221	867	79	89	1256
60–64	167	683	102	49	1001
65–69	119	605	126	38	888
70–74	56	257	131	24	468
75–79	44	114	135	12	305
80 and over	28	81	184	4	297
Total	54672	21497	885	957	78011

Table 10.12 Male migrants by age and marital status: whole of Denmark, 1966

Age (years)	Single	Married	Widowed	Divorded	Total
less than 5	24821				24821
5– 9	11948				11948
10–14	8673				8673
15–19	30221	322			30543
20–24	46842	15174	4	178	62198
25–29	11247	16941	19	734	28941
30–34	3075	11459	33	768	15335
35–39	1636	7306	33	697	9672
40–44	1100	5373	48	651	7172
45–49	748	3960	85	545	5338
50–54	542	2943	130	497	4112
55–59	482	2201	180	346	3209
60–64	367	1474	210	215	2266
65–69	259	1238	272	166	1935
70–74	117	575	269	56	1017
75-79	80	249	270	39	638
80 and over	50	187	393	20	650
Total	142208	69402	1946	4912	218468

[2] Y. Blayo, 'La mobilité dans un village de la Brie vers le milieu du XIXᵉ siècle', *Population* (1970), **3**, pp. 573–605'

Direct measures

When change of residence is registered, statistics on departures and arrivals according to certain characteristics of the migrant can be obtained. Those available for Denmark are the most detailed (by sex, age, marital status, previous residence and new residence). Table 10.11 shows men who migrated in 1966 from rural districts. Table 10.12 is for the whole of Denmark, also the male sex.

3 Analysis of geographical mobility

As we have said before, we treat geographical mobility as a closed phenomenon although it is an open phenomenon. We treated nuptiality in an equivalent way, although its character as an open phenomenon is even more marked. As for other phenomena, this way of measuring mobility permits, or at least attempts, isolation of a pure phenomenon, that is to say one that is undisturbed by other factors, of which mortality, which cannot be eliminated, is the most important. Although this is the typical analytical approach, it may appear surprising in the case of migration, since the latter, insofar as it is motivated by local overpopulation, depends closely on other demographic phenomena.

But if we refer to chemistry, we realize that the concern there for breaking down compounds into elements, which is a little bit like that which motivates the demographer, is independent of the way these elements might exist in nature and of the fact that most of them do not actually exist in that state. In fact, analysis is inseparable from the scientific approach, and it has its place in the study of migration as in that of other demographic phenomena.

As we said before, we emphasize the point of view of departure. So we will be preoccupied essentially with the analysis of emigration. But of course, we shall also talk about immigration and about the net balance. Finally, let us specify that we are going to take the longitudinal perspective, that is to say, that we shall study migration by generations.

As in the case of other phenomena, we compute the basic indices as if the necessary statistics were always available, even if we have to settle later for other more accessible indices. This approach seems to be the only one which provides the necessary coherence and allows us to see exactly what is involved in the measures that we may be forced to use.

Migration and first emigration

Given the longitudinal approach, we must study emigration for a well defined cohort, for example, people born in Ain between 1890 and 1894. If we could study those persons throughout their lifetime, we would have to take into consideration all their successive moves. But this would raise serious problems because of the non-comparability of various kinds of migration.

We could also define the group in such a way that observation will cease with moves out of Ain. In this case, emigration is defined as departure from a *département*, and the phenomenon being investigated is the first emigration from Ain; the word 'first' means that there has not been any other since the formation of the cohort under study. If we are dealing with a cohort of adults, this does not exclude the possibility that some have already moved before the formation of the cohort.[3]

In the following, however, we shall take first migration in the strict sense of departure from the area, *département* or region of birth. The reason for this is that place of birth is asked in the census and that the tabulation of the responses yields information on net first migration.

a) Probabilities of first migration

Imagine to start with that there are no deaths, and consider a segment of the Lexis diagram, the parallelogram at age x for the cohort under consideration. x may be expressed either in single years or in age groups.

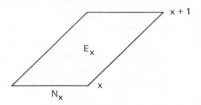

We will designate as N_x the number at their xth birthday of members of the cohort still living in the area (community, province, region) where they were born and as E_x the number of those who leave between their xth and their (x + 1)st birthday. The probability of first migration at age x, e_x, is obtained by dividing E_x by N_x. Thus, we have:

$$e_x = \frac{E_x}{N_x}.$$

In fact, there are always deaths at age x; let these be D_x. Some persons who died would have migrated, so that E_x should be increased by a certain quantity ε_x in order to apply the previous formula. To compute ε_x, we assume that those who died would, if they had lived, have migrated out to the same extent as the survivors. If all deaths D_x occurred immediately after the xth birthday, we would have:

$$\varepsilon_x = e_x D_x.$$

If all deaths D_x occurred immediately before the (x + 1)th anniversary, we would have:

$$\varepsilon_x = 0.$$

Since deaths occur throughout the year and are distributed fairly uniformly, we take:

$$\varepsilon_x = \frac{e_x D_x}{2}.$$

[3] Men born in 1901–5 present in Ain in 1921, for example.

So we have:

$$e_x = \frac{E_x + \varepsilon_x}{N_x} = \frac{E_x + e_x D_x/2}{N}$$

and therefore:

$$e_x = \frac{E_x}{N_x - D_x/2} \, . \tag{1}$$

Example:
Out of a total of 5000 young men born in the province where they are living, 200 leave at age 20 years whereas 60 die (mortality level in a historical population). The risk of first emigration is equal to:

$$\frac{200}{4970} = 40 \cdot 2 \text{ per thousand}$$

Without the correction, we would have obtained 40 per thousand, so in this case, the difference is insignificant.

Let us now imagine that the same conditions prevail over 5 years from age 20 to 24 years, i.e. that the mortality risk is 12 per thousand and the risk of first emigration is 40 per thousand. For the total of five years, the complete computation, on the basis of the five probabilities e_{20} to e_{24}, gives a probability of first migration of 185 per thousand. Over these five years, we observe 902 departures and 270 deaths.

Using formula (1) to evaluate the five-year probability gives:

$$_5e_{20} = \frac{902}{5000 - 135} = 185 \cdot 4.$$

Without the correction, we would have obtained $180 \cdot 4$ which differs from the true value by a quantity that is not entirely negligible. So it is when computing by age groups that the correction is necessary.

b) Number of non-emigrants

For the proportion e_x of people who leave the area where they were born, there is a corresponding proportion $r_x = 1 - e_x$ of people who stay there.

Consider the series $r_0, r_1 \ldots r_x$.

r_0 represents the proportion of people who in the absence of mortality would not have left the territory where they were born by the time of their first birthday. r_1 represents the equivalent proportion among those who continued to live in their area of birth through the year when they were age one. The product $r_0 r_1$ therefore represents the proportion of people in the generation being considered who were still living in their area of birth at the time of their second birthday.

By taking successively each term, we reach the product:

$$r_0 r_1 \cdots r_{x-1}.$$

If we take the initial size as a basis, the product represents the number of persons of the generation under study who, in the absence of mortality, would still be living in the territory of their birth at the time of their xth birthday. Designating this number as R_x, we have:

$$R_x = r_0 . r_1 \cdots r_{x-1}.$$

c) Non-emigration and survival

If we call the initial size N, and the number of departures and of deaths during the first year E_0 and D_0 respectively, the number N_1 at the first birthday is equal to:

$$N - E_0 - D_0 = N \left(1 - \frac{E_0}{N} - \frac{D_0}{N} \right).$$

We set:

$$\frac{E_0}{N} = e_0' \qquad \frac{D_0}{N} = q_0'.$$

From this we get:

$$N_1 = N(1 - e_0' - q_0')$$

and

$$q_0 = \frac{q_0'}{1 - e_0'/2} \qquad e_0 = \frac{e_0'}{1 - q_0'/2}$$

hence

$$e_0' = e_0 \left(1 - \frac{q_0'}{2} \right) \simeq e_0 - \frac{e_0 q_0}{2}$$

$$q_0' = q_0 \left(1 - \frac{e_0'}{2} \right) \simeq q_0 - \frac{e_0 q_0}{2}$$

and therefore:

$$1 - e_0' - q_0' \simeq 1 - e_0 - q_0 + e_0 q_0 = (1 - e_0)(1 - q_0).$$

Let's call the probability of survival to the first birthday under the conditions of mortality of the area of birth $_L S_1$. It is equal to $1 - q_0$; R_1, on the other hand, is the probability $1 - e_0$ of not emigrating. Therefore:

$$N_1 = N R_1 {}_L S_1.$$

The preceding demonstration is applicable at any age and we can write:

$$N_x = N_{x-1}(1 - e_{x-1})(1 - q_{x-1}).$$

It follows that:

$$N_2 = N_1(1 - e_1)(1 - q_1) = NR_1(1 - e_1)\,_LS_1(1 - q_1)$$

or:

$$N_2 = NR_2\,_LS_2$$

therefore by successive computation:

$$N_x = NR_x\,_LS_x.$$

This relationship can be interpreted as follows. At the xth birthday, the number of members of a generation who are still living in the territory where they were born is equal to the initial number multiplied by the product of the probability of surviving to age x under the mortality conditions of the area of birth, and the probability of not leaving that territory before age x, in the absence of mortality.

d) First emigration by marital status

The study of the relationships between mobility and marital status is interesting in itself, and it is also important from a theoretical point of view. Mobility is a disturbing phenomenon in relation to nuptiality, and the proportion single among the population at age x may depart significantly from the probability of remaining single at that age if the mobility of single people is very different from that of the entire population.

In addition to the relationships between mobility and marital status, there is a link between mobility and nuptiality stemming from marital migration. This happens when, say, a young girl leaves the community where she has been living since birth to join her husband in the community where he lives. Since the marriage often takes place in the community where the girl resides, the departure then occurs after marriage and consequently represents the departure of a married person. In the opposite case where a young man goes to live in the community where his wife lived before they married, the migration appears as that of a single person or a married person according to whether the change of residence is considered to have occurred before or after the marriage.

To avoid this and to maintain coherence between the statistics on population structure and those on change, it would be necessary to adopt the following rules:

1 a movement between the place of residence before marriage and the place where the marriage is celebrated is a movement of single persons: an emigration from the place of residence, an immigration into the place of celebration;

2 when the place of residence after marriage is different from the place of celebration, there is as well emigration from the former to the latter, and this emigration involves married people.

According to those rules, the young man who goes to the locality where his bride lives to get married and leaves again after the wedding to settle elsewhere, enters the single population of that locality by immigration and then leaves it by marriage; at the latter point he enters the class of married men and then leaves this again by his departure. The balance sheet is zero for each group and the desired coherence is ensured. In fact, those rules are inapplicable and unsuitable

Let's confine ourselves to the case of young people who have not yet left their place of birth and who are going to settle after their marriage in the husband's place of birth. If the marriage takes place there, we have a first emigration of a single woman; if the marriage takes place at the place of birth of the woman, we have:

a first emigration of a single man;
a return to the place of birth of a married man;
a first emigration of a married woman.

But since registration, where it exists, is limited to changes of residence, the departure and return of the man is not recorded. Even if it were, there would still be the drawback of having to deal with the emigration of a single woman or of a married woman depending on the place where the marriage occurred.

Imagine now that the marriage record is duplicated in the case of mixed marriages and that one copy is assigned to the residence of each of the partners before marriage. Marriage is assumed to have taken place simultaneously at both locations. In that case, there is no need to reckon with any movement other than the eventual transition from the residence before marriage to a different residence afterwards. This would always be a migration of married persons. Thus, in our example, both the man and the woman shift locally from the category of single to that of married persons; then the woman migrates as a married person.

Because of the embryonic state of migration statistics, these problems have thus far rarely been raised. They must be considered, however, if we analyse the results. In a monograph, it is possible to use marriage notices. They play approximately the same role as double registration, the only difference being a slight difference in date and the existence of a small proportion of notices that are not followed by a marriage.

Let's return to the example of the village in Brie. A boy recorded as single on the census list of 1856 who is not included on the list of 1861 is an emigrant. His departure is taken as that of a single person if his name is not included in the marriage notices between 1856 and the beginning of 1861 and as that of a married man in the opposite case. Conversely, a married woman included on the census list of 1861 and not on that of 1856 is an immigrant. Her entry is taken as that of a single woman if she figures in the marriage notices of the village from 1856 to the beginning of 1861 and is mentioned there as a resident of the village. On the contrary, she has entered as a married woman if she is not mentioned in these notices, or if she is mentioned as living in another community.

e) Probabilities of first emigration for single people

The same procedure is used as for the whole population, but now with two disturbing phenomena, death and first marriage. We keep the assumption that the single people who married or died would have had the same pattern of emigration as those who survived and did not marry, if they had not undergone death or marriage.

The probability of first emigration for single persons at age x, $_ce_x$, is then given by the formula:

$$_ce_x = \frac{_cE_x}{C_x - (_cM_x + _cD_x)/2}$$

where C_x represents the number of single persons in the generation being considered who were born in the area, and reach their xth birthday, and $_cE_x$, $_cM_x$, and $_cD_x$ designate departures, marriages and deaths respectively among these single persons between their xth and their $(x+1)$st birthday.

The correction factor $_cD_x/2$ is insignificant for an interval of one year and of small importance for a period of 5 years. The same is not true for $_cM_x/2$ which may be greater than 15% of C_x for one year and close to 50% of C_x for a period of 5 years. In the latter case, the result obtained will necessarily be very approximate.

f) Non-emigration, probability of remaining single and survival

By definition,

$$C_{x+1} = C_x - _cE_x - _cM_x - _cD_x$$
$$= C_x(1 - _ce'_x - _cn'_x - _cq'_x)$$

where $_ce'_x$, $_nn'_x$ and $_cq'_x$ designate respectively the ratios

$$\frac{_cE_x}{C_x}, \qquad \frac{_cM_x}{C_x}, \qquad \frac{_cD_x}{C_x}.$$

On the other hand, we have:

$$_ce_x = \frac{_ce'_x}{1 - (_cn'_x + _cq'_x)/2}$$

$$_cn_x = \frac{_cn'_x}{1 - (_ce'_x + _cq'_x)/2}$$

$$_cq_x = \frac{_cq'_x}{1 - (_ce_x + _cn_x)/2}$$

which can also be written:

$$_ce'_x \simeq _ce_x \frac{_ce_x}{2}(_cn_x + _cq_x)$$

$$_cn'_x \simeq _cn_x - \frac{_cn_x}{2}(_ce_x + _cq_x)$$

$$_c q'_x \simeq {}_c q_x - \frac{{}_c q_x}{2} \left({}_c e_x + {}_c n_x \right) .$$

Hence:

$$1 - {}_c e'_x - {}_c n'_x - {}_c q'_x = 1 - {}_c e_x - {}_c n_x - {}_c q_x + {}_c e_x \, {}_c n_x + {}_c e_x \, q_x + {}_c n_x \, {}_c q_x$$

and leaving third order terms out:

$$1 - {}_c e'_x - {}_c n'_x - {}_c q'_x = \left(1 - {}_c e_x \right) \left(1 - {}_c n_x \right) \left(1 - {}_c q_x \right).$$

Hence:

$$\frac{C_{x+1}}{C_x} = \frac{{}_c R_{x+1}}{{}_c R_x} \cdot \frac{{}_L \Gamma_{x+1}}{{}_L \Gamma_x} \cdot \frac{{}_{cL} S_{x+1}}{{}_{cL} S_x} .$$

$_{cL}S_x$ designates the probability of survival for single persons under local conditions.

$_c R_x$ is the probability that a single person will not migrate before age x in the absence of marriage and mortality.

$_L \Gamma_x$ is the probability that a non-emigrant will remain single in the absence of mortality.

g) The proportion of non-emigrants at age x

Call the probability of surviving to age x for the whole generation, including emigrants, S_x. The number at age x is NS_x, and the proportion ρ_x of non-emigrants is then:

$$\frac{NR_x \, {}_L S_x}{NS_x} = R_x \, \frac{{}_L S_x}{S_x}$$

which can be reduced to R_x when $_L S_x$ and S_x are equal, that is to say when the mortality of non-emigrants is equal at each age to that of the entire group of members of the generation in question.

Migration occurs mostly in early adulthood. Up to this point, the difference in mortality between those who remain at home and the emigrants will not cause $_L S_x$ to depart from S_x. After that, the effect of mortality differences will be small at first because mortality is low in early adulthood. So, we may accept that the proportion of non-emigrants is of the same order of magnitude as R_x well into adulthood.

Consider now the proportion of non-emigrants at two ages, x and y $(y > x)$. On the one hand, we have:

$$\rho_x = R_x \cdot \frac{{}_L S_x}{S_x} \quad \text{et} \quad \rho_y = R_y \cdot \frac{{}_L S_y}{S_y} .$$

If S and $_L S$ were equal, we would get the probability of emigration between age x and age by computing:

$$\frac{\rho_x - \rho_y}{\rho_x} = 1 - \frac{\rho_y}{\rho_x}$$

since that would be equal to $(R_x - R_y)/R_x$.

What does the same computation yield when S is different from $_LS$?

$$\frac{\rho_y}{\rho_q} = \frac{R_y}{R_x} \cdot \frac{_LS_y}{_LS_x} \cdot \frac{S_x}{S_y}.$$

If mortality is very low for the two categories between x and y, or if it is the same, ρ_y/ρ_x differs little from R_y/R_x, or is equal to it. It is also true that if R_y/R_x is small compared to S_y/S_x, that is to say if migration is heavy compared to mortality, a fairly marked difference in mortality between those who remain at home and the emigrants would not have a great effect.

Example:

Suppose that R_x falls from 1000 at age 15 to 800 at age 25 years, and that we have:

$$\frac{_LS_{25}}{_LS_{15}} = 940 \qquad \frac{S_{25}}{S_{15}} = 952.$$

We have:

$$\frac{\rho_x}{\rho_y} = 0.8 \times \frac{940}{952} = 0.790$$

and the probability of first emigration between 15 and 25 years would be 0.210 instead of 0.0200.

h) The proportion of non-emigrants among single people of age x

This time, we must compare:

$$N \ _cR_x \ _{Lc}S_x \ _L\Gamma_x$$

with $N \ _cS_x \ \Gamma_x$
which gives a ratio $_c\rho_x$ such that:

$$_c\rho_c = \ _cR_x \frac{_{Lc}S_x}{_cS_x} \frac{_L\Gamma_x}{\Gamma_x}$$

and we have:

$$_c\rho_x = \ _cR_x.$$

when the *mortality* and *nuptiality* of the single people who did not emigrate are equal at each age to the mortality and nuptiality of all single people. The fear inevitably arises that this condition will not be realized, even in an approximate way.

G

i) The proportion single among non-emigrants

The number of non-emigrants at age x is equal to $NR_x {}_LS_x$ whereas the number of single non-emigrants is $N {}_cR_x {}_L\Gamma_x {}_{Lc}S_x$.

The ratio c_x is given by:

$$c_x = \frac{{}_cR_x}{R_x} \cdot \frac{{}_{Lc}S_x}{{}_LS_x} \cdot {}_L\Gamma_x$$

${}_{Lc}S_x/{}_LS_x$ is close enough to 1, particularly for women.

So we have:

$$c_x \simeq \frac{{}_cR_x}{R_x} {}_L\Gamma_x.$$

In order for c_x to be a good indicator of local nuptiality, it is necessary that ${}_cR_x$ and R_x differ little. In other words, the emigration of single people at each age must be similar to the emigration among the entire generation. Without a study of migratory movement by marital status, we don't know by how much ${}_cR_x/R_x$ diverges from unity.

Note:

We must not confuse conditions under which R_x and ρ_x are equal with the hypotheses on which the computation of first emigration probabilities are based.

These hypotheses are equivalent to assuming that the probabilities of dying and of leaving are independent for a non-emigrant. This implies, for example, that mobility is the same in social circumstances where mortality is low and in those where mortality is high. Thus, no comparison between non-emigrant and emigrant whatsoever is made.

The equating of ρ_x and R_x supposes, on the contrary, that mortality is the same among non-emigrants and among emigrants; so it compares the two. This condition does not postulate independence but continuity. The phenomenon being observed, migration, must not modify the disturbing phenomenon, mortality.

j) The problem of return migration

The preceding is meant, among other things, to facilitate the analysis of statistics where persons of a certain age, born in a given area, are classified according to the place where they are residing at the time of the census. But this does not cover all first emigrations; during the period between birth and a census or between two censuses, every departure which is followed by a return is cancelled, in a way, by this return.

Yet, to cancel a departure by a return which often occurs a long time later, has the drawback of either ignoring the departure or revealing it, depending on whether the period observed includes both the departure and the return, or whether it does not happen to cover the return. It is preferable to consider that a return is the equivalent, at least in a certain way, of the omission of a departure and that the aggregate of E_x first departures and U_x first returns is equivalent to $(E_x - U_x)$ first departures.

If we call $(e-i)_x$ the probability of net first emigration corresponding to $E_x - U_x$, we write:

$$(e-i)_x = \frac{E_x - U_x}{N_x - D_x/2}.$$

It is then natural also to write:

$$i_x = \frac{U_x}{N_x - D_x/2}$$

that is to say to define a probability of return migration. e_x and i_x are now defined separately, and we can therefore extend the concept to cases where i_x is larger than e_x. We would then have a probability of net first emigration which is negative.

An emigrant who comes back to the place of birth may leave again and we may then consider that this new departure cancels a return. We successively introduce all the departures and all the returns relating both to the cohort and to the area under consideration. e_x and i_x then designate the probabilities of emigration and immigration for this cohort-area complex.

On the basis of these probabilities, either positive or negative, we may also define $_n r_x = 1 - _n e_x$. $_n r$ will be greater than 1 when returns exceed departures. In the same way, we define $_n R_x$ so that:

$$_n R_x = {}_n r_0 \; {}_n r_1 \cdots {}_n r_{x-1}$$

and we always have:

$$N_x = N \; {}_n R_x \; S_x.$$

1) Applications

We are now equipped to interpret certain data from the 1901 and 1911 French censuses in the light of the above observations.

$_L S$ and S being little different, say, up to 40 years, we say that among men born in 1871–5, the probability of net non-emigration (non-emigration, or emigration followed by return before 1901) was close to 0·74 (see table 10.7).

We may estimate the probabilities of net emigration between 1901 and 1911 as well, and this is more interesting. They are as shown in table 10.13 by cohort.

2) Another application

Among the women born in 1930–37 who were living in the Paris region in 1954 and were enumerated in 1962, 95 per thousand were not living in the Paris region any more at the latter date. The probability of emigration not followed by return between 1954 and 1962 was approximately 95 per thousand if we use the perfectly acceptable hypothesis that the probabilities of surviving $_L S$ and S were little different.

Table 10.13 Probabilities of net emigration for males by cohort: France, 1901 to 1911

Cohort	Age in 1901 (years)	e_x per thousand
1896–1900	0– 4	62
1891–1895	5– 9	95
1886–1890	10–14	148*
1881–1885	15–19	130
1876–1880	20–24	70*
1871–1875	25–29	28
1866–1870	30–34	5

*In order to calculate these probabilities, the observed proportions at 20–24 years have been replaced by proportions estimated by interpolation; the purpose is to eliminate the extraneous effect of military service.

3) The problem at older ages

Returning to the tables for the male sex in 1901 and 1911, the proportions of men born in a *département* who had been enumerated there for the birth cohorts aged 40 to 49 years in 1901 are shown in table 10.14.

Table 10.14 Proportion enumerated in *département* of birth per thousand males of selected ages: France, censuses of 1901 and 1911

Age in 1901 (years)	1901	1911
40–44	735	749
45–49	743	765
50–54	765	788
55–59	783	805

The proportion increases a little between 1901 and 1911. This could be due to return migration to the area of birth which was continuous and weak, but it could also be due to excess mortality among the emigrants. Because of the feeble strength of the movement, it is impossible to settle the issue. All we can do is assume that excess mortality among emigrants is not very likely in this period and that therefore return migration is more convincing.

Note:
In theory, the emigration probabilities are defined in such a way as to eliminate the extraneous influence of mortality. A probability of return U_x should be defined in the same way; it would be given by the following ratio (except for a correction factor):

$$u_x = \frac{U_x}{NS_x - NR_x \, _\mathscr{L}S_x}$$

so that, without mortality, we would have a number of returns, U'_x equal to:

$$u_x N(1 - R_x)$$

and i_x would be replaced by:

$$i'_x = \frac{U'_x}{NR_x} = u_x \frac{1 - R_x}{R_x} = u_x \left(\frac{1}{R_x} - 1 \right)$$

whereas we had written:

$$i_x = \frac{U_x}{R_x \, _LS_x} = u_x \frac{S_x - R_x \, _LS_x}{R_x \, _LS_x} = u_x \left(\frac{S_x}{_LS_x} \frac{1}{R_x} - 1 \right)$$

i_x and i'_x are equal only if S_x and $_LS_x$ are equal.

The way in which i_x is computed therefore implicitly assumes that the mortality of non-emigrants is the same as that of the whole population. So the introduction of net migration puts us in the position of behaving as though the condition of continuity holds, whereas it is possible that it does not. For the time being, we do not have enough information on the mortality differential between migrants and non-migrants to evaluate the error involved.

Overall view of migration

a) Introduction

1) Example of a cohort
Up to this point, we have been considering a cohort of persons born in a given area during a certain period, and the migration that relates both to this cohort and to this area. After starting with first departures only, we extended the study to all departures and returns, of whatever order. Thus, there are no other migrations that involve both the cohort and the area. The other migrations of the cohort concern other areas; these are migrations of the second and higher orders which are not return migrations to the area left at the time of first departure. To study them would be equivalent to following the movements of a cohort throughout its lifetime. This is not really feasible today, except through retrospective observation.

2) The case of an area
Up to now we have given priority to the cohort, the first element in the cohort-area pair. But some studies may demand that we focus exclusively on the territory. In that case, it is necessary to consider all the inhabitants of that area. We are not concerned any longer about a cohort defined once and for all by original events occurring in a well defined period, but about a population that is constantly being reshaped by births, deaths, immigration, and emigration.

If the area is small. only moves in and out of that area are usually considered; in other words, immigration and emigration, which are one component of population change.

In a large territory, we may also consider internal migation despite the heterogeneity of movements originating in different communities. When dealing with a nation that is not greatly affected by international migration, there is scarcely anything left except internal migration, and its study becomes a study of events which involve the population without modifying its size and age distribution. And since a person may move several times, just as a woman may have several children, there are analogies between internal mobility for an entire population and the fertility of an adult population.

b) Net migration, gross migration

The difference between entries and departures is called net migration or residual migration. It is called net immigration if the entries are more numerous, net emigration in the opposite case. It is also possible to treat net migration as an algebraic quantity. It is then considered positive when immigration is larger, since in that case the balance of migration increases the population. The sum of entries and exits is called gross migration. The United Nations demographic dictionary does not indicate clearly whether this may include movements inside the area in question; if so internal migrations should be counted twice, once as an arrival and once as a departure. This approach is justified when change of residence is registered at the point of departure and at the point of entry. But this could be a source of confusion if one wanted to include movement within communities also, since these can only be recognized as moves (and not as arrivals or departures). A retrospective survey inquires in an analogous way about moves rather than about arrivals and departures. In fact, the usage is not settled, and it is necessary to specify exactly what is to be understood by gross migration.

Yearly migration rate

This rate is obtained by relating the migration of one year, either gross or net, to the average population of the area in question during that year. Table 10.15 gives an example based on Copenhagen, in 1966 (figures are in thousands).

Table 10.15 Yearly migration in thousands: Copenhagen, 1966

Average population	Immigration	Emigration	Migratory balance	Gross migration
670·5	39·0	50·9	−11·9	89·9

The rates are as follows:
Net emigration: 17·6 per thousand
Gross migration: 133·2 per thousand

For Denmark as a whole, we may present the results in two different ways according to whether or not internal migration is included.

Table 10.16 Yearly migration in thousands excluding internal migration:
Denmark, 1966

Average population	Immigration	Emigration	Migratory balance	Gross migration
4793	29·8	28·1	1·7	57·9

Table 10.17 Yearly migration in thousands including internal migration:
Denmark, 1966

Average population	Immigration	Emigration	Migratory balance	Gross migration
4793	489·9	488·2	1·7	978·1

1 Without internal migration (see table 10.16).
Net migration rate: 0·4 per thousand
Gross migration rate: 12·1 per thousand.

2 With internal migration (see table 10.17).
Net migration rate: 0·4 per thousand
Gross migration rate: 204·1 per thousand.

When internal migration alone is considered, the number, which this time is a number of moves, can also be related to the total population. This is practiced in Sweden for instance. The rate obtained in this way could perhaps be called the internal mobility rate in order to distinguish it from gross migration.

c) Internal mobility rates by sex and age

By relating the annual number of internal moves of persons of a selected sex and age to the average population for that sex and age in that year, we obtain the corresponding internal mobility rate for the year.

As an example, table 10.18 shows the computations for Swedish females in 1966.

Mobility by generations

The foregoing rates relate to one year. To make up a similar table for a generation or a group of five generations, it would first be necessary to assemble yearly tables covering a century, and this is not possible at present. Since these tables are established on the basis of age groups, they would then have to be modified to extract the data by generations or groups of generations.

So the only means of obtaining mobility by birth cohort is the retrospective survey. Since moves occur at all ages, old people would have to be interviewed, but in so doing the risk of bias (selection by death) would be increased. For a single survey, the best thing is to interview persons at the end of their adult years, but repeated surveys among people at all ages would be preferable.

Table 10.18 Internal mobility rates for females by age: Sweden, 1966

Age group (years)	Average population	Internal migration	Mobility rate per thousand
	thousands		
0– 4	280·1	31·1	111·0
5– 9	254·2	16·3	64·1
10–14	260·5	11·3	43·4
15–19	297·5	31·6	106·2
20–24	306·9	65·5	213·4
25–29	237·4	34·4	144·9
30–34	217·2	17·9	82·4
35–39	232·7	12·8	55·0
40–44	259·6	10·2	39·3
45–49	266·5	8·3	31·1
50–54	259·8	6·4	24·6
55–59	255·1	5·4	21·2
60–64	227·3	4·5	19·8
65–69	193·2	3·6	18·6
70–74	153·4	2·2	14·3
75–79	108·9	1·5	13·8
80	96·7	1·4	14·5
Total	3907·0	264·4	67·7

A survey was conducted in France by INED in 1961 as an experiment. An analysis was done by cohort for people living in the countryside at the time of the survey.[4] Table 10.19 shows the mobility rates for three cohorts, sexes combined, starting at 15 years of age; moves prior to that age were not recorded.

Table 10.19 Example of mobility rates for three cohorts: France, survey of 1961

Age (years)	Cohort		
	1890 and earlier	1891–1895	1896–1900
	per thousand	per thousand	per thousand
15–19	39	46	24
20–24	98	75	93
25–29	52	75	76
30–34	47	53	31
35–39	31	34	32
40–44	30	24	22
45–49	18	15	17
50–54	24	3	15
55–59	18	16	23
60–64	19	18	
65–69	13		

[4]G. Pourcher, 'Un essai d'analyse par cohorte de mobilité géographique et professionnelle', *Population* (1966), **2**, pp. 355–73.

Random fluctuations are clearly important. The importance of the error resulting from the fact that only survivors are interviewed is not known, and there is no certainty that the proportion of the latter is not higher or lower among the migrants than for the whole population.

d) Cumulative mobility, average number of moves

Suppose however that this error is minor and that the foregoing rates are pure mobility rates without the extraneous influence of mortality.

By adding the rates after 15–19 years (and multiplying by five since we are dealing with annual rates and 5-year age groups), we obtain the cumulative mobility between age 15 years and successively, 20, 25 . . . 70 years (see table 10.20).

Table 10.20 Cumulative mobility for three cohorts: France, survey of 1961

Age (years)	Cohort		
	1890 and earlier	1891–1895	1896–1900
	Cumulative mobility per thousand		
20	195	230	120
25	685	605	585
30	945	980	965
35	1180	1245	1120
40	1335	1415	1280
45	1485	1535	1390
50	1575	1610	1475
55	1695	1625	1505
60	1785	1705	1665
65	1880	1795	
70	1945		

If the mobility rates had been computed on the basis of continuous observation of the generations in question, the cumulated mobility up to age x would not necessarily be equal to the average number of moves after age 15 of the persons interviewed at age x. It would be lower if the non-migrants were less susceptible to death, higher if they were more susceptible than the migrants.

The model implies that for the survivors cumulative mobility and the average number of movements are identical. But the same is not true for the whole population, survivors and deceased together, unless the relationship between mobility and mortality is weak.

We have already encountered an analogous situation in the study of fertility. But in that case, available measures showed that cumulative fertility differs little from the average number of children for women or couples who have survived to that age or that duration of marriage.

e) First moves, successive moves

If there were a strong link between mortality and mobility, it would be

G*

necessary to study mobility on the basis of the probabilities of migration for each order, analogous to those we have defined for first emigration. If, on the contrary, the relationship were weak, it would be possible to study migration of whatever order by relating the moves of that order to the total survivors, whatever their number of moves might be. One would thus study first migration by relating first moves to the total survivors of the cohort being considered, instead of relating them to all members who have not yet emigrated. The 'first moves column of the table' would thus be obtained instead of the 'probabilities of first emigration' from the same table of mobility of the first order.

With a single retrospective survey, this is the only possible way to proceed. But the mobility rates for first moves obtained in this way are representative of the entirety of the group of cohorts only if the link between mortality and mobility is weak. Let us assume that this is the case. It is then possible to compute, from the mobility rates for first moves, the number of non-emigrants R_x and the probabilities of first emigration. In table 10.21, we present the cohorts previous to 1900, both sexes together, as an example.

f) Number of moves

It is possible to classify the respondents according to the number of moves, in the same way as completed families are classified according to the number of children. Here is the tabulation for the INED survey converted to a total of 1000 (generations before 1900, from 15 to 50 years old).

No change	266
1	302
2	187
3	122
4	72
5 and over	51
Total	1000

The average number of moves is 1·59.

Probability of a first or a new move

We proceed in the same way as for parity progression ratios. We cumulate the relative frequencies from the bottom up and relate each cumulated number to the one above (see table 10.22).

g) Intervals between moves

The number of moves that a person may achieve in a given time (between ages 15 and 50 years for example in the INED survey) is inversely related to the length of the interval between moves. So we find ourselves in the same situation as in studies of the family: the variation in the intervals according to the order of the move must be studied for groups of persons having the same total number of moves. When working this way, intervals should be computed as differences in the mean ages at the time of the moves of each order. In table

Table 10.21 Computation of the number of non-migrants and the probabilities of first migration per thousand, cohorts born prior to 1900: France, survey of 1961

| Age (years) | Mobility rate | | Exact age x | Non-emigrants at age x R_x | Probabilities $5^e x$ per thousand |
| | Annual | in 5 years | | | |
	per thousand				
15–19	34	170	15	1000	170
20–24	66	330	20	830	398
25–29	25	125	25	500	250
30–34	7	35	30	375	93
35–39	10	50	35	340	147
40–44	3	15	40	290	52
45–49	1	5	45	275	18
50–54	2	10	50	270	37
55–59	4	20	55	260	77
60–64	1	5	60	240	21
65–69	3	15	65	235	64
			70	220	

Table 10.22 Computation of the probability of moving by order of move, cohorts born prior to 1900: France, survey of 1961

Moves	Frequency	Cumulation	Desired probability
0	266	1000	734
1	302	734	589
2	187	432	567
3	122	245	502
4	72	123	415
5	51	31	

Table 10.23 Mean ages at moves before age 50, cohorts of 1910 and earlier: France, survey of 1961

| 1 move only | 2 moves | | 3 moves | | |
	1st	2nd	1st	2nd	3rd
26·2	24·2	34·4	21·8	28·8	37·3

Table 10.24 Intervals between moves before age 50, cohorts of 1910 and earlier: France, survey of 1961

| 2 moves | 3 moves | |
Interval 1–2	Interval 1—2	Interval 2—3
10·2	7·0	8·5

10.23, we present the ages at moves before age 50 years for the cohorts of 1910 and earlier. The corresponding intervals in years to one decimal place are given in table 10.24.

4 The destination of migrants

Up to now we have used almost the same approach to migration as to another demographic phenomenon, either nuptiality among the single or female fertility, according to whether we are talking about first migration or all moves. In doing so, we have left aside that which is specific to migration, the fact that a person leaves a place to settle in another one. Because of this, migration is not defined only by its intensity; it is also a question of destination. The latter may be defined more or less precisely, but one is always limited by the need to end up with tables that would not be too awkward to use.

Example of a particular area

Let's turn our attention to a particular *département*, say Creuse. A look at the tables for the census of 1901 in which the native born of each *département* are classified according to the *département* where they were enumerated shows that, leaving Creuse itself alone, the natives of Creuse are settled primarily in neighbouring *départements* and in Seine, Rhône and Loire.

We may then, for Creuse, summarize the table as in table 10·25, in absolute numbers and per thousand Frenchmen born in Creuse and enumerated in 1901.

Table 10.25 *Département* of residence of French citizens born in Creuse: France, census of 1901

Département of residence	Number enumerated	Per thousand	
Creuse	231 589	749	749
Haute-Vienne	6585	21	
Indre	2752	9	
Cher	1301	4	
Allier	4301	14	59
Puy-de-Dôme	2257	7	
Corrèze	1202	4	
Seine	31 530	102	102
Rhône	5806	19	
Loire	2041	6	25
Other *départements*	19 939	65	65
Total	309 303	1000	1000

Dividing by the total, we obtain a proportional distribution of the whole according to the place of enumeration. This may be further condensed by regrouping the neighbouring *départements*, on the one hand, and Rhône and Loire on the other. The above procedure has the obvious drawback of burying the interesting part of the data under the weight of those who stayed at home. One might instead, or at least in addition, produce a table such as table 10.26 which gives the proportional distribution of the emigrants only.

Table 10.26 Distribution of emigrants from Creuse by residence: France, census of 1901

Area where emigrants are enumerated	Per 1000 emigrants
Neighbouring *départements*	235
Seine	406
Rhône et Loire	100
Other *départements*	259
Total	1000

Note that the class 'other *départements*' is not negligible and there may be reason to study it in detail to simplify or organize it.

Here is another example, concerning internal migration in Sweden in 1966. It relates to people who left the city of Stockholm for one of the 24 other territorial subdivisions, called *län*.

Limiting ourselves to the *län* which received at least 500 immigrants coming from the city of Stockholm, we get the results given in table 10.27.

Table 10.27 Distribution of emigrants from the city of Stockholm: Sweden, 1966

Län	Absolute numbers	Per 1000	Per 1000 population of Stockholm **
*Stockholm**	23 896	670	30·4
Uppsala	889	25	1·1
Södermanland	911	26	1·2
Östergötland	660	19	0·8
Malmöhus	1297	36	1·7
Göteborg et Bohus	866	24	1·1
Västmanland	635	18	0·8
Kopparberg	626	18	0·8
Gävleborg	744	21	0·9
Västernorrland	608	17	0·8
Norbotten	547	15	0·7
Others	3950	111	5·1
Total	35 629	1000	45·5

*Reference here is to the *län* of Stockholm, a unit distinct from the city.
**The average population of Stockholm in 1966 was 784 811.

A whole country

In this instance, those simplifications which are appropriate for one subdivision are not appropriate for most of the others, and a contingency table has to be set up giving the distribution in absolute numbers, and then other tables giving proportional distributions or mobility rates. If the subdivision used is fairly detailed, such a table is difficult to handle. In France, if the *département* is taken as the subdivision, the end result is a table containing 8100 cells.

We give in table 10.28 the left hand section of the table for Sweden in 1966, showing internal mobility rates per thousand.

Table 10.28 Segment from table showing the destination of emigrants by place of origin: Sweden, 1966

| Destination | Subdivision of departure | | | |
	City of Stockholm	Stockholms *län*	Uppsala *län*	Södermanlands *län*
City of Stockholm	—	18·6	3·8	3·6
Stockholms *län*	30·4	—	9·8	7·8
Uppsala *län*	1·1	2·8	—	1·9
Södermanlands *län*	1·2	2·4	1·7	—
All destinations	45·4	43·2	40·5	35·4

The subdivision of France into 22 planning regions leads to a table of about the same size. The relative frequency (per thousand) by area of residence in 1962 for each region of residence in 1954 can be adopted as an index to measure the internal migration which occurred between 1 January 1954 and 7 April 1962 (census date) and lasted until the latter date.

The left hand part of that table is as shown in table 10.29.

The total of the relative frequencies in one column is equal to 1000. The above

Table 10.29 Segment of table showing the proportional distribution of place of residence in 1962 by place of residence in 1954: France, census of 1962

| Region of residence in 1962 | Region of departure (1954) | | | |
	Paris region	Champagne	Picardie	Haute-Normandie
Paris region	925·8	27·9	43·1	33·2
Champagne	2·8	903·0	9·5	1·0
Picardie	6·1	10·1	899·9	8·3
Haute-Normandie	4·3	1·5	6·9	920·0
Total	1000	1000	1000	1000

table is a probability matrix. If it were multiplied through by the vector 'enumerated population in 1962 according to the region in 1954', the vector 'population of 1962 according to the region of residence in 1962' would be obtained.[5] Thus, it is a matrix of transitional probabilities relative to the population at a certain date, t, classified according to residence at a prior date, t_0. It leads to the same population classified according to residence at date t. t can be a future date, and then the matrix in question permits conversion of regional projections, excluding internal migration, to projections for the same date inclusive of internal migration.

Thus, among the matrices giving internal migration indices for a period of one year or several years, the best is the one giving relative frequencies, for *each category of residence at the beginning of the period*, by class of residence at the end of the period. This table may be accompanied by another one giving the proportional distribution of migrants from each region of origin according to the region of destination. The latter would be in effect a summary of the tables of this kind made for each particular region. In this table, the main diagonal remains empty.

Note 1:
The table of internal mobility rates for Sweden in 1966 could be transformed into a matrix of probabilities by adding in the main diagonal the complements of the rates for all destinations which are given at the bottom of the corresponding column, for example 954·6, which is the complement of 45·4 in cell 1–1. But this matrix does not have the same properties as the preceding one. It does not provide transitional probabilities relating the distribution by residence at the beginning of the year to the distribution by residence at the end of the year. The difference is rather minor, however, when migration itself is relatively moderate.

Note 2:
To obtain the transition matrix for one year, it would be necessary to ask at the beginning of each year the residence at the beginning of the preceding year. This could be done in a periodic survey. But if, as in Sweden, changes of residence are registered, such a survey would be a useless expenditure if the registration of moves yields equivalent figures. But does it?

Consider one subdivision A and the remainder of the country B; suppose to begin with that there is no return migration. Let's call the population of A at the beginning of the year, P; the deaths in that population during the year, whether they occur in A or in B, D; the number of departures during the year from A to B, E; and the deaths that occur in B among the E immigrants coming from A, D_e. The proportion of emigrants remaining at the end of the year in the population which inhabited A at the beginning is equal to:

$$\frac{E - D_e}{P - D}.$$

If mortality is the same among emigrants as in the whole population, we may

[5]See appendix 1.

write the following, designating the common value of the probability of dying as q:

$$D = qP$$

$$D_e = q\frac{E}{2}$$

since emigrants have been exposed only half a year on the average to the risk of dying in B.

The proportion of remaining emigrants thus is written:

$$\frac{E}{P}\frac{1-q/2}{1-q} \simeq \frac{E}{P(1-q/2)}.$$

But $P(1-q/2)$ is the average population of A in the absence of migration. If the mortality of migrants and of the whole initial population of A are the same, the registration of moves does lead to the same result as the proposed periodic survey, provided that the moves are related to the average population in the absence of migration and not to the true average population (the arithmetic mean of the populations at 1 January and 31 December of the year).

Except by accident, the mortality of migrants can be the same as that of the whole population only at the same ages, since migrants are much younger on the average. Transition matrices established on the basis of mobility rates should thus be by age group. But the same is true for matrices established on the basis of net migrants. As long as projections are almost always made by sex and age and as long as emigration depends heavily on age, the matrices making the transition from a future population exclusive of migration to a future population that takes migration into account should be established for each age group. For the same reason, the sexes must also be distinguished.

When mortality is very low, the condition of equality, which refers in fact to probabilities of survival, is met. In this case, the transition matrix for all ages may be established on the basis of moves at all ages. But that matrix, like any index for all ages together, such as birth, death, or nuptiality rates, depends on the age composition of the population, for the entire country and by geographical subdivision.

5 Return and serial migration

Because these two types of migration exist, the following question must be raised: 'Is it better to operate through a survey asking about residence x years before the survey, or to register changes of residence?'

Return migration

Here, two extreme types are probably the most important:

    1 the fairly quick return to the country, province, or village which he left of the migrant who did not adapt

2 the return at the end of his working life of a retired person who left his previous residence a long time ago.

Call the place of departure A, the place of destination from which the return originates B, and imagine zero or negligible mortality up to an advanced age; suppose moreover that returns of type 1 reach their maximum after m years of absence, m being on the order of several years.

In the case of a survey, we question the people in A and those in B about their residence x years before. When x is larger than m, nobody in A who migrated between A and B with a return of type 1 will answer that he was living in B x years before the survey. In B, however, persons will turn up who migrated between A and B less than x years ago and who are still in B. Some of them will go back to A but that return migration will not turn up in any later survey if x remains larger than m. When x is less than m, some people who left A for B and came back to A will be identified as living in B, x years before.

At first glance, the first case (x larger than m) seems unfavourable, since return migration is missed entirely. To use this approach, x should be as small as possible so that no one can escape, which comes to the same thing as continuous registration. But after some thought, it becomes clear that the first case meets the objectives of analysis better than the second, since the question asked plays the role of a net with a mesh large enough to separate two types of migration which remain mixed in variable proportion in the second case. This would not matter if the mixture raised no problems, but it does. Take continuous registration, which is the equivalent of the case where x is very small. The return from B to A becomes a migration from B to A indistinguishable from others, and we have only a mobility rate e_{BA}. But that rate is the sum of two terms:

e'_{BA} for actual mobility between B and A

e''_{BA} for return mobility.

If we designate U_{BA} the return during a certain unit of time, a year in practice, we have for that year:

$$e''_{BA} = \frac{U_{BA}}{P_B}.$$

But U_{BA} depends, in a complex way, on the previous arrivals in B of persons coming from A, and on the proportion of these persons destined to go back to A. This proportion is normally independent of the population of A. The same is not true for arrivals in B of persons coming from A, since their number depends both on the mobility rate between A and B and *on the population of A*.

Thus, indices computed on the basis of registered moves have the drawback of leading to mobility indicators which still depend on the numbers, or rather on the relationship between the numbers of A and of B. They do not correspond to the analytical objective at its most elementary, the elimination of the influence of population size.

Still, m cannot always be determined, if only because there is a return migration of type 2. So it is really necessary to study return migration as a separate topic.

Serial migration

Imagine a woman from Creuse who migrates to Paris in two stages. First she spends some time in Limoges, then migrates permanently from Limoges to Paris. To the extent that this person intended, from the start, to go to Paris, emigration from Limoges to Paris depends on the number of migrants from Creuse who stay in Limoges before going on to Paris; that number in turn depends on the population of Creuse. Thus, stages produce an effect analogous to returns, in the sense that the emigration rate for a population, here that of Limoges, depends on another population.

Imagine now that every emigrant from Creuse to Paris passes through Limogenes and resides there just over one year. In a survey on residence one year before, no migration from Creuse towards Paris will appear, since the move requires more than one year to be completed. It would be quite different with a survey asking about residence five or ten years before. In that instance, like returns migration, surveys on residence x years before are preferable to continuous registration. However, it would again be preferable to study serial migration in and of itself.

11

Natural Increase of a population

When there is no migration, the increase of the population is termed natural; it consists only of entries by births and exits by deaths.

1 The crude rate of natural increase

This is the difference between the crude birth rate and the crude death rates. It is positive if there is an excess of births over deaths, zero if deaths are equal to births and negative if deaths exceed births. It is often expressed as a percentage.

The evolution of a population with a constant rate of natural increase

Let's call the constant rate of increase r, and the initial size of the population P_0. After one year the population has increased by rP_0; to become equal to $P_0 + rP_0 = P_0(1 + r)$ it was multiplied by $(1 + r)$. Since the rate of increase remains constant, the number $P_0(1 + r)$ will, in its turn, be multiplied by $(1 + r)$ in the course of the second year, so at the end of this second year it will be equal to $P_0(1 + r)^2$, and so on. At the end of year k the size will be $P_0(1 + r)^k$. Thus, a population with a constant rate of natural increase increases in geometric progression. If r is positive, the population increases; if r is negative, it decreases.

Doubling time

When dealing with developing countries in particular, the doubling time of the population is often used to indicate a certain positive rate of natural increase. Table 11.1 gives some doubling times corresponding to round values of the rate of natural increase.

A population increasing constantly by 2% per year would double in 35 years, quadruple in 70 years, and be multiplied by 8 in 105 years, or in a little over one century.

2 Reproduction

Reproduction of the generations

The process of reproduction aims to ensure the survival of the species by the continuous replacement of deaths by new life. However, to ensure

Table 11.1 Doubling times corresponding to
selected rates of natural increase

Rate of natural increase	Doubling time (years)
0·1 %	690
0·5 %	140
1 %	70
1·5 %	46·5
2 %	35
2·5 %	28
3 %	23·5
3·5 %	20
4 %	17·7

reproduction it is not sufficient for births to be more numerous than deaths over a certain period. Thus, a group of couples having only one child each does not provide for its own replacement, even though as long as these couples are young, the births will exceed the deaths by quite a bit. This example shows that in this area, as in many others, structural effects obscure the essential situation. The net reproduction rate originated in the effort to eliminate structural effects. Rather than attempting to define it at first, let us look at examples of its computation.

We will take first the generations of women born around 1881. The proportion surviving to the middle of each age group and the fertility for those groups are shown in table 11.2.

Table 11.2 Computation of the net reproduction rate, cohort born about 1881

Age group (years)	Survivors per 1000 at birth (1)	Fertility rate per thousand (2)	Product (1) × (2) (3)	Product (3) × (5)
15–19	714	25	18	90
20–24	692	135	93	465
25–29	670	147	98	490
30–34	648	92	60	300
35–39	626	52	33	165
40–44	605	22	13	65
45–49	582	2	1	5
				1580

The product of these two quantities gives an average number of children per year brought into the world by women born around 1881, per thousand of these women at their birth. Each of these products multiplied by 5 gives approximately the number of children born in 5 years, for an *initial* cohort size of 1000. The sum of these last products gives the total number of children born to the female generation of 1881, for an initial size of this generation of 1000. By multiplying this number of 0·49, the total number of children is replaced by the total number of girls, and that is 770.

At their birth, the girls born to women in the generation of 1881 were clearly less numerous than members of their mother's generation were at their own birth. Thus, the generation of 1881 fell far short of reproducing itself, if we count from birth to birth. It was not so far short if we consider the generation of 1881 when it was 15 years old and look at the number of girls born to this generation who reached age 15 years themselves. It turns out to be 850 for an initial number (at 15 years of age this time) in the 1881 generation equal to 1000. When mortality is decreasing, the concept of reproduction of a generation is not so easy to comprehend, so we must be wary of jumping to conclusions.

Period net reproduction rates

Consider the fertility rates for the period 1931–5 and the proportion of women surviving at various ages which correspond to the mortality of that same period. With these two series, we may take the same computation as previously. It is shown in table 11.3.

Table 11.3 Computation of the net reproduction rate: France, period 1931–5

Age (years)	Survivors per 1000 at birth (1)	Fertility rate per thousand (2)	Product (1) × (2)	Product (1) × (2) × 5
15–19	890	30	27	135
20–24	873	126	110	550
25–29	854	123	105	525
30–34	835	85	71	355
35–39	815	48	39	195
40–44	792	17	13	65
45–49	765	2	2	10
				1835

By multiplying 1835 by 0·49, we come up with 900 girls per thousand women. Thus, a population having both the age-specific female fertility rates and the mortality of the period 1931–5 would not reproduce itself. But before concluding that the population from which these observations were taken is itself threatened by depopulation, we must ask whether the conditions of the period 1931–5 are likely to continue. Between the two world wars the enthusiasm for the net reproduction rate was such that this question was rather forgotten.

Until the last war, the net reproduction rate was only calculated for the female portion of the population because there were illegitimate children to be accounted for. Just after the war, the possibility of estimating the age distribution of the fathers of these children was demonstrated and, hence, of computing a net reproduction rate for the male portion of the population.

This rate is generally not the same as that for the female portion (see the following paragraph), but it is not possible to give a long term interpretation of these rates if they contradict each other. It can happen that one of the net period reproduction rates is below 1 (indicating decline) whereas the other one is over 1 (indicating increase). This is especially likely to be so in a period of major imbalance between the sexes following a war, a situation which is in itself unstable and does not lend itself well to projection.

3 Stable and stationary populations

Lotka studied the evolution of a closed population with a *constant* fertility and mortality. He showed that whatever its initial distribution by age, this population would finally increase at a constant rate and would achieve an unchanging age distribution, the latter depending only on fertility and mortality.[1]

In a stable population, the net reproduction rates of the two portions, feminine and masculine, are different since the average age of fathers at the birth of their children is higher than the average age of mothers. The rates of increase for each of these two segments are the same since the sex distribution of the population does not change. Since $\log(1 + r)$ is very close to $\log R_0/\bar{a}^2$, (R_0 is the net reproduction rate, $\bar{a}$ is the mean age of the parent considered, whether father or mother), R_0 is higher for the male sex because $\bar{a}$ is higher. Note that here it is impossible to have the kind of contradictions observed for real populations: if one reproduction rate is above 1, zero, or lower than 1, the other one must follow, since we always have:

$$\frac{\log R_0}{a} = \frac{\log R_0'}{a'}$$

(the terms with a prime being those of the males, the terms without prime those of the females).

Stationary populations

A stationary population is a stable population with a growth rate of zero. Births are equal to deaths and all the generations have the same initial size. Any organization with constant recruiting that is equal to the total of retirements is likewise a stationary population.

In practice, stationary populations in the strict sense are never encountered. Nevertheless, one may have to deal with problems where the properties of

[1] More recently, it has been demonstrated that several populations with an initial age distribution that is different end up with identical age distributions at any given time if they are subjected indefinitely to the same fertility and the same mortality, whether those are constant or variable. In the first case, the common age distribution is unchanging, in the second case, it changes through time.

In practice, differences in the initial age distribution perpetuate themselves for scarcely more than one or one and a half centuries. So a population does not show traces in its present age distribution of the imbalances of all kinds to which its age pyramid has been subjected as a result of events going back further than 150 years. See also chapter 13, section 1.

[2] See chapter 13, p. 220.

stationary populations are relevant. Moreover, stationary populations serve as an implicit point of reference more often than one would think. Although frequently untrue, their study should certainly not be overlooked.

Properties of stationary populations

a) Size of the population

Let N be the *constant* annual number of births. The population at age x at any time (N being constant over any given year) is approximately equal to:

$$N \frac{S(x+1)+S(x)}{2}$$

where $S(x)$ designates the probability of surviving between birth and age x.

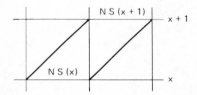

Thus we have:

$$P = N\left[\frac{1+S(1)}{2}+\frac{S(1)+S(2)}{2}\right]+ \cdots$$

$$= N\left[\frac{1}{2}+S_1+S_2+ \cdots\right] = Ne_0.$$

So the size of a stationary population is equal to the product of the annual number of births and the expectation of life in years. Or more generally, it is equal to the product of the number of entries (yearly, monthly or daily) by the average length of stay, in years, months, or days.

b) Expectation of life

Conversely, the expectation of life in years is equal to the total population, which is constant, divided by the annual number of births, also constant. In general, the average length of stay is equal to size divided by the number of entries per unit of time.

Example:
The number of patients present in a group of hospitals on 1 January of one year is 12 807. The number of admissions per year is 141 618. If the sick population of these hospitals could be considered stationary, the average length of stay would be 0·09 years (0·09 = 12 807/141 618).

Actually the number of patients in a hospital depends on seasonal factors among other things. In the most favourable case, it could only be considered as stationary on an average basis. It is not sufficient to know the population on one single date; it is necessary to know it for a sufficiently large number of dates to be able to compute an average population (see below).

c) The average age of the population

Among biths that occur during a very short span of time, 30 years before a census, we select the people who will live just 40 years; they have ten years to live after the census. We do the same for the births that occur ten years before the same census, during a short span of time equal to the former; these people have 30 years to live after the census.

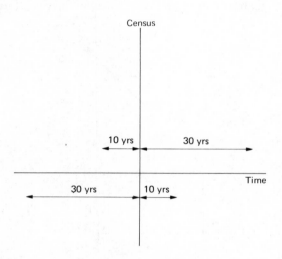

Since the population is stationary, there are as many of the latter as of the former. Thus, we can find for any group at age x with an expectation of life y, a corresponding group of the same size at age y with an expectation of life x. This illustrates the following property: the mean age of a stationary population at any given moment is equal to the mean of the expectations of life (as of the age reached at the moment in question) for the persons making up that population. Twice this mean age is therefore equal to the mean length of life of the individuals enumerated. The latter is greater than the expectation of life at birth, since the average length of life of a group which has reached a certain age—the sum of that age and the expectation of life at that age—is greater than the expectation of life at birth for the generation to which the group belongs.

It can happen under conditions of very high mortality that the average age of a presumably stationary population and its expectation of life at birth are nearly the same. But it would be a serious mistake to attribute this equality to anything other than luck. In general, the average age of a stationary population is not equal to the expectation of life and in most cases it is lower.

d) The crude birth rate and the crude death rate

These are equal and their common value is equal to $1/e_o$, the reciprocal of the expectation of life at birth.

e) The identity of cross-sectional and longitudinal observations

All cohorts have the same history:[3] they have the same initial size and numbers at each age, the same distribution according to any characteristic or set of characteristics and the same number of vital events at each age and duration.

It follows that the observations made in the course of one year are equivalent to the observations that would be made through the life of a generation. In this case, the period measures, which are unchanging, are also cohort measures.

f) Proportionality of observed deaths and of the death column of the life table

The deaths at age x are equal to $Nd_x/10\,000$, where d_x represents the life table deaths per 10 000 births. It might then be possible to follow the compiler of the first life table, the astronomer E. Halley, who constructed a life table based only on the deaths by age for the city of Breslau in 1687–91. But this famous example is not to be imitated, since the conditions required to apply that method are almost never fulfilled.

Stationary population 'on the average'

a) Seasonal factors

Let us go back to the example of patients in a hospital. Their number is obviously subject to seasonal fluctuation. Imagine, for the time being, that this is the only influence operating: the number of admissions and the number of patients are each the same at any two dates one year apart. The number of admissions and the average number of patients over one year or over a period of a whole number of years are constant. These two numbers and the average duration of stay for the average patient (or the average duration of stay for all the patients admitted in the course of a year) are linked by the same relations as in a true stationary population.

Indeed, consider the number E of admissions and the total J of hospital days through a year of 365 days. The mean hospital population P is equal to $J/365$. These J hospital days are classified in 3 categories according to whether they concern people

1. admitted before the beginning of the year of observation
2. admitted and discharged during that year
3. admitted during that year, but discharged after the year is over.

Because of the time pattern that we have assumed, the situation at the end of the year is identical to the situation at its beginning regardless of the aspect considered. The number of patients is the same and the number of days that

---

[3] As far as overall mortality and fertility are concerned. But it would be natural to assume that in fact all demographic characteristics are unchanging; in that case one could talk about absolutely stationary population.

they have remaining to spend in the hospital is the same. The number of days represented by the first category is therefore equal to that which people of the third group have remaining to spend in the hospital. Hence, J is equal to the number of days spent in the hospital by people admitted during one year. $J/365$ is the corresponding number of years; the mean duration of stay per patient is therefore equal to J/E if counted in years.

The observations made during one year are sufficient to trace the history of each 'cohort'. But this is not so for observations made during a period of less than a year, because they miss a part of the period of one year, when the events occur.

The mean rate of admission as well as the mean rate of discharge is equal to the reciprocal of the mean duration of stay.

b) Random factors

In the absence of trend in any direction at all, the number of patients is influenced by random factors, such as weather conditions or epidemics. The time pattern is broken but one can be sure that the same situation will be encountered from time to time at random intervals. What has been said above about one period is equally true for such an interval or a series of intervals. In reality, it will always be difficult to determine the intervals in question with any accuracy. But if we take a long period, the difference between category 1 and category 3 becomes insignificant, and the relationships between average population, admissions, and average duration hold.

c) Applications

The preceding relationships are interesting because they permit estimation of the average duration (of stay in a hospital, in a hotel, between purchase and sale, between purchase and manufacture) on the basis of an accounting of entries and of inventories of stocks or supplies as long as there are enough of the latter within the periodic cycle to allow an estimation of the average population. The problem of knowing whether it is legitimate to apply these relationships often persists. In demography, it is very rare to deal with stationary populations.

Note:
If we make a longitudinal study of a generation on the basis of surveys or censuses repeated at regular intervals of periodicity a, we are in the same situation as if we only enumerated persons at age x_0, $x_0 + a$, $x_0 + 2a$ in a stationary population having the same characteristics as that generation, (x_0 being the age at which the cohort in question was observed for the first time.)

If a is equal to 1, the longitudinal study of a birth cohort is equivalent to a census of a stationary population. If a is larger than 1 but not too great, approximately the same thing can be done by interpolation.

Truncated intervals

Let's take some event A and the cohort made up by persons who have experienced event *A* during a certain period. We are interested in a second event *B*, similar to *A* or different, and we want to study the distribution of the time interval between *A* and *B*; in particular, we would like to know the mean of that distribution.

In a good many cases, it is much easier to question people who are between *A* and *B* about the date of *A* than to follow a cohort between *A* and *B*. It is, for instance, much easier for a doctor to ask his female patient about the date of the beginning of their last menstrual period than to enter the same information in a file for each patient covering two or more successive periods.

The interval *AB* is then truncated by the survey, the census, or the medical consultation, in which the question about the date of *A* was asked. Only one portion of the truncated interval, the left one, *AQ*, is known. (*Q* designated the question asked about the date *A* at the time of the survey, census, consultation or any other occasion). We want to know what information on the distribution of *AB* can be drawn from the knowledge of the left hand portion of truncated intervals.[4]

The problem would be unsurmountable if nothing was known about the distribution of events *A* in time. But in certain cases it is legitimate to assume that there is, on the average, the same number of events *A* in each unit of time, or that the only fluctuation is seasonal. In this case, the question becomes equivalent to a question on the date of birth in a stationary population (or one that is stationary on the average). Determining the mean interval *AB* from the distribution of *AQ* by duration is equivalent to determining the expectation of life at birth according to the age distribution of the stationary population.

We know (properties 1 and 2 of stationary populations) that the average interval *AB* is obtained by dividing the number of intervals *AQ* (population) by the number of events *A* (births) by unit of time. But here this latter number, corresponding to the number of births, is not known. It has to be estimated, as well as possible, from the distribution of *AQ* by duration.

Example:

Returning to the menstrual cycle, the number of women whose period begins on a certain day is the same, whatever the day, if the group is large enough. So we are in a case equivalent to that of a stationary population. On the other hand, there might be some selection:

1 if women consult a doctor more or less often at the time of their period;

2 if women who have markedly shorter or markedly longer cycles than the average visit their doctor more often than other women.

These difficulties may be overcome if the question on the date of the last period can be asked at the time of a compulsory medical examination made by appointment.

Imagine that such is the case and that the duration of the menstrual cycle in days is distributed as in table 11.4.

[4]The term left hand portion has been adopted because of the custom of orienting all horizontal axes, and in particular that representing time, from left to right.

Table 11.4 Distribution of the duration of the menstrual cycle among 1000 women in a hypothetical population

Duration in days	Frequency	Cumulative frequency	Duration in days	Frequency	Cumulative frequency
0 to 17	0	1000	34	26	125
18	2	1000	35	18·	99
19	3	998	36	14	81
20	4	995	37	11	67
21	7	991	38	9	56
22	8	984	39	8	47
23	17	976	40	8	39
24	42	959	41	7	31
25	80	917	42	6	24
26	111	837	43	5	18
27	127	726	44	4	13
28	138	599	45	3	9
29	106	461	46	2	6
30	79	355	47	2	4
31	66	276	48	1	2
32	48	210	49	1	1
33	37	162	50 and over	0	

Since the question relates to the date of the beginning of menstruation, the duration of the menstrual cycle above is given as a difference between dates. The result is that a cycle of 18 days may last from 17 days, 0 hours to 18 days, 24 hours. Its mean duration is thus 18 days and not 18 and a half days, which would be the case if we were counting in completed days. The average duration of the cycle is 29·068 days, rounded out to 29·07, with a standard deviation of 4·413.

The column headed 'cumulative frequency' gives the sum of the relative frequencies starting from the longest durations; each entry shows the number of cycles with a duration equal to, or greater than, the duration for that line. Thus, the number of cycles per thousand observations with a duration equal to, or greater than, 25 days is 917.

Imagine now that our observation is made on 22 October and that it relates to a population where 2000 menstrual periods begin every day. Among the 2000 cycles that started 49 days before, or on 3 September, 2 are incomplete on 22 October at 0 a.m. Since medical examinations take place towards the middle of the day, we shall operate as if they occurred at noon on 22 October. Assuming that the beginning of menstruation is uniformly distributed over the day, there will still be one cycle which started on 3 September. Among those that started on 4 September, the two which are due to end on 23 October will still be incomplete and half of the two which are due to end on 22 October; this gives a total of three, the mean of twice the cumulated frequency at 49 days and twice the cumulated frequency at 48 days.

Moving back in this way to each preceding line, the tabulation (shown in table 11.5) of cycles remaining incomplete at noon on 22 October is obtained by their duration in days (difference of dates). Only half of the cycles beginning on 22 October are there, because of the postulated hour of the examination.

Table 11.5 Distribution of incomplete cycles observed in a hypothetical population at the time of observation

Duration	Incomplete cycles	Duration	Incomplete cycles	Duration	Incomplete cycles
0	1000	17	2000	34	224
1	2000	18	1998	35	180
2	2000	19	1993	36	148
3	2000	20	1986	37	123
4	2000	21	1975	38	103
5	2000	22	1960	39	86
6	2000	23	1935	40	70
7	2000	24	1876	41	55
8	2000	25	1754	42	42
9	2000	26	1563	43	31
10	2000	27	1325	44	22
11	2000	28	1060	45	15
12	2000	29	816	46	10
13	2000	30	631	47	6
14	2000	31	486	48	3
15	2000	32	372	49	1
16	2000	33	287	50	
			Total		58 136

In practice, the number of unfinished cycles observed at duration 0 will be markedly different from 1000 because of the concentration of absences at the beginning of menstruation (absences for duration 0 are not corrected[5]). We will substitute for this half of the mean number of cycles remaining observed at short durations (for instance durations of 1 to 15 days). Dividing 58 136 by 2000, we again obtain 29·068.

We have shown (property 3 of stationary populations) that the left hand portion of a truncated interval is equal, on the average, to the right hand portion (on the average $AQ = QB$). This is based on intuition, and when confronted with a distribution of fractions of intervals AQ it is tempting to compute the average value and multiply by two to obtain the average value for the intervals AB truncated by Q and then to use this average for the one required, that for all intervals AB, whether they are truncated or not. But this would be a mistake.[6]

The average value of truncated intervals $\bar{y}$ is above the average value of all intervals, $\bar{\imath}$. $\bar{y}$ and $\bar{\imath}$ are linked by the relation:

$$\bar{y} = \bar{\imath}(1 + \gamma^2)$$

[5]This detail is important. If the examination can be made over a period of several days at the choice of the women, those who aren't feeling well at the beginning of their period will not be interviewed at duration 0 or 1 but at higher durations. If they have an appointment for a given day with the possibility of coming several days later (but not earlier), this drawback is diminished providing that the report is classified as of the day of the appointment and that no record is kept of those among the absentees whose menstruation started on the very day of their appointment (see also latter part of this section).

[6]The error is committed because one does not see, under the guise of different phraseology, the analogy with the stationary population and, in the absence of registration of event A, there appears to be only one distribution which could be studied by conventional methods. See Mindel C. Sheps and Evelyn LaPierre-Adamcyk, *On the Measurement of Human Fertility: Selected Writings of L. Henry* (Amsterdam: Elsevier, 1972), p. 84.

where γ is the coefficient of variation of the distribution of all intervals, that is to say the ratio of the standard deviation to the mean. Here, the mean value of intervals AQ is 14·87, which makes 29·74 the mean duration of menstrual cycles truncated by an examination. γ is equal to 0·152 and γ^2 to 0·023. Since i is equal to 29·07, $i(1 + \gamma^2) = 29·07 \times 1·023 = 29·74$.

The difference between the two average values 29·07 and 29·74 is not very great in this case, but a larger error might be made if we were dealing with very scattered distributions.

Other examples:
We shall not go into them in depth, but it is useful to mention them.

1) Breastfeeding
It is possible to ask women whether they are still nursing their babies. As long as the means of feeding, by breast or bottle, adopted by women and the frequency of medical consultation are independent, and the observations are repeated often enough during the year to eliminate eventually the effect of seasonality of births, such a question would yield a stationary subpopulation of breastfed children classified by age. The average duration of breastfeeding is the ratio of the total 'population' of durations to the corresponding 'births' (children born in a unit of time to the women interviewed). If we double the mean age of breastfed children, the result obtained is too high for this mean duration.

2) Temporary migration
Certain questions asked in surveys in Africa about residents who were temporarily away provide a population of temporary absentees classified according to the length of time since their departure. To the extent that distortion due to seasonal movements can be corrected (and these biases are important in this case), and to the extent that there are no major cyclical fluctuations of long-term trends, the problem faced is analogous to the preceding ones. The most difficult thing here is to estimate the number of departures per unit of time, especially if many absences are of very short duration.

Note:
It is certainly preferable to study phenomena that have achieved a certain stability through continuous observation, with or without retrospective questions. But it is natural to try to extract the maximum from isolated or discontinuous cross-sectional observations when possible. Experience shows that there is considerable risk of coming up against a dead end. This is one of the reasons which has led us to consider truncated intervals at some length.

There's another reason for drawing attention to them. The concern for distinguishing clearly between the longitudinal and cross-sectional approaches has arisen only recently, and all the consequences of that distinction have undoubtedly not yet been realized. But truncated intervals, at least with respect to their left hand portion, belong in the domain of the cross-sectional, whereas the study of intervals in their entirety belongs in the area of longitudinal analysis. To confuse them is to continue confusing what is cross-sectional and what is longitudinal.

This confusion is further encouraged by illusions that must be dispelled. For instance, it is imagined sometimes that by increasing the frequency of surveys, it will be possible to catch all the intervals, however small, and that in this way the difference between truncated intervals and other intervals will disappear, since all will be truncated. But if surveys were close enough to one another to catch all the intervals, it would still be true that longer intervals would be found more often than short ones, since the probability of catching an interval in a survey is proportional to the duration of that interval. To avoid this problem, each interval would have to be individualized and counted only once. One might as well have continuous observation.

4 Populations with variable characteristics

Variation in the characteristics

We have already indicated in connection with stable populations that the distribution by sex and age of a population does not depend on the distant past of that population, whether its characteristics are variable or constant. For populations with variable characteristics this means that variations in these characteristics have an effect on the age distribution only to the extent that they occurred in the not too distant past. Fluctuations that go back more than one century, or at the extreme one and a half centuries, have almost no influence on the age distribution. However, they do have an influence on the size: to visualize this, it is enough to imagine two populations having the same characteristics continuously up to a certain date, when a catastrophe reduces one of them to a fraction k of its former size without modifying the age distribution or any other characteristic except total size. From then on, the total size of that population stays equal to k times the total size of the other one, no matter how far away in time the catastrophe occurred.[7]

Observed variations

For thousands of years, the human race lived in a mortality situation which was extremely irregular with intermittent times of extreme excess mortality caused by famines or particularly destructive epidemics, such as plague. In normal circumstances, mortality was far from even, but the variation from year to year remained moderate compared to the peaks of excess mortality. This prevalent mortality has been termed normal, as opposed to the mortality of catastrophes or crises. Often the peaks of excess mortality were accompanied by decreases of fertility, particularly during subsistence crises, either immediately or as a consequence of a decline in nuptiality.

The situation changed with progress in the economic and health spheres. This happened a long time ago in Western Europe, more recently in developing countries. In general, mortality declined before, sometimes long

[7]This assumes that the characteristics of those populations do not depend on the total size. Otherwise, the losses due to the catastrophe could not possibly leave the other characteristics of the population unchanged.

before, fertility. In developed countries, the fertility decline dates back everywhere at least half a century; in developing countries, either it has hardly started or is still to come.

In developed countries, Western Europe in particular, these changes were accompanied by fundamental changes in age composition. There was a definite increase in the proportion of old people (age 60 years and over, or 65 years and over, according to the definition used) and, at least up to the last war, a decrease in the proportion of children (age less than 15 years) or of young people (age less than 20 years).

This phenomenon has been called the 'ageing of the population'. Its causes were misunderstood at first, and it was attributed to the decline in mortality. Because of the similarity in words, it was thought that the decline had increased the proportion of aged people in the population because it had increased the proportion in each generation reaching old age. In fact, this verbal similarity is misleading. The decline in mortality as it has occurred up to now would not have been sufficient in itself to age Western populations. The cause of the ageing observed is the decline in fertility, the consequence of birth control.

When projections are made where mortality is declining as it has in the West, one notices that this decline by itself results in a slight increase in the proportion of young people. Table 11.6 shows an example.[8] Mortality decreases in the same way in both variants: once with unchanging fertility, once with declining fertility. Ageing occurs only if fertility declines.

Table 11.6 Effect of fertility and mortality decline on the age structure of a hypothetical population

Age	Original age structure	One hundred years later, with declining mortality	
		and constant fertility	and declining fertility
0–14 years	45·0	48·0	23·7
15–64 years	53·4	49·9	67·3
65 years and over	1·6	2·1	9·0
Total	100·0	100·0	100·0

The decline of mortality thus far has not resulted in the ageing of the population. However, future declines could contribute to ageing. This is because little progress remains to be made at the younger ages, but there is much to be accomplished at the older ages. It is this kind of progress that would age the population.

[8]Taken from *Le Tiers Monde*, Travaux et documents de l'INED (1961), **39.**

Part II Models

12

Introduction

The use of models in demography is almost as old as the science itself. The first life table published by Halley in 1692 was constructed by assuming that the population concerned, that of Breslau in 1688–91, was stationary or, in other words, that it conformed to a model.

The subsequent development of demography turned primarily toward the improvement of data collection, census and vital registration, and of methods of analysis and measurement. The use of models tended to be forgotten. Aside from Lotka's theory, which was elaborated between the two world wars, models have taken their rightful place in demography only in the last 25 years, and it is even more recently that they have been considered as distinct from analysis.

Let us go over the sequence of operations in order to see the role of models clearly.

1) Observation
This is the collection of raw data in the form of absolute numbers of persons or events, classified in various ways. It is the ore that will have to be worked over to extract the metal and get rid of the slag.

2) Analysis
This involves the treatment of the raw data in order to separate each phenomenon from what is extraneous to it, that is to say the influence of size, of structure and of other phenomena.

These refining operations already take up a good deal of the demographer's time and talent, but he would be wrong to accept their result as the end.

1 Causes of the phenomena

The search for causes of the phenomena and of their variations in time is the point of departure for a difficult undertaking. Demographers are sometimes accused of restricting themselves to the description of nuptiality, fertility, mortality and migration, without bothering to look for the causes of these phenomena and of their fluctuations. This accusation is not fair. It is not enough to want to find the causes of phenomena to be able to do so. One needs to be well equipped to succeed. An impatient person who fails to equip himself well before setting out usually does not get anywhere, or he ends up with nothing but illusory relationships. Demographers are aware of this and, no doubt for this reason, they are cautious. In addition, demographic phenomena have two types of causes, internal and external.

Internal causes

Internal causes are those which are themselves demographic. Thus, the decline of births in France between 1915 and 1919 (hollows in the age distribution) is an internal cause of the reduction in marriages during the years 1930–39. This severe decline in births created a strong imbalance between boys born just before the first world war and girls born during the war, that is to say between the male and female generations from which a majority of the marriages would have to come. So the decline in births is an internal cause of the changes in nuptiality provoked by this imbalance.

External causes

On the other hand, an external cause comes from outside demography: it belongs to economics, biology, history, or custom. Take the example of the unequal chances of death among the various social classes. Mortality is higher at the bottom of the social ladder than at the top; in other words, the poor die more than the rich. This phrasing suggests, however, that poverty is the immediate cause of the excess mortality of the underprivileged classes. As proof one would have to be able to make an experiment consisting of a comparison of the mortality of two groups that were alike in every respect except one, income per head. This experiment, like many others, cannot be carried out since we are dealing with human beings. Nevertheless, it is useful to describe it for it tells us under what conditions observations can be substituted for the experiment that we cannot do.

By definition, external causes are outside the area of demography, and we must look for them with the help of other disciplines. Here is an example: it has been known since 1890 at least that influenza epidemics often cause a decline in the birth rate and that this happens approximately nine months after the epidemic. There are various possible reasons—a decrease in the frequency of sexual intercourse, temporary sterility of one sex or the other, or an increase in early spontaneous abortions. The answer cannot be found without the help of medical knowledge.

Knowing in order to act and knowing before acting

Like any science, demography must help man to behave more effectively and to modify the course of events. To achieve this one must recognize external causes. To explain excess infant mortality among coal miners, one must know whether it results from lack of money, ignorance or indifference. It does not make sense to go into this, however, unless one is really sure that there is excess infant mortality among coal miners. In this instance, this is an easy matter to assess since methods for observing and computing infant mortality are well established today.

This is not always the case, and it may happen that an external cause is blamed for something that is really the result of internal causes. The risk is considerable when one is hurrying to explain a phenomenon in terms of external causes that may seem obvious, without having examined demographic connections and their consequences. In other words, the cautious approach is to make sure that internal causes play no role before looking for external causes.

Internal causes and models

Internal causality implies that a present demographic phenomenon follows from earlier demographic phenomena. One could just as well say, starting with an earlier phenomenon, that the present phenomenon is a projected consequence of the previous phenomenon. But projections are models, since they indicate how the population will evolve under certain conditions of fertility, mortality, and migration.

Thus models represent the third phase of demography, after observation and analysis, in between the latter and the eventual search for external causes.[1]

2 Other aspects of the models

There are other opportunities to make use of models, however, and models might be defined more generally as the study of numerical relationships for the purpose of tracing causes, untangling the complexities of a set of non-independent data, and justifying methods of measurement or techniques for correcting errors. In many cases they replace experiments which cannot be carried out or observations which are inaccessible.

In the following pages, we shall not study all existing models. We shall concentrate on the following:

Models of population dynamics: Lotka's theory and subsequent developments, the properties of populations with constant fertility and of populations with invariable age distributions. These are taken up in chapter 13.

Models of family formation following marriage are the subject of three chapters—14, 15 and 16. Chapter 14 will deal with fecundability and its measurement, chapter 15 with the influence of intra-uterine mortality on fecundity at the beginning of marriage, and chapter 16 with models which involve all births, first together, then by birth order.

Finally, chapter 17 will give a brief discussion of nuptiality models.

These chapters deal with subjects which have already been touched on in part I, but from another point of view. For this reason, we have not attempted to eliminate all repetition.

---

[1] Models are sometimes only an extension or a further stage of analysis; it is convenient however to maintain the distinction, if only because in many cases models are clearly differentiated from analysis.

13
Models of population dynamics

We are not going to deal with all models of this kind, but only with some of them:

1 Lotka's theory and its later developments, because of their importance, but without going into detail
2 Certain aspects of populations with constant fertility and of populations with unchanging age distributions.

1 Lotka's theory and later developments

A general view of Lotka's theory

The essence of Lotka's theory[1] concerns the evolution of a female population subjected forever to constant overall fertility and age-specific mortality. No recognition is given to marriage. The latter is of no importance in the stable state: nuptiality is constant then, and therefore overall all fertility is too. However, it is important in the initial phase, when population is fluctuating in search of its equilibrium. Because of these fluctuations, there are imbalances in the size of male and female cohorts whose ages make them suited to marry each other; nuptiality and consequently fertility fluctuate as well.

Since we are dealing with a female population only, fertility includes girls only. It follows that for purposes of computation the usual overall fertility, which refers to both sexes together, must be converted into fertility 'in terms of girls only'. This can be done by multiplying current overall fertility by 0·485 (sex ratio of 106) or by 0·490 (sex ratio of 104).

Lotka's essential conclusion is as follows. A population that has been exposed for ever to unchanging conditions of overall fertility and age-specific mortality tends toward a population with an unchanging age distribution and growth rate. They depend on the fertility and mortality conditions, but not on the initial age distribution. This population at the limit is characterized as stable. It is entirely unchanging except for its size which increases or decreases at a constant rate, that is to say in geometric progression. When even the size remains constant, the stable population is called stationary (see chapter 11 for the properties of stationary populations).

[1] A. Lotka, *Théorie analytique des associations biologiques*, second part (Paris: Hermann and Cie, 1939), 149 pp.

As a first approximation, the rate of increase of a stable population or intrinsic rate of natural increase, r, depends only on the net reproduction rate, R_0, and on the average age, $\bar{a}$, of the net fertility distribution. Calculated as a discontinuous process, the relationship is expressed as follows: (see third section below)

$$\log(1+r) = \frac{\log R_0}{\bar{a}}$$

If these results are valid for the female population, they can be applied to the whole population. The sex ratio of a stable population is unchanging and the two parts, masculine and feminine, grow at the same rate.

Later development

a) Other solutions

Because it was so important, Lotka's theory stimulated research. The results often made the theory more rigorous or reached the same conclusion by different routes such as matrix algebra and characteristic functions.[2]

b) The introduction of nuptiality

Right after the war, net reproduction rates were computed in England for the male sex, and it was noted that these rates were sometimes incompatible with those for the feminine sex. This led P. Karmel to try to introduce nuptiality into Lotka's theory. The attempt has remained theoretical because there were no models of nuptiality at that time, but it at least had the virtue of identifying the cause of the 'conflict between male and female measures of reproduction'.[3] Lotka's essential finding survives: the population tends toward a stable population with a rate of increase and an age distribution which are independent of the initial state.

c) Size

We can restrict ourselves to the absolute number of births (the population is derived from that by simple computations). This number increases or decreases in geometric progression. It actually depends on the initial conditions, but when the process has been going on for a long time, it is the product of two terms: one of the form $(1+r)^t$, which only depends on time t, and another which is not dependent on time, but is a constant dependent on the initial conditions. This relationship has been studied by P. Vincent[4] and H. LeBras.[5]

[2] P. H. Leslie, 'On the use of matrices in certain population mathematics', *Biometrika* (November 1946), **33,** part iii, pp. 183–212.

[3] P. Karmel, *Population* (1949), **3,** pp. 471–94.

[4] P. Vincent, *Potentiel d'acroissement d'une population* (Paris: Berger-Levrault, 1946), 26 pp.

[5] H. LeBras, 'Retour d'une population à l'état stable après une "catastrophe" ', *Population* (1969) **5,** pp. 861–95.

For a population segment composed of N women born at the same moment, the constant in question is equal to N/μ_1 where μ_1 is the mean age of child-bearing in the stable population that descends from this segment (μ_1 is different from $\bar{a}$ and, in a growing population, smaller).

d) Migration

Lotka's theory can be applied to a population subjected to constant rates of mobility by in- or out-migration: the probability of survival in the equations is replaced by the probability of surviving and being present at the same time. Instead of taking one population in isolation, it is possible to consider together all populations which exchange individuals by migration. H. LeBras has recently shown that this aggregate tends toward a state of equilibrium where all the populations increase at the same rate and have a constant relationship to the total population, whatever the initial conditions were.[6]

e) Variable conditions

Lotka's theory supposes that overall fertility and mortality do not change. The case of variable conditions has been studied, long after Lotka, by A. Lopez,[7] J. Bourgeois-Pichat[8] and A. Coale,[9] and H. LeBras.[10]

The first of these authors showed that a population subjected indefinitely to conditions of fertility and mortality which varied but were independent of the size of the population would, after a fairly long time, reach a variable age distribution and a variable growth rate independent of the initial size and age distribution. In other words, a population forgets its initial state, whether its fertility and its morality are constant or variable. This is only true, in the latter case, if mortality and fertility are not a function of size.

J. Bourgeois and A. Coale studied populations with constant fertility but with a mortality declining, as it has in Europe over almost two centuries and more recently elsewhere. They showed that in that case the age distribution of the population changed little. Consequently, any ageing of the population would be primarily due to the decline in fertility, at least as long as mortality declined mostly at young ages (the story would be different if the decline occurred mostly in old age). They called such populations quasi-stable. An example is given in part I, at the end of chapter 11.

H. LeBras has concerned himself with a special set of variable conditions, the catastrophes and crises which afflicted the populations of the most developed countries of today from the origins of mankind up to the eighteenth century. He investigated periodic crises first, and then those which occur at

[6]H. LeBras, 'Equilibre de populations soumises à des migrations', *Theoretical Population Biology* (1971), **2**, no. 1, pp. 100–121.

[7]A. Lopez, *Problems in Stable Population Theory* (Princeton: Office of Population Research, 1961), 120 pp.

[8]J. Bourgeois-Pichat, 'Dans quelle mesure peut-on limiter le vieillissement de la population?', *Trois journées pour l'étude scientifique du vieillissement de la population* **2**, pp. 63–75.

[9]A. J. Coale, 'The effects of changes in mortality and fertility on age composition,' *Milbank Memorial Fund Quarterly* (January 1956), **34**, pp. 79–114.

[10]*Op. cit.* and 'Eléments pour une théorie des populations instables', *Population* (1971), **3**, pp. 525–72.

random intervals. In the latter case, it is possible to define a mean rate of increase which depends on fertility, on normal mortality, and on the frequency and intensity of the crises. The age distribution has periodic or pseudo-periodic fluctuations. The initial state is forgotten, as in the previous case, since crises are only one particular aspect of the general case. Note that in every case the convergence takes place, for all practical purposes, in less than 150 years.

Lotka's equation in discrete form

Set Z_a as the probability of surviving from birth to 1 January after the ath birthday, and f_a as the annual overall fertility in terms of girls, between one 1 January and the next, for women who reach age a during that year.

If the year in question is designated by t, the year of birth of these women is $t - a$. Their initial number is B_{t-a}, the number of female births during the year $(t-a)$. On 1 January, the number is $B_{t-a}Z_{a-1}$; on 31 December, it is $B_{t-a}Z_a$. The average size is therefore:

$$B_{t-a}\frac{Z_{a-1}+Z_a}{2}.$$

$(Z_{a-1}+Z_a)/2$ differs little from 1_a, the probability of survival to the ath birthday. The average number of women in the generation $(t-a)$ therefore is $B_{t-a}1_a$. The number of girls born during the year t is equal to:

$$B_{t-a}1_a f_a.$$

The total number of births B_t for the year t is therefore such that:

$$B_t = \sum_{a_1}^{a_2} B_{t-a}1_a f_a$$

a_1 is the lowest fertile age, a_2 the highest (a_1 is on the order 15 years, a_2 on the order of 50 years). We may replace the product $1_a f_a$ by m_a (net fertility rate in terms of girls) and write:

$$B_t = \sum_{a_1}^{a_2} B_{t-a}m_a.$$

At the limit, B_t increases or decreases according to a geometric progression with a common ratio $1 + r$ (r being the rate of increase). We therefore have:

$$B_t = B_{t-a}(1+r)^a$$

$$B_{t-a} = \frac{B_t}{(1+r)^a} = B_t(1+r)^{-a}$$

and hence:

$$B_t = \sum_{a_1}^{a_2} B_t(1+r)^{-a}m_a = B_t\sum_{a_1}^{a_2} (1+r)^{-a}m_a$$

or:

$$1 = \sum_{a_1}^{a_2} (1+r)^{-a} m_a.$$

Let's isolate $(1+r)^{-a}$ where $\bar{a}$ is the average age defined as

$$\bar{a} = \frac{\sum a m_a}{\sum m_a}.$$

It follows that:

$$1 = (1+r)^{-\bar{a}} \sum_{a_1}^{a_2} (1+r)^{\bar{a}-a} m_a.$$

If we expand $(1+r)^{\bar{a}-a}$, we obtain:[11]

$$(1+r)^{\bar{a}-a} = 1 + (\bar{a}-a)r + \frac{(\bar{a}-a)(\bar{a}-a-1)}{2} r^2 + \cdots$$

hence (leaving out the terms containing powers of r higher than 2):

$$\sum (1+r)^{\bar{a}-a} m_a = \sum m_a + r \sum (\bar{a}-a) m_a +$$

$$+ \frac{r^2}{2} \sum (\bar{a}-a)^2 m_a - \frac{r^2}{2} \sum (\bar{a}-a) m_a.$$

The terms containing $(\bar{a}-a)$ are zero because of the definition of $\bar{a}$. So, designating $\sum m_a$ by R_0, $\sum (\bar{a}-a)^2 m_a$ is the product of R_0 and V_a, the variance of a. We are left with:

$$\sum (1+r)^{\bar{a}-a} m_a = R_0 \cdot \left(1 + \frac{r^2}{2} V_a\right).$$

Hence we have:

$$1 = (1+r)^{-\bar{a}} R_0 \cdot \left(1 + \frac{r^2}{2} V_a\right)$$

and by taking the logarithms:

$$o = -\bar{a} \log(1+r) + \log R_0 + \log\left(1 + \frac{r^2}{2} V_a\right).$$

If we disregard the term containing r^2, we have:

$$\bar{a} \log(1+r) = \log R_0$$

$$\log(1+r) = \frac{\log R_0}{\bar{a}}.$$

[11]See appendix 2, part 3, for an explanation.

If we don't, we have:

$$\log(1+r) = \frac{\log R_0 + \log(1+r^2/2\,V_a)}{a}$$

which permits the computation of r by successive approximation, each time replacing r^2 by the square of the preceding approximation of r.

2 The relationship between the number of births and the number of women in a population with fertility which remains constant

In the absence of ups and downs in births or deaths, the numbers of women are almost in arithmetical progression from 20–24 years to 40–44 years of age and even from 15–19 years to 45–49 years. Births between t and $t+5$ are a number B such that:

$$B = \sum_i F_i f_i, \tag{1}$$

F_i being the average size of the age group i in the period from t to $t+5$, and f_i the fertility of that age group. To say that F_i varies in arithmetic progression with i means that it can be put in the form:

$$F_0 - iA$$

where F_0 is the size of an age group taken as the origin, for instance 15–19 years, A is a constant, and i is the number of age groups starting with 15–19 ($i = 0$ for 15–19, $+1$ for 20–24, $+2$ for 25–29 . . . , $+6$ for 45–49 years).

Equation (1) can thus be written:

$$B = \sum(F_0 - iA)f_i = \sum F_0 f_i - \sum iAf_i$$

or also:

$$B = F_0 \sum f_i - A \sum if_i$$

Substituting a variable $\bar{i}$ such that:

$$\bar{i} = \frac{\sum if_i}{\sum f_i}$$

$$B = F_0 \sum f_i - \bar{i}A \sum f_i$$

$$= (F_0 - \bar{i}A)\sum f_i \tag{2}$$

$F_0 - \bar{i}A$ is the size of the age group $\bar{i}$, $\bar{i}$ being the mean value of i in the distribution of the fertility rates f_i. If we call it the mean age group and designate its size by $\bar{F}$, (2) can be written:

$$B = \bar{F} \sum f_i$$

hence:

$$\frac{B}{\overline{F}} = \sum f_i = \text{constant} \tag{3}$$

In a population with constant fertility, the ratio of the births for 5 years to the number of women in the mean age group remains constant.[12] Thus, if mortality decreases, the ratio of girls at ages 0–4 to the corresponding number of births, and therefore to the number of women in the mean age group, will increase.

Example:
Take as values of F_i the numbers shown in table 13.1, which are proportional to the female population of France in 1791.

Table 13.1 Relationship between the numbers of births and of women in a population with constant fertility

Age (years)	i	F_i	$F_0 - iA$	f_i	$F_i f_i$	$(F_0 - iA)f_i$	if_i
15–19	0	965	965	20	19·3	19·3	—
20–24	1	889	887	313	278·3	277·6	313
25–29	2	806	809	608	490·0	491·9	1216
30–34	3	726	731	670	486·4	489·8	2010
35–39	4	646	653	587	379·2	383·3	2348
40–44	5	570	575	301	171·6	173·1	1505
45–49	6	497	497	18	8·9	8·9	108
Total		5099	5117	2517	1833·7	1843·9	7500

A is one-sixth of the difference between 965 and 497, that is to say, one sixth of 468, or 78. We have $887 = 965 - 78$, $809 = 965 - 2 \times 78 = 965 - 156$ and so on. It is clear that the series which progresses arithmetically, $F_0 - iA$, differs very little from the series F_i. The mean value of i is 2·98 (7500/2517) which corresponds to age 32·4 years ($17·5 + 5 \times 2·98$). The corresponding mean size is: $F_0 - 2·98A = 965 - 2·98 \times 78 = 733$.
The ratio of 1843·9 to 733 equals 2·516.

Let us try basing the ratio on the actual number corresponding to $\bar{i}$. This is the age group $29·9 - 34·8$, of a size equal to 728 (98 % of 726 and 2 % of 806). The ratio of 1833·7 to 728 is equal to 2·519.

Conclusion:
The age pyramid of a population where fertility does not change is subject to one constraint: the ratio of births to the number of women at a fixed age, close to 30 years, is invariable. The actual age and ratio depend only on fertility.

---

[12] If f_i is overall fertility in the normal sense, that is to say, for both sexes together, B designates all births. If f_i designates fertility only in terms of girls, B includes only female births. The latter case is the one that applies to the example.

3 Populations with unvarying age distributions

Properties

When fertility remains constant without major ups and downs in mortality, the age distribution varies little. This is why we are interested in studying the properties of populations with unchanging age distributions.

Consider two consecutive years t and $t+1$. Let:

P_a be the number at age a on 1 January of t,

B the number of births of the year t,

k_a the prospective risk of dying at age a during the year t,

k_N the probability of dying between birth and 1 January of $t+1$, during the year t,

Z_a the probability of survival as of 1 January following the ath birthday, taken from the life table for the year t.

r the annual rate of increase for the year t.

Let $P'_a, B', k'_a, k'_N, Z'_a, r'$ be analogous quantities for the year $t+1$. Here is the corresponding Lexis diagram:

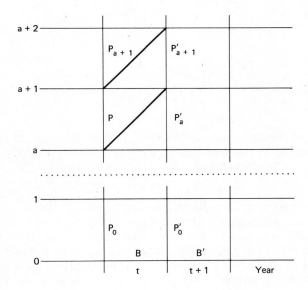

Since the age distribution does not change, the total numbers at the beginning of the year $(t+1)$ are equal to $(1+r)$ times the numbers at the beginning of the year t, *whatever the age a.*

$$P'_{a+1} = (1+r)P_{a+1}.$$

And since the people aged $a+1$ in $t+1$ are the survivors of people aged a in t, we also have:

$$P'_{a+1} = (1-k_a)P_a$$

which gives:

$$(1+r)P_{a+1} = (1-k_a)P_a$$
$$(1+r)P_a = (1-k_{a-1})P_{a-1}$$
$$\cdots\cdots\cdots\cdots\cdots\cdots\cdots$$
$$(1+r)P_1 = (1-k_0)P_0$$

and consequently:

$$(1+r)^{a+1}P_{a+1} = (1-k_0)\cdots(1-k_0)P_0. \tag{1}$$

Moreover:

$$P_0' = (1-k_N)B = (1+r)P_0$$

or:

$$P_0 = \frac{(1-k_N)B}{1+r} \tag{2}$$

From the whole series of relations (1) and (2), it results that:

$$(1+r)^{a+1}P_{a+1} = \frac{(1-k_N)(1-k_0)\cdots(1-k_a)B}{1+r}$$

that is to say:

$$(1+r)^{a+2}P_{a+1} = Z_{a+1}B. \tag{3}$$

In a stable population with a growth rate of r, the number P_a in the age group a at the beginning of the year (i.e. people who were born during the year $t-1-a$ when the births numbered B_{t-1-a}) is such that

$$B_{t-1-a}Z_a = B(1+r)_{-a-1}Z_a.$$

This is the equivalent of the preceding formula.

The following conclusion emerges: at the beginning of each year, a population with an unchanging age distribution must have the age distribution of the stable population corresponding to its mortality and its growth rate for that year. It follows that the age distribution at the beginning of the year $t+1$ must correspond also to the characteristics of the year $t+1$, which means that

$$P_a' = B'(1+r')^{-a-1}Z_a' = (1+r)P_a$$
$$\cdots\cdots\cdots\cdots\cdots\cdots\cdots\cdots$$
$$P_0' = B'(1+r')^{-1}Z_0' = (1+r)P_0.$$

It follows that:

$$B'(1+r')^{-a-1}Z_a' = (1+r)B(1+r)^{-a-1}Z_a$$
$$\cdots\cdots\cdots\cdots\cdots\cdots\cdots\cdots\cdots$$
$$B'(1+r')^{-1}Z_0' = (1+r)B(1+r)^{-1}Z_0$$

which is to say:

$$B'(1+r')^{-a-1}Z'_a = B(1+r)^{-a}Z_a$$
$$B'(1+r')^{-a}Z'_{a-1} = B(1+r)^{-a+1}Z_{a-1}$$

which gives:

$$\frac{Z'_a}{Z'_{a-1}} \cdot \frac{1}{1+r'} = \frac{Z_a}{Z_{a-1}} \cdot \frac{1}{1+r}$$

that is to say:

$$\frac{1-k'_{a-1}}{1+r'} = \frac{1-k_{a-1}}{1+r}$$

$$\frac{1-k'_0}{1+r'} = \frac{1-k_0}{1+r}$$

and

$$B(1-k_N) = \frac{B'(1-k'_N)}{1+r'} \tag{4}$$

Following the first birthday, this set of conditions comes down to the following proposition: the ratio of the probabilities of survival from one 1 January to the next for two consecutive years is independent of age and equal to the ratio of the multipliers $(1+r)$ and $(1+r')$ of the population during those years

$$\frac{1-k'}{1-k} = \frac{1+r'}{1+r}.$$

This gives:

$$k'-k+k'r-kr' = r-r'$$

$(k'-k)$ is small compared to k, so that if $k'r$ is replaced by kr, the resulting error is insignificant; hence:

$$k'-k = r-r'-kr+kr' = (r-r')(1-k)$$

and also:

$$\frac{(1-k)-(1-k')}{1-k} = r-r'.$$

The relative variation of the probability of surviving $(1-k)$ from one 1 January to the next is the same for all ages in completed years and is equal to the absolute variation in the rate of natural increase from the year considered to the following year.

Let's go back to k_N. Suppose that fertility is constant. Since f_a is the fertility rate of women who have reached age a during a year, we have:

$$B = \sum f_a \frac{P_a + P'_{a+1}}{2}$$

$$B' = \sum f_a \frac{P_{a'} + P''_a + 1}{2} + 1$$

if we call P'' the population at the end of the year $t + 1$. The series P' is equal to the series of P multiplied by $1 + r$. The series of P'' is equal to the series of P' multiplied by $1 + r$.

It results that:

$$B = \frac{\sum f_a P_a}{2} + \frac{\sum f_a P_a (1 + r)}{2}$$

$$B' = \frac{\sum f_a P'_a}{2} + \frac{\sum f_a P'_a (1 + r')}{2}$$

$$B = \left(1 + \frac{r}{2}\right) \sum f_a P_a$$

$$B' = \left(1 + \frac{r'}{2}\right) \sum f_a P'_a = \left(1 + \frac{r'}{2}\right)(1 + r) \sum f_a P_a$$

hence:

$$\frac{B'}{B} = (1 + r) \frac{1 + r'/2}{1 + r/2}$$

and therefore, according to (4):

$$\frac{1 - k_N}{1 - k'_N} = \frac{1 + r}{1 + r'} \cdot \frac{1 + r'/2}{1 + r/2}$$

which, insofar as r and r' are small, can be written:[13]

$$\frac{1 - k_N}{1 - k'_N} = \frac{1 + r/2}{1 + r'/2}$$

and this can be rewritten as before:

$$\frac{(1 - k_N) - (1 - k'_N)}{1 - k_N} = \frac{r - r'}{2}.$$

---

[13]See appendix 2.

The relative variation of $1 - k_N$ is equal to half the absolute variation in the rate of natural increase. The relative variations of $1 - k_N$ are half the relative variations of the other probabilities of survival.

Comparison with real life

Populations where fertility is constant but mortality declines maintain an age distribution that changes little. The small variations which can be observed, however, are systematic. The proportions of young and old people increase, the proportion of adults decreases. One inevitably wonders what relationship there is between these deviations and those existing between the real decline in mortality, and the decline that would exist if the age distribution were to remain constant in the absence of any change in fertility.

To examine this point, let us compare the female mortality of the model life tables of the United Nations for levels 20 ($e_0 = 30$) and 40 ($e_0 = 40$). Table 13.2 gives the various values of the survival probabilities between one age group and the next, that is to say for 5 years, and the probability of surviving from birth to 1 January which is the boundary of the five-year period considered (Table V of the UN publication, *Population Studies*, no. 25).

Table 13.2 Comparison of the actual differences in survival probabilities implied by a given decline in mortality and those which would be required to keep the original age distribution unchanged, female sex

	Life table			
Age group (years)	Level 20	Level 40	Increase per thousand	
	Probability of surviving $1 - k$		actual	necessary
Birth	0·724	0·797	73	10
0– 4	0·857	0·911	54	23
5– 9	0·952	0·971	19	26
10–14	0·954	0·970	16	26
15–19	0·939	0·959	20	25
20–24	0·926	0·950	24	25
25–29	0·917	0·946	29	25
30–34	0·908	0·942	34	24·5
35–39	0·899	0·937	38	24
40–44	0·888	0·929	41	24
45–49	0·869	0·914	45	23·5
50–54	0·841	0·891	50	23
55–59	0·798	0·854	56	21·5
60–64	0·736	0·797	61	20
65–69	0·649	0·715	66	17·5
70–74	0·533	0·603	70	14
75–79	0·396	0·469	73	11

Source: Table V of the UN publication, *Population Studies* **25.**

For a population like that of France around 1790, such a mortality decline causes an increase in the five-year growth rate of 0·027 (it goes from 0·020 to 0·047). The increase in the survival probabilities necessary to maintain the age distribution $[0·27/2(1 - k_N)$ and $0·27 (1 - k)]$ is given in the column on the right.

Figure 13.1, which illustrates this table, shows how much the real series of increases differs from the other: the first decreases when the other one rises and vice-versa, so that the second series is at its maximum at the ages where the first reaches a minimum. It is hardly astonishing, therefore, that the age distribution of populations with constant fertility changes to some extent. It is actually surprising that it doesn't change more.

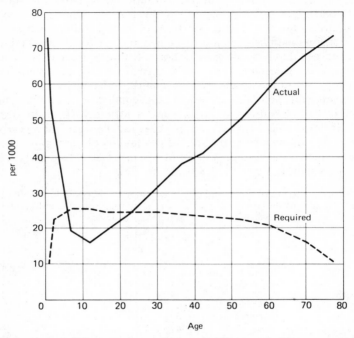

Figure 13.1   Actual differences in survival probabilities and differences required to maintain an unchanged age distribution when mortality declines from level 20 to level 40 of the UN model life tables

Let us add that if we were to choose tables corresponding to lower levels of mortality, it could well happen that the increase necessary to maintain the age distribution would exceed at 5–9 years and 10–14 years the greatest increase that could possibly be observed (the difference between 1 and the survival probability from the table taken as the point of origin). In order to maintain the age distribution, mortality would have to be negative or there would have to be in-migration at the ages where mortality is lowest, which amounts to the same thing.

14

Models of family building starting with marriage—general comments, fecundability

1 The models

The observed facts

These models are based on the following commonly observed facts:

1 Conception is random: even outside of periods of pregnancy, breastfeeding or temporary sterility, it is not an unavoidable consequence of sexual intercourse.

2 Every conception prevents another conception for a certain time.

3 Every pregnancy does not lead to a live birth.

4 Various kinds of temporary sterility exist other than that following conception.

5 A couple may be completely sterile from the beginning of marriage. Others become sterile sooner or later and all, or almost all, are sterile by the time the wife reaches the age of 50 years.

6 Human intervention reduces fertility, by means of contraception and induced abortion.

Their mathematical translation

In order to use these observations in model building, it is necessary to manipulate them, to translate them into concepts or notions which lend themselves to mathematical treatment or numerical computation. Here is that translation:

1 The random character of conception is accounted for by introducing a probability of conceiving per menstrual cycle, excepting non-susceptible periods (see below). This probability is called *fecundability*; the term was introduced in 1924 by C. Gini. He considered this notion applicable only in the absence of contraception, but this restriction is not essential, and today we talk about fecundability as natural (in the absence of contraception) or residual (that which persists despite contraception).

2 The period following conception during which a new conception is impossible is called the non-susceptible period. The non-susceptible period lasts from conception to the recurrence of ovulation after the end of pregnancy if sexual relations have been resumed before ovulation recurs, or from conception to the resumption of sexual intercourse if ovulation recurs before that happens. The non-susceptible period may vary in length, and in models it

takes the form of a probability of not having terminated the non-susceptible period within a certain time after conception.

3 In order to take the risk of death of the embryo or the foetus into account, the probability that a conception will result in a live birth is also introduced. This requires the knowledge of intra-uterine mortality.

4 Temporary sterility, due either to anovulatory cycles or to other causes, plays a separate role only if the risk of sterility for one cycle depends on the situation in the preceding cycle. Up to now, these risks have been treated as though they were independent.

5 Complete sterility is the same thing as zero fecundability from a certain age, a certain length of marriage or a certain number of pregnancies on. It can be introduced explicitly or accounted for by the variation of fecundability with age.

6 Contraception and abortion are linked to the number of children that the couple wishes not to exceed. Thus, there are at least two stages in married life— before the last wanted birth, and after that birth. Actually, contraception is often practised before the last unwanted pregnancy, but with less effectiveness,[1] in order to space births somewhat, or to postpone the first conception. To take these intentions into account, delays in conception and desired spacing patterns must be introduced, as well as residual fecundability for the various stages (for example, before the first birth, between the first and the second birth, or after the second birth if it is the last one desired).

2 Fecundability

Fecundability varies from one married woman to another. However, we will begin by studying it in homogeneous groups; models for heterogeneous groups are obtained from the sum of homogeneous groups.

Homogeneous groups

Fecundability was defined on the basis of the menstrual cycle. But the length of the latter varies from one woman to another and for the same woman. The notion of fecundability therefore had to be expanded to refer to a period of constant length, such as a month. This extension is legitimate only if the basic relationships implied in the definition of fecundability in its strict sense, (i.e. for the menstrual cycle) are maintained. We shall spend some time examining whether or not this is the case.[2]

a) Fecundability per menstrual cycle

1) Constant fecundability

Let us call fecundability p and its complement q. Table 14.1 gives the proportionate number of conceptions, during successive cycles, in a group of women not yet pregnant at the beginning of the first cycle, when the size of the group is taken as unity. The table also includes the series of proportions of women not pregnant at the beginning of each cycle. This series is identical to that of the powers of q.

[1] The efficacy of contraception was defined in chapter 7, p. 101.

[2] This point, as well as the influence of the time of marriage in the cycle and of the duration of pregnancy, has been studied by P. Vincent in *Recherches sur la fécondité biologique. Etude d'un groupe de familles nombreuses* (Paris: PUF, 1961), 278 pp.

Table 14.1 Proportion of conceptions and of women not yet pregnant by menstrual cycle, constant fecundability

Cycle number	Conceptions during the cycle	Women not yet pregnant at beginning of cycle
1	p	1
2	pq	q
3	pq^2	q^2
4	pq^3	q^3
5	pq^4	q^4
.	. . .	. .

The average number of ovulations before conceiving:

Ovulation necessarily preceds conception. The number of ovulations before conception therefore is equal to 1 for women who conceive during the first cycle, to 2 for those who conceive during the second cycle, and so on. So the average number is equal to:

$$p + 2pq + 3pq^2 + \cdots + (n+1)pq^n + \cdots$$

that is to say to p multiplied by:

$$1 + 2q + 3q^2 + \cdots + (n+1)q^n + \cdots$$

which is a derivative of:

$$q + q^2 + \cdots + q^{n+1} + \cdots = (1 + q + \cdots + q^n + \cdots)$$

and also the derivative with respect of q of:

$$q \, \frac{1}{1-q} = \frac{q}{1-q}$$

This derivative is equal to:

$$\frac{1}{(1-q)^2} = \frac{1}{p^2}.$$

The average number of ovulations before conception is therefore equal to:

$$p \, \frac{1}{p^2} = \frac{1}{p}$$

There is another proof which may be preferable because it demands less knowledge of mathematics and because it is analogous to the computation of life expectancy.

The number of women who become pregnant during the 1st cycle is equal to $1 - q$, the number of those becoming pregnant during the second cycle equals $q - q^2$, and so on. The mean number of ovulations for which we are looking is therefore:

$$1 - q + 2(q - q^2) + 3(q - q^3) + \cdots$$

or if we simplify:

$$1+q+q^2+q^3+\cdots.$$

This geometric series with the common ratio q adds up to:

$$\frac{1}{1-q}=\frac{1}{p}.$$

The delay in conception:
Taking the duration of a cycle as the unit of time, the mean number of cycles which separate the first ovulation from conception is equal to $1/p-1$, since the number of ovulations is larger by one than the number of intervals of duration equal to one cycle beginning from the first ovulation. The average delay to conception starting from a point M situated k cycles before the first ovulation is equal to $(1/p-1)+k$.

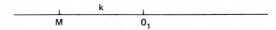

2) Varying fecundability
Let's designate the successive fecundabilities by $p_1, p_2, p_3, \ldots, p_n$ and their respective complements by $q_1, q_2, \ldots, q_n$. Table 14.1 is now replaced by table 14.2.

Table 14.2 Proportion of conceptions and of women not yet pregnant by menstrual cycle, varying fecundability

Cycle number	Conceptions during the cycle	Women not yet pregnant at beginning of cycle
1	p_1	1
2	$p_2 q_1$	q_1
3	$p_3 q_1 q_2$	$q_1 q_2$
4	$p_4 q_1 q_2 q_3$	$q_1 q_2 q_3$
5	$p_5 q_1 q_2 q_3 q_4$	$q_1 q_2 q_3 q_4$
.	. . . .	. . . .

The average number of ovulations before conception becomes:

$$1+q_1+q_1 q_2+\cdots+q_1 q_2\cdots q_n+\cdots.$$

b) Fecundability by month

The menstrual cycle is often equated with the month, without much concern as to whether it is legitimate to substitute a period of fixed duration for a period of variable duration, such as the menstrual cycle. We shall first examine the variation in the duration of the cycle from one woman to another, and then the variation in this duration for the same woman. We assume that fecundability is constant.

1) Variation in the duration of the cycle among women

Consider women with a cycle of duration d days, the fixed period or basis that we intend to substitute for the cycle of duration b days. After bd days, we have b cycles and d months and there remain q^b women who are not yet pregnant.

If there also exists a constant fecundability p_1 by month, we have:

$$q_1^d = q^b \tag{1}$$

q_1 being equal to $1-p_1$. If q_1 exists, it is then defined by relation (1), but in practice, it is computed by relation (2):

$$\log q_1 = \frac{b}{d} \log q. \tag{2}$$

Degree of accuracy:

We wonder whether the value of q_1 thus obtained corresponds exactly or in an approximate way to what we are looking for. To find out, we first compare values of q_1 extracted from (1) to those that can be observed directly.

Let us assume that $b/d = 1+a$

$$p_1 = 1-q_1 = 1-q^{1+a} = 1-(1-p)^{1+a}.$$

If p is small enough, we may neglect the terms that include p^2 and write:[3]

$$p_1 = 1-[1-(1+a)p] = (1+a)p.$$

Let's compare these results with those that are obtained by the direct observation of a group of women with ovulations uniformly distributed in time.

First, when b is greater than d—since A is the origin, the segment AA' is of length d and the segment AB' is of length b.

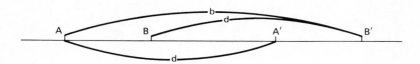

All the women in question have one and only one ovulation in AA'. Since the cycle has a fixed duration d, women who ovulate between A and B ($BB' = d$) and who do not become pregnant ovulate a second time between A' and B'. We have:

$$\frac{AB}{AA'} = \frac{b-d}{d} = a$$

$$\frac{BA'}{AA'} = \frac{b-2(b-d)}{d} = \frac{2d-b}{d} = 1-a.$$

[3]See the justification given in appendix 2.

Table 14.3 Comparison of fecundability by month and by menstrual cycle of 24 days

Unit of time	Cycles of 24 days					
	Conceptions			Not yet pregnant		
	in 6 days	per cycle	per month	per 60 000	per 10 000	$10\,000\,q_1^n$ *
	(1)	(2)	(3)	(4)	(5)	(6)
1	4500			60 000	10 000	10 000
2	4500	18 000				
3	4500		21 150			
4	4500					
5	3150					
6	3150	12 600		38 850	6 475	6 403
7	3150					
8	3150		13 860			
9	2205					
10	2205	8 820				
11	2205			24 990	4 165	4 100
12	2205					
13	1543·5		9 040			
14	1543·5	6 174				
15	1543·5					
16	1543·5			15 950	2 658	2 625
17	1080·5					
18	1080·5	4 322	5 866			
19	1080·5					
20	1080·5					
21				10 084	1 681	1 681
22						
23						
24						
25						
26						
27						
28						
29						
30						

*n = number of months.

The number of conceptions following ovulations occurring between A and A' is equal to p. Added to these we have the conceptions following the second ovulations during $A'B'$. They come to pq (q being the number of women not pregnant during the first ovulation between A and B). The total number of conceptions is thus:

$$p(1+aq) = p(1+a) - ap^2.$$

Second, when b is smaller than d—the figure is as follows:

Women who ovulate between B and A' do not ovulate during AB; the others have one and only one ovulation.

$$\frac{BA'}{AA'} = \frac{d-b}{d} = -\alpha$$

$$\frac{AB}{AA'} = \frac{d-(d-b)}{d} = 1 + \alpha.$$

The number of women becoming pregnant is $p(1+\alpha)$.

Table 14.4 Comparison of fecundability by month and by menstrual cycle of 36 days

Unit of time $(n+1)$	Cycles of 36 days					
	Conceptions		Not yet pregnant			
	in 6 days	per cycle	per month	per 60 000	per 10 000	10 000 q_1^n *
	(1)	(2)	(3)	(4)	(5)	(6)
1	3000			60 000	10 000	10 000
2	3000		15 000			
3	3000	18 000				
4	3000					
5	3000					
6	3000	———		45 000	7 500	7 429
7	2100					
8	2100		11 400			
9	2100	12 600				
10	2100					
11	2100			33 600	5 600	5 519
12	2100	———				
13	1470		8 610			
14	1470					
15	1470	8 820				
16	1470			24 990	4 165	4 100
17	1470					
18	1470	———	6 468			
19	1029					
20	1029					
21	1029	6 174		18 522	3 087	3 046
22	1029					
23	1029		4 836			
24	1029	———				
25	720·3					
26	720·3			13 686	2 281	2 263
27	720·3	4 322				
28	720·3		3 602			
29	720·3					
30	720·3			10 084	1 681	1 681

*n = number of months.

We can see that the number of conceptions in the first month is equal to the first approximation of p in the one case and that it differs by $-\alpha p^2$ in the other.

This means that the value of q_1, defined by (1) or (2), is at best an approximation of what we are looking for.

We must now test with models whether this approximation is sufficient. Since the mean durations of cycles for any woman almost all fall between 24 and 36 days,[4] it is sufficient to look at cycles of 24 days and cycles of 36 days. For this, we can take 6 days as unit of time. The computations are done as indicated in tables 14.3 and 14.4 for a fecundability of 0.3 and a number of ovulations equal to 60 000 per cycle (15 000 per period of 6 days for a cycle of 24 days and 10 000 per period of 6 days for a cycle of 36 days).

The values of q^n in columns (6) do not differ by much more than 1 % from the true values in columns (5) and this is an insignificant difference. It follows that for a constant fecundability per menstrual cycle of fixed duration there is also a corresponding constant fecundability per month.

2) Variation in the duration of the cycle for the same woman

This can only be studied by means of models. We take the following distribution of cycle durations (according to Gunn) applicable for any mean (table 14.5 gives, as an example, the distribution for a mean length of cycle of 28 days).

Table 14.5 Distribution of durations of menstrual cycles with an average duration of 28 days

Days		Frequency
In relation to mean duration d	for a mean length of cycle of 28 days	
$d-6$	22	1
$d-5$	23	1
$d-4$	24	3
$d-3$	25	4
$d-2$	26	10
$d-1$	27	19
d	28	25
$d+1$	29	18
$d+2$	30	9
$d+3$	31	5
$d+4$	32	3
$d+5$	33	1
$d+6$	34	1
Total		100

The next step is to calculate the number of ovulations of order 1, 2, . . . starting from a certain point, in the absence of fecundation (i.e. order starting from the point considered and not starting from puberty). We assume, as a start, that ovulation occurs an equal number of times on each day. The only exception to this hypothesis is at the beginning of marriage because the date of marriage may be chosen in such a way as to avoid the menstrual period.

[4] According to observations by Gunn quoted by P. Vincent, 'Données biométriques sur la conception et la grossesse, *Population* (1956), p. 73.

Table 14.6 gives one part of the computation for an average cycle of 28 days and 1000 ovulations per day. The number of women is 28 000.[5]

Table 14.6 Computation of the number of ovulations by order for a cycle of 28 days mean duration and 1000 ovulations per day in the absence of conceptions

Month	Day	Ovulations of the following order starting from day 0		
		Order 1	Order 2	Order 3
0	0	1000		
	1	1000		
	....			
	21	1000		
	22	990	10	
	....			
	28	370	630	
	29	190	810	
1	30	100	900	
	31	50	950	
	....			
	57		282	718
	58		178	822
	59		107	893

After one month (30 days), there are 27 820 1st order, 2180 2nd order and no 3rd order ovulations. 180 women (28 000 − 27 820) have not ovulated since the start, 25 640 (27 820–2180) have ovulated only once (since this was not followed by a second ovulation) 2180 have ovulated twice (since there was no ovulation of highest order).

These numbers are used to derive the number of women who are not yet pregnant after 30 days, shown in table 14.7.

Table 14.7 Computation of the number of women not yet pregnant after 30 days

Number of ovulations	Number of women	Coefficient	Women not pregnant
0	180	1	180
1	25 640	0·7	17 948
2	2 180	0·49	1 068
	28 000		19 196

The 180 women who have had no ovulation have not become pregnant, whatever the fecundability, hence the coefficient 1. With a fecundability of 0·3, 70 % of the women who have ovulated only once have avoided pregnancy; hence the coefficient 0·7. Among the 2180 women who would have ovulated twice if they had not become pregnant, 30 % became pregnant after the first

[5]During a very long period of duration T, each woman has T/d ovulations, d being the mean duration of the cycle. The mean number of ovulations per day and per woman is therefore equal to $1/d$. For N women, it is equal to N/d. Here $N/d = 1000$; hence $N = 1000\,d$, or 28 000 for $d = 28$.

ovulation; only 70 % ovulated a second time and, among those, 70 % escaped pregnancy. Hence, the coefficient is 0·49 for women who had two ovulations in the month and did not become pregnant. If we multiply the number of women who would have had 0, 1 or 2 ovulations in the absence of fecundation, by the appropriate coefficient, we obtain the number of women not yet pregnant after one month. An analogous computation gives 13 142 after two months. By dividing 19 196 and 13 142 each by 28 000, we obtain 0·685 and 0·469. 0·469 is the square of 0·685.

A similar computation was made (by periods of 4 days to shorten the computations) for cycles averaging 24 days and 36 days in duration, and was continued over ten months. The monthly risk of pregnancy, or ratio of the conceptions for one month to the women who have not yet conceived at the beginning of the month, departs rather little from a constant value.

The finding holds if we introduce variations in the distribution of ovulations owing to a choice of the date of marriage so that it will not fall during menstruation. Instead of distributing ovulations uniformly over a duration d equal to that of the cycle, we substitute a distribution where there are no ovulations for 4 days, and which is otherwise uniform over the rest of the first d days after marriage. To select the 4 days without ovulation, we assume that ovulation precedes menstruation by, say, 14 days.

Conclusion:

These studies lead to the conclusion that cycles of variable duration may be replaced by the average month which has a fixed duration close to the average duration of menstrual cycles. Thus, we can actually work with months in the same way as we would with menstrual cycles of unchanging length. Of course, fecundability per month differs from fecundability per cycle, to the extent that the mean duration of the cycles considered differs from the month. This fecundability by month is close to $p \times 30·4/d$ (p being the fecundability per cycle, d the average duration, in days, of the cycles considered, and 30·4 the average number of days in a month), but not close enough to be able to use this approximation instead of the exact duration, especially when d is smaller than one month.

c) From conception to birth

It is extremely difficult to obtain data on conceptions. Their date is uncertain and a fraction of their total goes completely unnoticed. Live births, on the contrary, are easily observed, and they can be classified by duration of marriage with as much precision as is necessary. Since it is also possible to observe populations where marriage usually coincides with the beginning of sexual relations for the couple (because the frequency of premarital conceptions is low), the attempt has been made to determine fecundability on the basis of the tabulation of first birth by duration of marriage in completed months.

In doing this, there is danger that the results will be biased because of:

1 the choice of the date of marriage in such a way as to avoid the presumed time of menstruation

2 variations in the duration of pregnancy, even when we are dealing with live births

3 intra-uterine mortality as a result of which one or more spontaneous abortions and the ensuing non-susceptible periods may intervene between marriage and the first live birth.

We shall come back later to intra-uterine mortality. For the moment, we will discuss the other two sources of bias.

1) Choice of the date of marriage

Naturally an effort is made to avoid the menstrual period. Since the date of marriage is determined several months in advance, prudence suggests selecting the middle between the dates foreseen for the preceding and following menstrual periods. Variations in the duration of the cycle themselves enlarge the span where the marriage will fall in the cycle. Other considerations (work in the fields, religious calendar, invitations, holidays) interfere with this factor and further spread the final location of marriage in the cycle. Moreover, according to the work of P. Vincent, marriage occurs more often after ovulation than before. This finding suggests that we should study a model

Table 14.8 Distribution of durations of 1000 pregnancies,* counting from the first day after the last menstruation

Duration in months	Duration in days	Number of pregnancies (per 1000 total)
7	220–224	1
	225–229	2
	230–234	3
	235–239	5
8	240–244	9
	245–249	14
	250–254	25
	255–259	37
	260–264	53
	265–269	82
9	270–274	113
	275–279	160
	280–284	166
	285–289	142
	290–294	97
	295–299	52
10	300–304	23
	305–309	11
	310–314	4
	315–319	1
	Total	1000

*Pregnancies terminated by at least one live birth.

where marriage is uniformly distributed over 25 days in a cycle of 30 days; the choice of 5 days with no marriage, rather than 4, is required by the subdivision into groups of 5 days of duration of pregnancy in the available statistics. If we count from the first day of menstruation, we have the following 5 periods of 5 days of marriage: 5–9, 10–14, 15–19, 20–24, and 25–29 days.

2) Duration of pregnancy

Table 14.8 gives the relative frequency for durations of pregnancy computed starting from the first day of the previous menstruation period, which is the conventional measurement of duration.

We assume that ovulation occurs on the 14th day and that women who get married in periods 15–19, 20–24, and 25–29 cannot become pregnant in that cycle. For the group of women marrying during days 5–9 who become pregnant at the first ovulation after marriage, the duration of marriage at delivery is equal to the conventional duration of pregnancy minus 5 to 10 days. For the group marrying during days 10–14, this conventional duration is decreased by 10 to 15 days. For the group marrying during days 15–19, pregnancy cannot occur until the following cycle; duration of marriage at their first birth therefore exceeds the duration of pregnancy by 10–15 days for the ones who become pregnant at the time of the first ovulation after marriage. For the group marrying during days 20–24, duration of pregnancy is exceeded by 5 to 10 days; for the group marrying during days 25–29, by 0 to 5 days. The following table summarizes these figures, while the diagram expresses them graphically.

Days of the marriage	Duration of marriage-duration of pregnancy
5– 9	− 5 to −10
10–14	−10 to −15
15–19	+10 to +15
20–24	+ 5 to +10
25–29	0 to + 5

	days 5–9	days 10–14	days 15–19	days 20–24	days 25–29	
					Menses	
				Menses		
			Menses			
		Menses				
	Menses					
Marriages	days 5–9	days 10–14	days 15–19	days 20–24	days 25–29	
					Menses	
				Menses		
			Menses			
		Menses				
	Menses					

The result is that for 1000 conceptions which follow immediately after marriages on days 5–9, the number of first births at 7 months of marriage includes all frequencies up to duration 240–244, that is 20, for the marriages at the beginning of the period, and up to duration 245–9, that is 34, for marriages at the end of the period of 5 days. The number of births at 8 months of marriage is obtained in an analogous way by adding the frequencies from 245–9 to 270–74 days, which gives 324, then from 250–54 to 275–9 days, which gives 470, and so on. And we end up with the figures given in table 14.9.

Table 14.9 Distribution of first births by period of marriage during the menstrual cycle and by marriage duration

Duration of marriage (months)	Period of marriage									
	5–9		10–14		15—19		20–24		25–29	
	begin-ning	end	begin-ning	end	begin-ning	end	begin-ning	end	begin-ning	end
6	—	—	—	1	—	—	—	—	—	—
7	20	34	34	58	1	3	3	6	6	11
8	324	470	470	611	58	93	93	143	143	220
9	640	491	491	329	611	716	716	760	760	730
10	16	5	5	1	329	188	188	51	91	39
11					1					

From this we finally get the distribution, by duration of marriage in months, of first births following conception at the first ovulation after marriage.[6]

Duration of marriage in months	Frequency
6	1
7	176
8	2 625
9	6 244
10	953
11	1
Total	10 000

Let us now compute first births by month of duration of marriage for fecundability 0·35. For 10 000 marriages, we have 3500 conceptions at the first ovulation. Since we have a model with zero intra-uterine mortality, they are distributed like the 10 000 conceptions above. At the next ovulation, that is to say, one month later, we have 2275 (0·35 × 6500) conceptions which are again

[6] Placing ovulation at the end of the 14th day is sufficient to make the latest marriages during days 10–14 precede ovulation.

distributed like the 10 000 conceptions but stepped down by one additional month. The pattern is as shown in table 14.10. The number of women who have not yet delivered after 6 months, 7 months . . . , the number of births in the month and the ratio of this number to that of the women (i.e. the monthly probability of giving birth) are as given in table 14.11.

Table 14.10 Distribution of births resulting from conceptions at the time of ovulation by order of ovulation after marriage

Duration of marriage at birth (months)	\multicolumn{8}{c}{Order}								Total
	1	2	3	4	5	6	7	8	
6	—								
7	62								62
8	919	40							959
9	2185	597	26						2808
10	334	1421	388	17					2160
11		217	923	252	11				1403
12			141	600	164	7			912
13				92	390	107	5		594
14					60	254	69	3	386

Table 14.11 Computation of the monthly probability of giving birth by month after marriage

Month	\multicolumn{2}{c}{Number of}		Monthly probability of giving birth
	women who have not yet delivered	first births	
6	10000	—	—
7	10000	62	0·006
8	9938	959	0·096
9	9979	2808	0·313
10	6171	2160	0·350
11	4011	1403	0·350
12	2608	912	0·350

Thus, in a homogeneous group and with no intra-uterine mortality, the monthly probability of giving birth calculated on the basis of first births would be equal to fecundability from 10 months on. This finding has a theoretical justification. We ignore the frequencies at 6 and 11 months of marriage in table 14.10, and call the frequencies at 7, 8, 9 and 10 months A, B, C and D respectively. Table 14.10 can then be written as shown in table 14.12.

Table 14.12 Theoretical distribution of births resulting from conceptions at the time of ovulation by order of ovulation after marriage

Duration of marriage at birth (months)	Order					Total
	1	2	3	4	5	
7	Ap					Ap
8	Bp	Apq				$p(B+Aq)$
9	Cp	Bpq	Apq^2			$p(C+Bq+Aq^2)$
10	Dp	Cpq	Bpq^2	Apq^3		$p(D+Cq+Bq^2+Aq^3)$
11		Dpq	Cpq^2	Bpq^3	Apq^4	$pq(D+Cq+Bq^2+Aq^3)$

From duration 10 on, the total is in the form pq^nK where:

$$K = D+Cq+Bq^2+Aq^2.$$

The number of women who have not become pregnant by the beginning of the tenth month is equal to:

$$\sum pq^n K = pK\sum(1+q+\cdots+q^n+\cdots) = \frac{pK}{p} = K.$$

The monthly probability of giving birth is thus equal to $pK/K = p$. The same is true for the following months. Note that K is constant for a given fecundability, in the sense that it does not depend on duration of marriage; but K does depend on fecundability.

Heterogeneous groups

a) Constant fecundability

A heterogeneous group may be treated as the sum of homogeneous groups with fecundabilities

$$p_i(i = 1, 2, \ldots, k, \ldots)$$

and sizes a_i.

In this group, conceptions during successive months number:

$$\sum p_i a_i, \sum p_i q_i a_i, \ldots \sum p_i q_i^n a_i,$$

The number of women not yet pregnant at the beginning of each month is similarly:

$$\sum a_i, \sum q_i a_i, \ldots, \sum q_i^n a_i.$$

By dividing conceptions by the corresponding numbers of non-pregnant women, we obtain the successive monthly probabilities of conception:[7]

$$f_i = \frac{\sum p_i a_i}{\sum a_i}$$

---

[7]Similar probabilities were defined previously on the basis of first births, but the same idea holds for conceptions.

$$f_2 = \frac{\sum p_i q_i a_i}{\sum q_i a_i}$$

The first monthly probability of conception is equal to the mean fecundability before any conception. The second, f_2, is an average of the fecundabilities p_i weighted by the values $a_i q_i$. These values are smaller than a_i (since $q_i < 1$) and decrease as p_i increases. So f_2 is smaller than f_1, since high fecundabilities are proportionately less well represented in the former than in the latter. The same inequality prevails between f_2 and f_3 ... etc. so that we have:

$$f_1 > f_2 > f_3 > \cdots > f_{n-1} > f_n > \cdots.$$

Note that f_2 is also a mean fecundability, that of the women who remain, numbering $a_i q_i$ in each group, after removing the women who became pregnant during the first month. The higher the fecundability of the group, the greater the proportion removed: there is selection in favour of groups with low fertility which remain in observation longer. But when we talk about the mean fecundability of a heterogeneous group, without being more precise, we mean their fecundability before any selection has occurred, thus before anyone has conceived. This can scarcely be observed at any time other than the beginning of marriage, with the additional condition that premarital pregnancies should be rare.

1) Gini's index
C. Gini advocated the use of the ratio r of first births during one month to those of the preceding month. The same concept can be applied to conceptions:

$$r_1 = \frac{\sum p_i q_i a_i}{\sum p_i a_i}.$$

We have:

$$1 - r_1 = \frac{\sum p_i (1 - q_i) a_i}{\sum p_i a_i} = \frac{\sum p_i . p_i a_i}{\sum p_i a_i}.$$

$1 - r_1$ is thus the mean fecundability of women who become pregnant during the first month (numbering $p_i a_i$ in each group), always with no intra-uterine mortality.

2) The average number of ovulations before conception
This number is equal to $1/p_i$ for each component group. For the whole, it is equal to:

$$\frac{\sum 1/p_i a_i}{\sum a_i} = \frac{1}{p_h}$$

p_h is the harmonic mean of fecundabilities.

The harmonic mean of a distribution is always lower than the ordinary mean. It follows that the average number of ovulations before conception is greater in a heterogeneous group of mean fecundability $\bar{p}$ than it would be in a homogeneous group with fecundability $\bar{p}$.

3) The delay in conceiving
Counted from marriage, the delay in conceiving is equal to the mean number of ovulations, including the first one, only if marriage occurs immediately after an ovulation O; otherwise it is shorter.

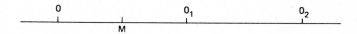

The average delay in conception c after marriage is such that:

$$c = \frac{1}{p_h} - \frac{OM}{OO_1}.$$

OM/OO_1 is usually replaced by $1/2$, which is a sufficiently close approximation.[8]

4) From conception to birth.
For each component group, we proceed as shown for a homogeneous group with fecundability 0.35 at the end of the earlier section, pp. 241–3. Take an aggregate composed of 7 groups with fecundabilities increasing by 0.10 starting from 0.05. The sizes of the groups are proportional to numbers 1 or 2 according to the following arrangement.[9]

Fecundability	Size proportional to
0·05	1
0·15	2
0·25	2
0·35	2
0·45	1
0·55	1
0·65	1

[8]The finding given on p. 232 reappears in a different form, since

$$\frac{OM}{OO_1} = \frac{OO_1 - MO_1}{OO_1} = 1 - k.$$

[9]This corresponds approximately to the true distribution of fecundabilities in a population of married women of ages 20 to 30 years.

Table 14.13 Monthly probability of birth, by duration of marriage, for heterogeneous fecundabilities

Duration of marriage (in months)	Monthly probability of conception per thousand	Duration from marriage to conception (in months)	Monthly probability of birth per thousand
6	0		
7	6		
8	88		
9	276	0	320
10	272	1	273
11	234	2	236
12	206	3	207
13	183	4	185
14	165·5	5	167
15	151	6	152
16	139	7	139
17	128	8	128
18	120	9	119
19	112	10	111
20	105	11	105

The monthly probabilities of conception are given in the left hand part of table 14.13. On the right, we have the monthly probabilities of birth for the same aggregate. Computing births on the basis of conceptions eliminates the influence of the location of marriage in the cycle[10] and the influence of the duration of pregnancy.

The final result is equivalent to that observed for homogeneous groups. After 10 months duration of marriage, the monthly probabilities of giving birth are the same as those that would be observed if pregnancy had a uniform duration of 9 months. But the similarity, although very good, is not total in this case. The difference is due to the fact that although the first births number $p_i q_i^n K_i$ in each group, K_i, which is independent of n, depends on the fecundability and therefore varies from one group to another. The similarity remains good, however, because for central values pf p_i the number of women who are not pregnant after one month, $(A+B+C+D)q_i = q_i$, is almost proportional to the number of women who are not yet mothers after 10 months of marriage (months 0 to 9 included), a number that is equal to:

$$A+B+C+D-(A+B+C)p_i-(A+B)p_iq_i-Ap_iq^2_i$$

that is to say to:

$$Aq^3_i+Bq^2_i+Cq_i+D.$$

Here are the values of the ratio:

$$\alpha = \frac{(A+B+C+D)q_i}{Aq^3_i+Bq^2_i+Cq_i+D}$$

[10]Since we are substituting the month for the cycle by virtue of our earlier findings.

for various values of q_i:

q_i	a
0·95	1·015
0·90	1·02
0·80	1·04
0·70	1·05
0·60	1·05
0·50	1·04
0·40	1·02
0·30	0·97

b) Variable fecundbility

The case of heterogenous groups where the fecundability of each woman varies with age or duration of marriage does not deserve special attention. It amounts to the same thing as adding together homogeneous groups where the fecundability of each woman varies. The preceding studies would have to be redone in the light of such an endeavour, but it has not yet been done, and it is implicitly accepted that the simplifications which are acceptable when fecundability is constant continue to be so when fecundability varies.

15

Models of family building starting with marriage – intra-uterine mortality and fecundability

1 Problems of the influence of intra-uterine mortality on fertility

The subject of intra-uterine mortality, whether for the purposes of measuring it or of studying its role in fertility, has been neglected for a long time. The study by French and Bierman[1] changed this situation and stimulated research into the influence of intra-uterine mortality on fertility in particular.

This influence is twofold.

a) Given the same fecundability, the lower intra-uterine mortality is, the higher the number of live births. Inversely, an equal number of births can be generated by the combination of high fecundability and high intra-uterine mortality or by the combination of lower fecundability and lower intra-uterine mortality. Among such combinations, there is one which associates the lowest fecundability of all with zero intra-uterine mortality. This suggests that intra-uterine mortality could be considered as a factor which simply reduces fecundability. To take intra-uterine mortality into account, it would be sufficient to replace overall fecundability, comprising all conceptions, by effective fecundability, where only those conceptions that lead to live births would be included.

b) It would be possible to use this approach if spontaneous abortion occurred only very early in pregnancy. This is not the case, and conceptions which lead to spontaneous abortions are accompanied, at least for the most part, by a non-susceptible period of a duration which cannot be ignored.

Deaths in the intra-uterine life table

The nonsusceptible period is at least as long as the duration of gestation at the time of the spontaneous abortion. The distribution given in table 15.1 of deaths in the intra-uterine life table according to the conventional measurement of pregnancy length is sufficient to show that the non-susceptible period should not be ignored.

[1]*Op. cit.*, see chapter 9, note 5.

Table 15.1 Distribution of deaths in the intra-uterine life table

Duration of pregnancy (months)	Deaths in the table		Duration of pregnancy (months)	Deaths in the table	
	Per 1000 pregnancies	Per 100 deaths[2]		Per 1000 pregnancies	Per 100 deaths [2]
0	0	0	6	2·4	1
1	108·1	46	7	2·3	1
2	62·4	26	8	2·3	1
3	37·2	16	9	2·5	1
4	10·5	5	10 and over	3·0	0
5	6·6	3	Total	237·3	100

Source: After French and Bierman, *op. cit.*

Very early intra-uterine deaths

French and Bierman's observations start at 4 weeks conventional duration of pregnancy (approximately at 2 weeks since conception). Very early intra-uterine deaths are excluded, and this is the reason why the above table has a zero frequency for conventional durations of less than 1 month.

Such very early intra-uterine deaths are a reality none the less and some authors even think that there are a great many of them, either before or during implantation. But it is questionable whether an intra-uterine death before implantation influences the woman's organism at all or causes a non-susceptible period. The same may well be true of deaths during or very soon after implantation. So very early deaths have the highest probability of not precipitating any non-susceptible period or of precipitating only an insignificant one. The results in one study,[3] have confirmed this assumption.

In consequence, very early intra-uterine deaths do have as their main, if not their only, effect the reduction of apparent fecundability (that which can be measured in terms of live births).[4]

2 The computation of a distribution of intra-uterine deaths suited for models

The distribution given above is by true conventional duration, that is to say counted from a clearly defined origin, the beginning of the last menstrual period. For the purpose of models, that kind of distribution has to be replaced by a distribution which gives the number of events *B*, following a previous event *A*, that occur in the same unit of time as event *A*, in the subsequent unit of time, and so on.

Here *A* designates conception and *B* intra-uterine death. Since we are trying to study the changes brought about by intra-uterine mortality in the

[2]French and Bierman presented their data grouped by periods of 4 weeks. We have given them by month for convenience. To compensate, we have compressed the percent distribution slightly by giving a frequency of 0 to the last period (ten months and over).
[3]Louis Henry, 'Mortalité intra-utérine et fécondabilité', *Population* (1964), **5,** pp. 899–940.
[4]They would also decrease fecundability measured in terms of conceptions since those conceptions which end in a very early intra-uterine death usually remain unknown.

distribution of first live births by marriage duration, the unit of time is the month of duration of marriage. The distribution that we want must tell us how many intra-uterine deaths occur in the same month (of marriage duration) as conception, in the following month, in the month after that, and so on.

Let us consider the same situation that we had earlier: marriages are uniformly distributed through 25 days out of a cycle of 30 days, omitting the first day of the menstrual period and the next 4 days. Under this hypothesis, 2/5 of marriages occur before ovulation and 3/5 after.

For the two fifths where marriage occurs before ovulation, the pregnancy of women who become pregnant at the first ovulation after marriage is conventionally counted starting with an origin R_0 which precedes marriage by 5 to 15 days.

For the other three fifths, the pregnancy of women who became pregnant at the first ovulation after marriage is counted starting from an origin R_1 located from 0 to 15 days after marriage.

Since five days is one sixth of a month, the distribution of duration of pregnancy at the time of the intra-uterine death must first be subdivided by

Table 15.2 Distribution of pregnancy duration at the time of an intra-uterine death

Sixths of month	Deaths	Sixths of month	Deaths
0	0	18	3·5
1	0	19	3·1
2	0	20	2·8
3	0	21	2·6
4	0	22	2·2
5	0	23	1·8
0–5	0	18–23	16·0
6	9·6	24	1·4
7	8·7	25	1·0
8	8·0	26	0·7
9	7·3	27	0·7
10	6·6	28	0·6
11	5·8	29	0·6
5–11	46·0	24·29	5·0
12	5·0	30	0·6
13	4·8	31	0·6
14	4·5	32	0·5
15	4·2	33	0·5
16	3·9	34	0·4
17	3·6	35	0·4
12–17	26·0	30–35	3·0

sixths of months. This can be done graphically, and the results are as shown in table 15.2.

We return now to marriages and take up those which occur from 5 to 10 days after the beginning of menstruation. For those which occur exactly 5 days after, the duration of marriage at the time of an intra-uterine death following a conception in the course of the first month is exactly one sixth of a month less than the conventional duration of pregnancy. For those which occur exactly 10 days after, the duration of marriage is two-sixths of a month less than the conventional duration. The differences appear in table 15.3 as displacements upwards by 1 row for 5 days and 2 rows for 10 days. The sum of the two columns is proportional to the distribution by duration of marriage of spontaneous abortions that follow conceptions occurring at the first ovulation after marriage. For marriages which occur 10 to 15 days after the beginning of menstruation, the displacements are two-sixths of a month for 10 days, and three sixths for 15 days; again the sum is proportional to the distribution by duration of marriage in sixths of months, of spontaneous abortions that follow conceptions occurrring at the first ovulation after marriage.

The total of these two sums is proportional to the similar distribution for all marriages from 5 to 15 days. This comes to the same thing as taking the sum of the two extreme distributions, one sixths' and three sixths' displacement, plus twice the intermediate distribution, two sixths' displacement (columns (1) to (4) in table 15.3. For marriages which occur after ovulation, the displacements are in the opposite direction from the preceding ones and are from 0 to 5, 5 to 10, 10 to 15, according to whether the marriages precede menstruation by 0 to 5, 5 to 10, or 10 to 15 days. Here we have three sums and their total represents the distribution by duration of marriage of spontaneous abortions that follow conceptions occurring at the first ovulation after marriage. It comes to the same thing as taking the sum of the two extreme distributions, no displacement and three sixths' displacement, plus twice the two intermediate distributions, one sixths' displacement, plus twice the two intermediate distributions, one sixths' and two sixths' displacement (columns (5) to (9) of table 15.3).

For all marriages together, the distribution we want (column 10) is obtained by adding the two preceding totals. One is the sum of four distributions $(1 + 2 + 1)$, the other one of 6 $(1 + 2 + 2 + 1)$. This corresponds to the desired weights of 2/5 and 3/5.

Then all we need to do is to add the total for each month (column 11) and for the sake of simplicity to round off the distribution to two digits expressed on the basis of 100 (column 12).

For month 5, the result is 3 as in the distribution in table 15.1. For the following months, 6 to 9, we will also take the same frequencies, as in that distribution, or 1 for each of these months. The resulting distribution (7, 37, 27, 16, 6, 3, 1, 1, 1, 1) is that of spontaneous abortions per month for pregnancies following conception during the first months of marriage.[5] It is also the distribution of differences between the month (of marriage duration) when the spontaneous abortion occurred and the month when conception took place.

[5] Remember that by virtue of our earlier findings, we may operate as if the menstrual cycle were one month long, and consider therefore that conception during the first month is the same thing as conception at the first ovulation.

1*

Table 15.3 Computation of the distribution of intra-uterine deaths by difference (in months) between the marriage duration month of the death and the marriage duration month of the conception

Sixth of month	Marriages before ovulation 5d	10d	15d after menses	Total	Marriages after ovulation 0d	5d	10d	15d before menses	Total	All marriages per month Per sixth of month	Per thous-and	%	Month
	(1)	(2)	(3)	(4)	(5)	(6)	(7)	(8)	(9)	(10)	(11)	(12)	
0													
1													
2													
3			9·6	9·6						9·6	72·5	7	0
4		19·2	8·7	27·9						27·9			
5	9·6	17·4	8·0	35·0						35·0			
6	8·7	16·0	7·3	32·0	9·6				9·6	41·6			
7	8·0	14·6	6·6	29·2	8·7	19·2			27·9	57·1			
8	7·3	13·2	5·8	26·3	8·0	17·4	19·2		44·6	70·9			
9	6·6	11·6	5·0	23·2	7·3	16·0	17·4	9·6	50·3	73·5	370·3	37	1
10	5·8	10·0	4·8	20·6	6·6	14·6	16·0	8·7	45·9	66·5			
11	5·0	9·6	4·5	19·1	5·8	13·2	14·6	8·0	41·6	60·7			
12	4·8	9·0	4·2	18·0	5·0	11·6	13·2	7·3	37·1	55·1			
13	4·5	8·4	3·9	16·8	4·8	10·0	11·6	6·6	33·0	49·8			
14	4·2	7·8	3·6	15·6	4·5	9·6	10·0	5·8	29·9	45·5			
15	3·9	7·2	3·5	14·6	4·2	9·0	9·6	5·0	27·8	42·4	269·4	27	2
16	3·6	7·0	3·1	13·7	3·9	8·4	9·0	4·8	26·1	39·8			
17	3·5	6·2	2·8	12·5	3·6	7·8	8·4	4·5	24·3	36·8			
18	3·1	5·6	2·6	11·3	3·5	7·2	7·8	4·2	22·7	34·0			
19	2·8	5·2	2·2	10·2	3·1	7·0	7·2	3·9	21·2	31·4			
20	2·6	4·4	1·8	8·8	2·8	6·2	7·0	3·6	19·6	28·4			
21	2·2	3·6	1·4	7·2	2·6	5·6	6·2	3·5	17·9·	25·1	158·9	16	3
22	1·8	2·8	1·0	5·6	2·2	5·2	5·6	3·1	16·1	21·7			
23	1·4	2·0	0·7	4·1	1·8	4·4	5·2	2·8	14·2	18·3			
24	1·0	1·4	0·7	3·1	1·4	3·6	4·4	2·6	12·0	15·1			
25	0·7	1·4	0·6	2·7	1·0	2·8	3·6	2·2	9·6	12·3			
26	0·7	1·2	0·6	2·5	0·7	2·0	2·8	1·8	7·3	9·8			
27	0·6	1·2	0·6	2·4	0·7	1·4	2·0	1·4	5·5	7·9	58·1	6	4
28	0·6	1·2	0·6	2·4	0·6	1·4	1·4	1·0	4·4	6·8			
29	0·6	1·2	0·5	2·3	0·6	1·2	1·4	0·7	3·9	6·2			
30	0·6	1·0	0·5	2·1	0·6	1·2	1·2	0·7	3·7	5·3			
31	0·5	1·0	0·4	1·9	0·6	1·2	1·2	0·6	3·6	5·5			
32	0·5	0·8	0·4	1·7	0·5	1·2	1·2	0·6	3·5	5·2			
33	0·4	0·8	0·3	1·5	0·5	1·0	1·2	0·6	3·3	4·8	29·1	3	5
34	0·4	0·6	0·2	1·2	0·4	1·0	1·0	0·6	3·0	4·2			
35	0·3	0·4	0·2	0·9	0·4	0·8	1·0	0·5	2·7	3·6			

3 Computation of A. .V conceptions

This is what we shall call the conceptions of live born children that are preceded by at least one spontaneous abortion. The computation of A. .V conceptions may be done all together. But to start with, suppose that it will be done in steps and that AV, AAV, . . . , conceptions (i.e. conceptions preceded by one, two . . . , spontaneous abortions) will be calculated successively. Let's designate as C_0, C_1, C_2 . . . the first order conceptions which occur at marriage durations 0, 1, 2 . . . in months, as V_0, V_1, V_2 . . . the corresponding V conceptions and as A_0, A_1, A_2 . . . the corresponding A conceptions. If v is the probability (constant by hypothesis) that a conception will result in a live birth, we have:

$$V_i = v\, C_i$$
$$A_i = (1-v)\, C_i$$

and therefore:

$$A_i = (1-v)\,\frac{V_i}{v}, \qquad vA_i = (1-v)\, V_i$$

If d_0, d_1, d_2 . . . are the proportions of spontaneous abortions which occur in the month of conception, in the following month, in the month after that, and so on, if p is fecundability, which is constant according to our hypothesis, and q is the complement of p, then the table of spontaneous abortions according to the month of conception and the month of abortion combined is as shown in table 15.4.

Table 15.4 Theoretical number of spontaneous abortions by month of conception and month of abortion

Month of abortion	Month of conception					Probability of conceiving again during month 5
	0	1	2	3	4	
0	$A_0\, d_0$					$q^3\, p$
1	$A_0\, d_1$	$A_1\, d_0$				$q^2\, p$
2	$A_0\, d_2$	$A_1\, d_1$	$A_2\, d_0$			qp
3	$A_0\, d_3$	$A_1\, d_2$	$A_2\, d_1$	$A_3\, d_0$		p
4	$A_0\, d_4$	$A_1\, d_3$	$A_2\, d_2$	$A_3\, d_1$	$A_4\, d_0$	
5	$A_0\, d_5$	$A_1\, d_4$	$A_2\, d_3$	$A_3\, d_2$	$A_4\, d_1$	
.	. . .	. . .	. . .	. . .	. . .	
.	. . .	. . .	. . .	. . .	. . .	
Total	A_0	A_1	A_2	A_3	A_4	

Let's consider the case where women who abort during month i cannot become pregnant again before month $i+2$. AC conceptions (conceptions preceded by a spontaneous abortion) of month 5 originate from women having had a spontaneous abortion during month 0, 1, 2 and 3. Those women who aborted during month 3 are all exposed to conception during month 5 and a proportion p among them will conceive during that month. Those who aborted during month 2 were already exposed to a new conception during month 4, and a proportion q did not conceive; the proportions who will conceive during month 5 is therefore qp. In the same way, we have qp^2 for women who aborted during month 1 and qp^3 for women who aborted during month 0. These proportions are shown in the right hand column.

The number of AC conceptions in month 5 is thus equal to:

$$q^3\ pA_0\ d_0 +$$
$$q^2\ p(A_0\ d_1 + A_1\ a_0) +$$
$$qp(A_0\ d_2\ + A_1\ d_1 + A_2\ d_0) +$$
$$p(A_0\ d_3 + A_1\ d_2 + A_2\ d_1 + A_3\ d_0).$$

The number of AV conceptions can be deduced from the preceding by multiplying each term by v. Let us regroup the terms in A_0, in A_1, in A_2 and in A_3. The number of AV conceptions can be written as:

$$vA_0(q^3\ pd_0 + q^2\ pd_1 + qpd_2 + pd_3) +$$
$$vA_1(q^2\ pd_0 + qpd_1 + pd_2) +$$
$$vA_2(qpd_0 + pd_1) +$$
$$vA_3(pd_0)$$

which can also be written:

$$vA_0\ \gamma_3 + vA_1\ \gamma_2 + vA_2\ \gamma_1 + vA_3\ \gamma_0$$

if we designate by γ_i the sum of $i+1$ terms, $q^i\ pd_0 + \ldots + pd_i$.

If we replace vA_0 by $(1-v)\ V_0$, A_1 by $(1-v)\ V_1$, etc. the number of AV conceptions in month 5 becomes:

$$(1-v)\ V_0\ \gamma_3 + (1-v)\ V_1\ \gamma_2 + (1-v)\ V_2\ \gamma_1 + (1-v)\ V_3\ \gamma_0$$

or also, if we set $(1-v)\ \gamma_i = a_i$,

$$V_0\ a_3 + V_1\ a_2 + V_2\ a_1 + V_3\ a_0.$$

The following is a schematic summary of the computation of the γ's and of the AV conceptions:

Month		pq^n	γ		
0	d_3	p		V_0	α_3
1	d_2	pq		V_1	α_2
2	d_1	pq^2		V_2	α_1
3	d_0	pq^3	γ_3	V_3	α_0
4					AV
5					

The proportions d_0, d_1 are written starting from the bottom on a strip of paper which is placed on the left of pq^n. The sum of products $d_3 \ldots d_0\,pq^3$ is written on the line where d_0 has been placed (here line 4). The coefficients a_0, a_1, $a_2 \ldots$ are also written on a strip of paper starting from the bottom. We make a window in the paper strip below a_0. This makes a place to write the sum of products, for example, $V_0 a_3 + V_1 a_2 + V_2 a_1 + V_3 a_0$.

Table 15.5. Computation of the distribution of A. .V conceptions

Month i	pq_i	γ_i	a^i	V	AV	AAV	$AAAV$	$A..V$	$V+A..V$
	per 10 000				per 10 000 women				
0	3500	245	61	2625					2625
1	2275	1454	364	1706					1706
2	1479	1890	472	1110	16			16	1126
3	961	1789	447	721	106			106	827
4	625	1373	343	469	193			193	662
5	406	997	249	304	243	1		244	548
6	264	683	171	197	248	6		254	451

Table 15.5 gives numerical results for $p = 0.35, v = 0.75$; the series $d_0, d_1 \ldots$ is that given at the beginning of this section. The V column is that of the V conceptions which were not preceded by a spontaneous abortion. Since 10 000 pq^n is also the number of first conceptions per 10 000 women, the V column is deduced from the first column by multiplying it by 0.75. The same sort of calculations enable one to pass from V to AV on the one hand, and from AV to AAV on the other. Thus:

$$248 = \frac{469 \times 61 + 721 \times 364 + 1110 \times 472 + 1706 \times 447 + 2625 \times 343}{10\,000}$$

$$6 = \frac{193 \times 61 + 106 \times 364 + 16 \times 472 + 0 \times 447 + 0 \times 343}{10\,000}$$

As a result the sum, 254, is such that:

$$254 = \frac{662 \times 61 + 827 \times 364 + 1126 \times 472 + 1706 \times 447 + 2625 \times 343}{10\,000}$$

An analogous result would be obtained for a later month using V, AV, AAV and $AAAV$ this time. This means that we can obtain in one single computation the $A..V$ conceptions for any month i by adding products $a(V + A..V)$ of months $i-2, i-3 \ldots 0$.

4 Practical uses of the models

When the computations that we have just explained are completed, we know the monthly probability of giving birth for a homogeneous group at various levels of intra-uterine mortality. When these results are compared with the available observations (1549 intervals between marriage and maritally conceived first births taken from various historical demography studies), it is clear that real populations cannot be homogeneous with regard to fecundability and to intra-uterine mortality at the same time.

The distribution of fecundability

After correcting (graphically, guided by Vincent's models) for the effect of the timing of marriage on first births 9 months after marriage, the number of those is equal to $\overline{vp}$, whereas the number of first births 10 months after marriage is $\overline{vp} - \overline{vp}^2 (1 + c^2)$, where $\bar{v}$ is the mean value of the probability that a conception will result in a live birth, and $\bar{p}$ is the average value and c the coefficient of variation of fecundability. The difference $n_1 - n_2$ between the births in the 9th month and those in the 10th month is equal to $v\bar{p}^2 (1 + c^2)$.

From the two relationships

$$n_1 = \overline{vp}$$

$$\frac{n_1 - n_2}{n_1} = \bar{p}(1 + c^2)$$

it is easy to extract $\bar{p}$ and c, provided that $\bar{v}$ is known, even if only approximately.

For the 1549 observations mentioned above, we find values of $\bar{p}$ and c^2 on the order of 0·3.

Fecundability can vary from 0 to 1. Its frequency is nil for the extreme value 0^6 and probably also for the extreme value 1. It stands to reason moreover that the distribution has only one maximum (or mode). When this is so, it is or can be approximated by a Pearson type I distribution, one that is continuous and depends on two parameters, and therefore is determined when $\bar{p}$ and c^2 are known. For purposes of computation, we must replace this continuous distribution by a discrete one. The following highly simplified distribution will do for manual computations.

Fecundability	Frequency
0·05	1
0·15	2
0·25	2
0·35	2
0·45	1
0·55	1
0·65	1

Its average is 0·32 and the square of the coefficient of variation is 0·313.

The distribution of intra-uterine mortality

The inequality in the risk of spontaneous abortion (for the same order of conception) between women whose preceding pregnancy ended in a live birth and those for whom this pregnancy ended in a spontaneous abortion shows that heterogeneity with regard to intra-uterine mortality exists.

Let v_i be the probability that a conception will end in a live birth in homogeneous class i, and let a_i be the size of that class. The number of V conceptions (without previous conception) is equal to $v_i a_i$, and the number of A conceptions preceded by a V conception is $(1 - v_i)v_i a_i$. The number of A

[6]Women who are sterile from marriage on are excluded and constitute a separate group.

conceptions (without previous conception) is $(1-v_i)a_i$. That of A conceptions preceded by an A conception is equal to $(1-v_i)^2 a_i$.

The probability that the second pregnancy will end in a spontaneous abortion is equal to:

$$\frac{\sum (1-v_i)\, v_i a_i}{\sum v_i a_i} = \frac{\bar{v} - \bar{v}^2(1+\gamma^2)}{\bar{v}} = 1 - \bar{v} - \bar{v}\gamma^2$$

when the first pregnancy ended with a live birth, and it is equal to:

$$\frac{\sum (1-v_i)^2 a_i}{\sum (1-v_i)a_i} = \frac{1 - 2\bar{v} + \bar{v}(1+\gamma^2)}{1 - \bar{v}} = 1 - \bar{v} + \frac{\bar{v}^2\gamma^2}{1-\bar{v}}$$

when the first pregnancy ended with a spontaneous abortion ($\bar{v}$ being the mean of probabilities v_i and γ their coefficient of variation).

If A_1 and A_2 are measures of the first and of the second probabilities, we have:

$$A_2 - A_1 = \frac{\bar{v}^2\gamma^2}{1-\bar{v}} + \bar{v}\gamma^2 = \frac{\bar{v}\gamma^2}{1-\bar{v}}$$

$$1 - \bar{v} = \bar{v}A_1 + (1-\bar{v})\, A_2$$

hence:

$$1 - \bar{v} = \frac{A_1}{1 + A_1 - A_2}.$$

These formulae allow us to compute $\bar{v}$ and γ^2 on the basis of observations of second order conceptions. In actuality, there is a dearth of suitable observations on this point. From the few we have, the following simplified distribution has been extracted:

v_i	Frequency
0·65	1
0·70	1
0·75	1
0·80	2
0·85	2
0·90	2
0·95	1

5 Models and real life

Now that we have distributions for fecundability and intra-uterine mortality, we can compute monthly probabilities of giving birth for groups that are heterogeneous with respect to both factors or with respect to fecundability only (the case of groups that are heterogeneous with respect to intra-uterine mortality only is not of interest). It can be ascertained that there is little difference between a group that is heterogeneous with respect to intra-uterine mortality and a homogeneous group with a level of intra-uterine mortality equal to the mean for the preceding group. Thus heterogeneity with respect to intra-uterine mortality is of little importance, and we can limit ourself to models where intra-uterine mortality is the same for all women.

The comparison of these findings with real life lead to the following conclusions:[7]

When a pregnancy ends in a spontaneous abortion, the non-susceptible period scarcely exceeds the duration of pregnancy by more than one month.

Intra-uterine mortality, which is accompanied by a non-susceptible period (the only kind which raises particular problems), cannot attain values much higher than those which were observed in Kauaii starting at 4 weeks conventional duration of pregnancy.

It follows that:

1 Early intra-uterine deaths are not accompanied by a non-susceptible period or are accompanied only by an insignificant one.

2 Intra-uterine mortality was not markedly higher in the past than it is today (the observations relate for the most part to eighteenth-century populations). This fits in well with the medical observation that a substantial proportion of intra-uterine deaths are due to an anomaly in the chromosomes.

Observation:
This example shows the extent to which models can be useful. In this case, it is not only a matter of unravelling a complicated set of relationships; the model is sufficiently close to reality to be used in place of experimentation and to lead to fairly secure conclusions as to what that reality is and what it is not.

6 Mean interval between marriage and the first V conception

Let us call the delay from marriage to conception c_0, and the interval between an A conception and the subsequent A or V conception i_1. We assume that there is no relationship between fecundability and intra-uterine mortality and therefore that c_0 and i_1 are not dependent on v.

When the first V conception is also the first conception, the mean interval is c_0. When the first V conception is the second conception, the mean interval is $c_0 + i_1$. When it is the third conception, it is $c_0 + 2i_1$, and so on. In a homogeneous group, the first situation has a frequency of v, the second of $v(1-v)$, the third of $v(1-v)^2$, and so on.

The mean interval we are looking for is therefore equal to:

$$c_0[v + v(1-v) + v(1-v)^2 + \cdots] +$$
$$i_1[v(1-v) + 2v(1-v)^2 + \cdots].$$

The term in c_0 can also be written:

$$c_0 v[1 + (1-v) + (1-v)^2 + \cdots] = \frac{c_0 v}{1 - (1-v)} = c_0.$$

[7] *Op. cit.*, pp. 908–9, 916.

To compute the second term, set $1 - v = a$. The coefficient of i_1 is written:

$$(1-a)a + 2(1-a)a^2 + 3(1-a)a^3 + \cdots =$$

$$= a - a^2 + 2a^2 - 2a^3 + 3a^3 + \cdots$$

$$= a + a^2 + a^3 + \cdots = a(1 + a + a^2 + \cdots) = \frac{a}{1-a} = \frac{1-v}{v}.$$

So the desired mean interval is equal to:

$$c_0 + i_1 \frac{1-v}{v}.$$

For all intra-uterine deaths together, we end up with a mean interval equal to:

$$c_0 + i_1 \frac{1 - v_h}{v_h}$$

where v_h is the harmonic mean of v.

We have seen that c_0 is on the order of $1/p_h - 1/2$. As for i_1, it is equal to $1/p_h + g_a$ where g_a is the mean value of the non-susceptible period for spontaneous abortions. We know g_a is equal to 3 months, and $1/p_h$ is of the order of 6 months. The harmonic mean of v is on the order of 0·8 for first births. The mean interval is equal to:

$$5 \cdot 5 + \frac{0 \cdot 2}{0 \cdot 8} \times 9 = 5 \cdot 5 + 2 \cdot 25 = 7 \cdot 75.$$

Thus, the existence of intra-uterine mortality lengthens the interval between marriage and the first birth by approximately 2 months, and the delay to conception is increased by approximately 40%.

16

Models of family building starting with marriage—all births and relevant factors together

1 All births together

Up to now, we have been dealing with first order conceptions and births only. Among the basic factors affecting fertility, we have concentrated for the most part on fecundability and intra-uterine mortality and almost left aside the non-susceptible period; indeed, if the latter itself includes the influence of intra-uterine mortality, it intervenes only in a simplified form. We shall now deal with all conceptions together, then with all births. Here the non-susceptible period plays an important role.

The non-susceptible period

This is defined as the time during which one conception makes another conception impossible, because of the fact that ovulation stops during pregnancy and for some time after delivery, and because sexual relations may be interrupted for some time after the end of pregnancy. Under this definition, the non-susceptible period is affected by both physiological and behavioural factors.

The inhibition (frequent, but not universal) of ovulation by breastfeeding is included among the physiological factors. Its frequency and duration, which vary from one population to another and from one woman to another, are themselves a behavioural matter, so that even when there is no custom regulating the resumption of sexual intercourse after delivery, the non-susceptible period nevertheless depends on behaviour through the intervention of breastfeeding. The mechanism through which lactation suppresses ovulation has not been completely explained. External factors such as the woman's diet may play a role.

Breastfeeding was the general rule in the past and it is still widely practised in developing nations, although there are exceptions such as Bavaria in the last century.

a) **Variability of the non-susceptible period**

The non-susceptible period certainly varies from one woman to another, if only because with certain women ovulation recommences a short time after delivery even if they are nursing.

The non-susceptible period may also vary for the same woman:

1 Randomly—the child may die after a few days, weeks, or months; the interruption of breastfeeding due to that death shortens the non-susceptible period. The latter may also vary under the influence of unpredictable conditions (sickness, accidents) which may either shorten it (by interrupting breastfeeding) or prolong it (by temporary sterility).

2 With age or number of children—some doctors believe that nursing is more likely to inhibit ovulation after the second delivery than the first one and observations on historical populations seem to confirm that opinion. It has also been observed that the duration of post partum amenorrhea (the interruption of menstruation after delivery) increases with the woman's age. This steady increase is probably independent of the preceding one, which is limited to first births and therefore to the younger ages.

b) **The non-susceptible period in discrete models**

For discrete models, which conform best to reality, the definition of the non-susceptible period has to be adapted to the special characteristics of these models.

We assume that if there had been no non-susceptible period, there would have been a certain number of cycles between the one, 0, in which conception actually occurred and the one, 0_1, where the woman was once again subject to pregnancy (the first cycle where ovulation and sexual intercourse recur together). The duration of the non-susceptible period is by definition equal to the number of cycles which have been suppressed or made unnecessary by a conception in this way. Thus, in the diagram below, the non-susceptible period last 14 cycles, or 14 months since we have assimilated the cycle to the month.

Homogeneous groups

Only variations in the duration of the non-susceptible period for the same woman intervene within homogeneous groups. Because of such variations, women who conceived in a certain month x have non-susceptible periods of variable duration, so that at month $x + y$ some of these women are once again susceptible to pregnancy. But another fraction $K_{x, y}$ is still immune from the risk of conception, or, more simply is not at risk. If $K_{x, y}$ does not depend on x, we may write just K_y.

a) **Computation of K_y**

Normally a distribution like the one shown in table 16.1 is given for the duration of the non-susceptible period. To determine K_y, it is sufficient to observe that a woman who conceives during month x is not at risk during at least months $x+1$ and $x+2$; in month $x+3$, the portion for whom the non-susceptible period lasted only for 2 months is no longer not at risk, so $K_3 = 0.98$.

Table 16.1 Distribution of the duration of the non-susceptible period

Duration y (months)	Frequency	K_y	Duration y (months)	Frequency	K_y
1	—	1	17	1	0·62
2	2	1	18	1	0·61
3	8	0·98	19	1	0·60
4	8	0·90	20	2	0·59
5	2	0·82	21	4	0·57
6	—	0·80	22	6	0·53
7	—	0·80	23	7	0·47
8	—	0·80	24	9	0·40
9	3	0·80	25	9	0·31
10	6	0·77	26	7	0·22
11	4	0·71	27	6	0·15
12	1	0·67	28	4	0·09
13	1	0·66	29	2	0·05
14	1	0·65	30	1	0·03
15	1	0·64	31	1	0·02
16	1	0·63	32	1	0·01
			33	—	0·00

b) The basic equation

Consider a homogeneous group of married women whose number is taken as the base. We designate as C_x the number of conceptions in month x, and as p_x the fecundability, identical for all, of these women during month x.

C_x is equal to the product of p_x and the number of women exposed to conception. That number is equal to the total number minus the number of women not at risk. For the C_{x-y} women who conceived during month $x-y$, this number is equal to $C_{x-y}K_{x-y,x}$. For all the women who conceived between $x-G$ (G being the highest possible value for the non-susceptible period) and $x-1$, the number of women not at risk is equal to:

$$\sum_{y=1}^{y=G} C_{x-y}K_{x-y,y}.$$

If we take the total number of women as unity, the proportion of women exposed to conception during month x is:

$$1 - \sum_{y=1}^{y=G} C_{x-y}K_{x-y,y}$$

and we have:

$$C_x = p_x \left[1 - \sum_{y=1}^{y=G} C_{x-y}K_{x-y,y} \right]. \tag{1}$$

When $K_{x-y,y}$ is not dependent on x, equation (1) can be written more simply:

$$C_x = p_x\left[1 - \sum_{y=1}^{y=G} C_{x-y}K_y\right].\qquad(2)$$

Finally, if p_x itself were independent of x, we would have:

$$C_x = p\left[1 - \sum_{y=1}^{y=G} C_{x-y}K_y\right].\qquad(3)$$

c) Setting the computations

For convenience, we will take the quarter rather than the month and consider the case where the fraction K_y does not depend on x. We have the following distribution for the duration of the non-susceptible period, in quarters:

Duration Y (quarters)	Frequency	K_y
1	2	1
2	0	0·8
3	0	0·8
4	0	0·8
5	0	0·8
6	1	0·8
7	4	0·7
8	3	0·3
9	–	0·0

K_y, shown in the right hand column of the table, was computed as before.

Equation (2) allows us to compute the conceptions starting from marriage, provided the numbers of conceptions during the 8 preceding quarters are known. Consider the case where these numbers are zero (no premarital pregnancies). Table 16.2 shows how to proceed with the computations starting from marriage, when the value of p_x for each trimester is given. To compute the number not at risk, the values K_y are written starting from the bottom on a strip of paper and a window is made between line K_0 and the line below, as in the drawing to the right of table 16.2.

For example, we have:

$$6991 = 1823 \times 1 + 2460 \times 0·8 + 4000 \times 0·8.$$

d) Convergence

It can be demonstrated directly that the difference between any two possible solutions of equation (1) (stemming from any two possible sets of initial conditions) is a function which oscillates with duration of marriage and tends to zero when this duration increases indefinitely. The periodicity of the oscillations is less than G.

Table 16.2 Computation of the number of conceptions by duration of marriage

Duration of marriage (quarters)	p_x	Conceptions	Not at risk	Remainder	
0	0·400	4000			0·0
1	0·410	2460	4000	6000	0·3
2	0·420	1823	5660	4340	0·7
3	0·430	1294	6991	3009	0·8
4	0·440	915	7920	2080	0·8
5	0·450				0·8
6	0·460				0·8
7	0·470				0·8
8	0·480				0·8
9	0·490				1
10	0·500				

Thus, if there is one particular constant solution—which is the case for the form (3) of (1)—the other solutions appear as follows:

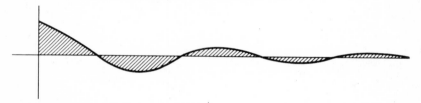

We could also write C_x in such a way as to return to one of Lotka's equations. In order to do so, it is enough to consider each conception as the birth of one particular being (the interval between conceptions) who dies in giving birth to the being which replaces him (the following interval). Then we write

$$C_x = \sum_{y=1}^{\infty} C_{x-y} f_{x-y,\, y}.$$

This equation belongs to the family of Lotka's equations, and plays the role of the period net reproduction rate. There is one difference from Lotka's equation, however: y, which is equivalent to the age of the mothers at the birth of their children, can vary from 1 to infinity. But in practice, $f_{x-y,y}$, the frequency of intervals y between two conceptions, is trivial as soon as y exceeds a few years. It is certainly possible to operate, even theoretically, as if y did not exceed a maximum y_M.

This brings us back to Lotka's equation where $f_{x-y,y}$ depends only on y, and to a more general equation where $f_{x-y,y}$ depends also on $x-y$. In both cases, there is convergence and, in the first case, that of a stationary population, the number of conceptions per month, quarter or year tends toward a constant. In a stationary population, this constant is equal to the product of the size of the population and the birth rate, the latter being equal to the reciprocal of the expectation of life. Here the size is the number of women. If we take this as unity, the number of conceptions per unit of time is equal to the reciprocal of the interval between conceptions, expressed in the same unit of time.

e) Limiting value of C_x in the stationary situation

In this case, p is constant and $K_{x-y,y}$ does not depend on x. The limiting value of C is such that:

$$C = p[1 - c\Sigma K_y]$$

but ΣK_y is equal to the average value $\bar{g}$ of the non-susceptible period. Therefore we have

$$C = p[1 - Cg]$$

and hence:

$$C = \frac{p}{1 + p\bar{g}}. \tag{5}$$

It follows that the average interval i between two conceptions, verifies the relation:

$$i = \frac{1}{p} + \bar{g} \tag{6}$$

i is called the *characteristic interval* for the homogeneous group being considered. The relation (6) can be demonstrated directly.

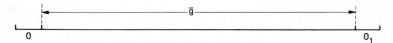

The first conception occurs in cycle 0, the second may occur starting with 0_1, and the mean duration between ovulation 0_1 and the following conception is equal to $1/p - 1$. If ovulations 0 and 0_1 are timed in the same way in relation to the month, the duration between 0 and 0_1 is equal to $\bar{g} + 1$. Hence:

$$i = \frac{1}{p} - 1 + \bar{g} + 1 = \frac{1}{p} + g$$

f) Some consequences of the existence of dampened oscillations

At short durations of marriage, the fertility rate depends heavily on the initial conditions. It is the equivalent of a crude birth rate and must be interpreted with the same caution as the latter. So it is useless to compute fertility rates by single year of age before 20 or even 25 years.

Some authors have thought that it would be better to compute fertility rates starting with V conceptions than starting with live births. This is a mistake. In a stationary situation, where C is a constant, the number of conceptions from marriage to month x (exclusively) is of the form $ax + b$, for large values of x. When there are no premarital conceptions, the total shaded area in the figure below is positive, because it is so for the pairs I and II, III and IV, etc.

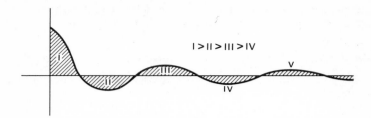

At short durations of marriage, the number of conceptions during the x first months of marriage is of the form $ax + b + \zeta_x$, where ζ_x is a dampened periodic term with a value which becomes smaller and smaller as x increases. The average number of conceptions per month in a period of x months from marriage is thus of the form:

$$a + \frac{b}{x} + \frac{\zeta_x}{x}$$

ζ_x/x soon becomes trivial, and the average number of conceptions per month, computed in this way, decreases as the duration of marriage increases.

The use of a similar measure in concrete situations has led some authors to conclude that fertility declines as the duration of marriage increases. Since this decline exists here even though the basic factors are held constant, the conclusion is suspect because it is not a good measure to use.

If one uses live births instead of V conceptions, the number of children born during the x first months of marriage is approximately proportional to x, as soon as the latter is large enough. The extraneous term b/x is completely insignificant and the mean number of live births per month during the x first month of marriage does not depend on x, except by way of the oscillating terms.

Heterogeneous groups

Consider a heterogeneous group composed of homogeneous groups, $1, 2, \ldots j$, $\ldots$ in the proportions $\alpha_1, \alpha_2, \ldots \alpha_j \ldots$. The results obtained previously hold for each of the groups. So there is still convergence and, in the stationary situation (where p and K_y are independent of x for each group), the limit of the number of conceptions per unit of time is a constant C such that:

$$C = \sum \alpha_j C_j$$

if C_j designates the constant limiting value of conceptions per unit of time in the component group j.

Since i_j is the characteristic interval of group j, $C_j = 1/i_j$, and therefore:

$$C = \sum \frac{\alpha_j}{i_j} = \frac{1}{i_h}.$$

In a heterogeneous group, the mean limiting number of conceptions per unit of time is equal to the reciprocal of the harmonic mean i_h of the characteristic intervals of the component groups. This harmonic mean is smaller than the arithmetic mean $\bar{i}$, and therefore we have

$$C > \frac{1}{\bar{i}}.$$

In other words, if we calculate the mean of the intervals of a heterogeneous group in such a way that each woman is represented by one and only one interval (1–2 for example), the reciprocal of this mean is smaller than the fertility rate.

The application of Lotka's theory to the heterogeneous group itself is complicated by the fact that f_y depends on the weight of the various component groups in C_{x-y}. But since C_{x-y} tends toward a constant as x increases, the weight of the component groups tends to become fixed. The same is true then of f_y and it follows that just as for a homogeneous group, C is the reciprocal of the mean interval between two conceptions.

This finding seems contradictory to the preceding one. But we are not dealing with the same mean intervals. The mean interval between two conceptions for the heterogeneous group is the mean of the intervals which separate a conception occurring during month x from the following conception. The conceptions in month x number $\alpha_1 C_1$ for homogeneous group 1, $\alpha_2 C^2$ for homogeneous group 2, . . . , $\alpha_j C_j$ for homogeneous group j, so that the interval which separates each from the following conception has an average value i^*, such that

$$i^* = \frac{\sum \alpha_j C_j i_j}{\sum \alpha_j C_j} = \frac{\sum \alpha_j}{\sum \alpha_j / i_j} = i_h.$$

The mean interval between conceptions in month x and the subsequent conceptions is therefore equal to the harmonic mean of the characteristic intervals of the component homogeneous groups, and consequently it is lower than the arithmetic mean of those characteristic intervals. This is the case because each group is represented in the conceptions for one month proportionately to both its size and its fertility ($1/i_j$), whereas in the arithmetic mean it is represented proportionately to its size only. In the first case, the higher a woman's fertility, and hence the smaller her characteristic interval, the more heavily she is represented in the mean. In the second case, all women have equal representation whatever their fertility.

2 Conceptions and live births by order

Errors in the interpretation of observations on birth intervals are frequently committed because of the failure to refer to models. In this area, models are an indispensable guide. In what follows, we assume that the basic functions do not depend on the order of the conception or birth. This hypothesis simplifies the computations but, if we rejected it, this would not lead to any fundamental change. We assume besides, that there are no conceptions before marriage.

The computation of first order conceptions

The number $C_{1,x}$ of first order conceptions during month x is equal to the product of fecundability p_x for that month and the number of women exposed to conception for the first time during that month.

This number is equal to the initial size, taken as basis, decreased by the number of women who have already conceived. It is thus equal to:

$$1 - \sum_{y=1}^{y=x} C_{1,x-y}$$

and then we get

$$C_{1,x} = p_x \left[1 - \sum_{y=1}^{y=x} C_{1,x-y} \right].$$

When p is constant, we have by iteration:

$$C_{1,0} = p$$
$$C_{1,1} = p[1-p] = pq$$
$$C_{1,x} = p\left[1 - \sum_{y=1}^{y=x} pq^{x-y} \right] = p[1 - p(1 + q + \cdots + q^{x-1})]$$

$$= p\left[1 - \frac{p(1-q^x)}{1-q} \right] = pq^x.$$

Computation of nth order conceptions

The number $C_{n,x}$ of nth order conceptions for month x is equal to the product of p_x by the number of women exposed to conception for the nth time. This number of women is equal to the number of women who have conceived $n-1$ times and not n times before month x, and are exposed to conceive an nth time.

The number of women who have conceived $n-1$ and not n times is equal to the number of conceptions of order $n-1$ before month x minus the number of conceptions of order n before month x. But among these women, some cannot conceive during month x. Those are the ones who are still in the non-susceptible period subsequent to the $(n-1)$th conception. We have therefore:

$$C_{n,x} = p_x \left[\sum_{y=1}^{y=x} C_{n-1,x-y} - \sum_{y=1}^{y=x} C_{n,x-y} - \sum_{y=1}^{y=g} C_{n-1,x-y} K_{x-y,y} \right]$$

Numerical example:

p is given as 0.5 and the values of K_y are the ones we made use of before; see table 16.3.

Computation of live births of first order

We will compute the first order V conceptions instead. Those are V conceptions which were not preceded either by any A or V conception, or by any V conception.

Table 16.3 Computation of nth order conceptions

Quarter	C_1	$\sum C_1$	$\sum C_1 K$	$\sum C_2$	Exposed	C_2
0	5000	0	0	0		0
1	2500	5000	5000	0	0	0
2	1250	7500	6500	0	1000	500
3	625	8750	7250	500	1000	500
4	312·5	9375	7625	1000	750	375
5	156	9687	7812	1375	500	250
6	78	9843	7906	1620	317	158·5
7	39	9921				
8	19·5	9960				

Their number is found by multiplying the number of women exposed to a first V conception by $p_x v_x$. It is equal to the initial size, taken as basis, decreased by the number of V_1 conceptions before month x and by the number of women who did not emerge from the non-susceptible period following an A conception which occurred in one of the $x - y$ months, and which was not preceded by any V conceptions. During month $x - y$, there were $V_{i,x-y}$ first order V conceptions. They represent the product of v_{x-y} and all conceptions in month $x - y$, which were not preceded by any V conceptions. So these conceptions number $V_{1,x-y}/v_{x-y}$, and the product of that number and $(1 - v_{x-y})$ represents the number of A conceptions of the month $x - y$ which were preceded by no V conception. The number of women who have not left the non-susceptible period following those A conceptions during the month $x - y$ is equal to:

$$\frac{1 - v_{x-y}}{v_{x-y}} V_{1,x-y} K_{A,x-y,y}$$

where K_A is the probability that one will still not be at risk y months after an A conception occurring in $x - y$.

Thus, we finally have:

$$V_{1,x} = p_x v_x \left[1 - \sum_{y=1}^{y=x} V_{1,x-y} - \sum_{y=1}^{y=G} \frac{1 - v_{x-y}}{v_{x-y}} V_{1,x-y} K_{A,x-y,y} \right]$$

Example:
$p = 0·35$, $v = 0·75$.
(The same data as in 'Intra-uterine mortality and fecundability', chapter 15, pp. 254–5.)

$$pv = 0·35 \times 0·75 = 0·2625 \qquad \frac{1-v}{v} = \frac{0·25}{0·75} = 1/3.$$

The values of K_A are: 1, 0·93, 0·56, 0·29, 0·13, 0·07, 0·04, 0·03, 0·02, 0·01, that is to say 1, $1 - d_0$, $1 - d_0 - d_1$, etc.

The computation is shown in table 16.4. The two small differences from the results obtained in connection with intra-uterine mortality by the method used in chapter 15, p. 255 are due to rounding.

Table 16.4 Computation of first order V conceptions

Month	V_1	$\sum V_1$	$\sum VK/3$	Exposed to risk
0	2625			10000
1	1706	2625	875	6500
2	1125	4331	1382	4287
3	827	5456	1394	3150
4	662	6283	1197	2520
5	548	6945	966	2089
6	452	7493	786	1721

Computation of nth order live births

The number $V_{n,x}$ of V conceptions in month x is equal to the product of $p_x v_x$ and the number of women exposed to an nth V conception. This number of women is equal to the number of women who have had $n-1$, and not n, V conceptions before month x, and who are exposed to having an nth V conception during month x. The number of women who have had $n-1$ and not n V conceptions is equal to the difference between the total number of V_{n-1} conceptions from month 0 to month $x-1$ inclusively and the total number of V_n conceptions.

Among these women, those who are in a non-susceptible period are not exposed to the risk of an nth V conception.

a) This non-susceptible period may follow a V_{n-1} conception. In that case, the number of women is equal to:

$$\sum_{y=1}^{y=G} V_{n-1,x-y} K_{V,x-y,y}$$

where $K_{V,x-y,y}$ represents the probability of not having left the non-susceptible period following a V conception in $x-y$, y months later.

b) This non-susceptible period may follow an A conception later than V_{n-1}, since this A conception would not have meant the removal of the woman from the group who have had $n-1$ and not n V conceptions.

Just as for V_1 conceptions, the number of those women is equal to:

$$\sum_{y=1}^{y=G} \frac{1-v_{x-y}}{v_{x-y}} V_{n,x-y} K_{A,x-y,y}$$

Hence, finally:

$$V_{n,x} = p_x v_x \left[\sum_{y=1}^{y=x} V_{n-1,x-y} - \sum_{y=1}^{y=x} V_{n,x-y} - \sum_{y=1}^{y=G} V_{n-1,x-y} K_{V,x-y,y} \right.$$

$$\left. - \sum_{y=1}^{y=G} \frac{1-v_{x-y}}{v_{x-y}} V_{n,x-y} K_{A,x-y,y} \right]$$

Births by order and by final family size

There are few observations on interbirth intervals by birth order and final family size. They are sufficient, however, to draw attention to the fact that the comparison of one interval with another, 1–2 and 4–5 for instance, is meaningful only if it relates to families who actually have both of these intervals, this is to say to families with 5 or more children. Since the last interval and, to a lesser extent, the next to last are significantly longer than the others, it would be better to compare intervals 1–2 and 4–5 only in families of the same final size. These comparisons raise problems of interpretation, so it is useful to extend the models to the computation of conceptions and births by order and by final family size.

Let's restrict ourselves to conceptions and take the example of a final number of 9 conceptions. We will have to compute among conceptions of order 1, 2, 3 ... 8, 9 in month x, how many will be followed by 8, 7 ... 1 and 0 conceptions between month x and month w, when the model ends.

This calculation can be done in various ways. With computers, the simplest is to compute for each month x, the number of conceptions of order 1, 2 ... 8, 9, *starting with* $x+1$, per, say, 10 000 conceptions in x (not to be confused with conceptions for 10 000 marriages in x, since the conceptions in x are followed by a non-susceptible period, and this is not true of marriages).

We will designate the results obtained as $10\,000 \sum\limits_{x+1}^{w} C_1, \ldots, 10\,000 \sum\limits_{x+1}^{w} C_9$; if

for 10 000 conceptions in x, we have $10\,000 \sum\limits_{x+1}^{w} C_1$ first order conceptions starting with $x+1$, there are $10\,000 \left(1 - \sum\limits_{x+1}^{w} C_1 \right)$ conceptions in x which have not been followed by any other conception. Similarly, there are:

$$10\,000 \left(\sum\limits_{x}^{w} C_1 - \sum\limits_{x+1}^{w} C_2 \right)$$

which were followed by only one conception, and so on up to:

$$10\,000 \left(\sum\limits_{x+1}^{w} C_8 - \sum\limits_{x+1}^{w} C_9 \right)$$

which were followed by 8 and only 8 conceptions.

Designate as $C_{1,x} \ldots C_{9,x}$ the conceptions of order 1, ..., 9 in month x. The number of those which belong to families where there are 9 and only 9 conceptions is equal to:

$$C_{1,x} \left(\sum\limits_{x+1}^{w} C_8 - \sum\limits_{x+1}^{w} C_9 \right),$$

$$C_{2,x} \left(\sum\limits_{x+1}^{w} C_7 - \sum\limits_{x+1}^{w} C_8 \right),$$

. . . .

$$C_{8,x}\left(\sum_{x+1}^{w} C_1 - \sum_{x+1}^{w} C_2\right),$$

$$C_{9,x}\left(1 - \sum_{x+1}^{w} C_1\right).$$

17

Nuptiality models

1 Marriages in general

In a monogamous society, especially, marriage creates a link between two populations, those of the marriageable men and women; the chance of finding a partner and the age at which one marries depend, other things being equal, on the size of the two populations which are confronted. In general, these sizes are not very different from one another, but major imbalances sometimes occur. Because of the upturn in the birth rate after 1946 in France, the 400 000 girls born each year immediately following the war had only 300,000 boys from which to choose in those generations which normally would have provided the most husbands for these girls, i.e. the generations born during the war. Such imbalance has to lead to changes in nuptiality and, in examining them, we shall consider whether they depend only on this imbalance, which is a structural factor, or whether other causes also intervene. Such a question cannot be answered with the existing nuptiality indices, since they are made up separately for each sex and do not take into account at all the ratio between the numbers presented to one another.

This problem arises particularly if one wishes to extend Lotka's theory to apply to both sexes simultaneously and hence, to nuptiality. P. H. Karmel presented a theoretical solution to the problem,[1] but it did not lead to progress in analysis; we still are not able to separate the effects of sexual imbalance from those due to other causes.

J. Bourgeois-Pichat suggested that the frequency of ultimate celibacy could be the result of local imbalances. The population would be made up of a large number of small and relatively isolated populations, and some imbalances would occur in a random way between the number of men and the number of women; such imbalances would reduce marriage for lack of partners, since isolation would prevent the excess of men in one place from compensating for the excess of women in another. However, the isolation of small populations cannot itself cause a reduction in marriage through local imbalances of the sexes. In an isolated population, there is an interrupted sequence of generations, and the imbalance which occurs between one or more cohorts can be compensated for by an imbalance in the opposite direction in others. Since it is impossible to draw a line between human generations,[2] Bourgeois-Pichat's idea must be modified if it is to be of any use.

[1] See, in particular, the article cited on p. 217.
[2] This is different from certain species, insects for instance, where mating is possible only between males and females born at the same time.

Everyday observation shows that, within a population, the forming of relationships is based on family, friendship and occupation, and that the people involved in these relations may form a group quite clearly separated from the rest of the population. We talk, in this sense, about members of a *circle*; it is said to be a closed circle if it includes few members and is not prepared to welcome new members. The equivalent exists among young people in the guise of cliques that are distinct and sometimes competitive. Such circles, or cliques, may bring together men and women, or boys and girls, and give rise to marriages stemming from these encounters. Generalizing from this observation, we see marriage as the result of encounters occurring within permanent or temporary groups, which we call endogamous circles, or simply, circles.

In order for the encounter to occur, the people concerned must already have joined the circle. Then the formation of a legal couple can be broken down into several stages.

1 At any given time, the category of marriageable people includes all those people who at that time are entitled to marry, whether they are consciously looking for a spouse, whether they are not concerned about it, or whether they have decided not to get married or remarry. But whereas girls, for instance, become marriageable when they reach age 15, the distribution of ages at marriage reaches a maximum around 20 years. Between these two ages, it would seem that marriageable girls, the majority of whom do not usually want to get married at the minimum age, become candidates for marriage at various ages and in increasing numbers as age increases. Seen this way, it is the candidates for marriage of each sex who actually get married, and not the people who are marriageable in the legal sense. The first stage therefore is to be a candidate for marriage. This involves each sex, independently of the other. In other words, if candidacy was a recognizable event, one would be entitled to make up tables for each sex separately without being concerned about what happened to the other sex.

For practical purposes, candidacy for marriage is not usually recognizable. The people involved themselves would not generally be able to say at what age they became more or less clearly aware that they could henceforth get married if the opportunity arose. It is still true, nevertheless, that at the time when they become marriageable in the legal sense and for a few years after, many young men and women envisage marriage only for later, whereas if they are not married 10 years after, they are worried and wish to find a wife or a husband, as the case may be. Between the two, at an age which remains vague in practice but which can be imagined as precise in theory, a change in attitude occurs which transforms a marriageable person into a candidate for marriage.

2 The candidate for marriage seeks to marry. For this purpose, he or she joins a circle of his choice. In practice, this step is not wholly conscious unless recourse is made to a marriage bureau of a group created to facilitate marriage. In most instances, the candidate does not have any relationships other than those of the group where he lives or works. But because he has become a candidate, this group or a part of it becomes, for the purposes of this theory, an endogamous circle. Like candidacy, membership in a circle relates to each sex independently of the other.

3 The formation of couples occurs within the circle according to rules that

may vary from one model to another—random formation (at least with regard to age); random combined with certain restrictions based on kinship, religion, height or colour; and deliberate choice. It is by means of these rules that the two populations, male and female, are transformed into one population of couples. The circle is in one sense the melting pot where the interaction occurs which leads to marriage.

4 The fourth stage is only the consecration or legalization of the outcome of the preceding phase. It must be distinguished however, because of the fairly long time which often separates the decision to get married from marriage itself.

Marriages at random

There can be no marriage if there has not first been an encounter and the latter is often fortuitous; one could even propose that luck alone presides over the formation of couples. This hypothesis, moreover, is not as extreme as it might seem, at least if we restrict ourselves to demographic characteristics. Of all the characteristics of the spouses, age is the one that interests demographers the most. There is definitely a certain correlation between ages of the spouses, but not a very strong one, and it can well be assumed that marriages occur within circles without taking age into account, as long as one allows a choice of circles which ensures the observed correlation between ages of the spouses.

For this it is sufficient to imagine that there are various kinds of circles; for example, circles of very young people, circles of people who are a little older and circles of mature or old persons, and that choice among these circles is tied to the age of the candidates. As a result, there will be a correlation between the ages of the men and women who belong to the same circle and it is possible to assume that the couples are formed without taking age into account within a circle. Wide possibilities of choice as to other characteristics then remain. But the choice is not complete: a rule that couples are formed randomly may imply that every one of eight female candidates confronted with 10 male candidates will get married. This is not necessarily the case with fully free choice. However, choice is not ruled out since one may imagine, for instance, that the women decide in a certain order: the first woman has a choice of ten male candidates, the second of nine, and so on, and the last has a choice of three.

In brief, if we are interested only in the age of spouses, the hypothesis of random formation of couples within circles implies:

a) that the age distributions of the men and women who make up couples are the same as those of all men and women in the circle at the same time

b) that the number of persons who do not get married within the circle they have joined is the same as if the formation of couples were random for all characteristics and not only for age.

Complete and transitory circles

In the example above, the eight women candidates all marry within the circle of 18 persons which they joined. In this case, we are talking about complete circles, as opposed to transitory circles which are ones where only some of the couples are formed out of those that could originate there (dance halls are concrete examples of transitory circles).

Up to now, there has been little study of transitory circles. For complete circles, two types must be distinguished:

1 The people who join a circle constitute a closed group, and those that do not find a partner there (under the rule of random marriage they belong to the sex in the majority) do not have an opportunity to join another circle but remain single or widowed. Circles like this have been termed unconnected. One complete unconnected circle of 10 boys and 8 girls will produce 8 couples and 2 bachelors under the rule of random marriage.

2 Those who have not found a partner in a circle have an opportunity to join other circles and they move from one circle to another until they have found a partner or until they give up further search because they are too old and reconcile themselves to the idea of remaining single or widowed. In this case, the circles are called intersecting. There are different kinds of intersecting circles according to whether the people who leave one circle all join the same one or are scattered among several.

a) Example of linked circles

A first circle of 10 boys and 8 girls produces 8 couples: the 2 boys in excess join a second circle including 9 more boys and 9 girls. Once again, there is an excess of 2 boys (who are not necessarily the same as in the preceding circle). They join a third circle with 11 other boys and 13 girls. The process stops because of the matched numbers and 13 couples are formed.

b) Example of non-linked circles

Instead of both joining the same circle, the 2 boys in excess in the first circle may each join a different circle. This scattering will happen in turn for boys and girls who are in excess in those circles.

Random celibacy

We call random celibacy that which is due to the unequal numbers of men and women occurring randomly in circles.

The study of models shows that the ability to be a candidate repeatedly modifies the frequency of random celibacy a great deal. With 16 persons per circle, this frequency is 20% for unconnected circles, whereas it is almost negligible for linked intersecting circles when each person has ten opportunities to be a candidate.

Since models with intersecting circles are certainly much closer to reality than those with unconnected circles, these results suggest that random celibacy could well be negligible, even among small populations.

Celibacy resulting from imbalance of the sexes

We are dealing here with that celibacy which may result from general inequalities such as are encountered after a war or are caused, because of the age difference between the spouses, by a sudden change of the birth rate. In this case, the possibility of being a candidate several times dilutes the excess of celibacy caused by the imbalance, so that it affects progressively a very large number of generations and remains almost imperceptible for each.

Similar circles

Members of an endogamous circle of Perpignan have no chance whatsoever to marry persons belonging to an endogamous circle in Lille. But if the age distribution of men and women is the same in those two circles, and if the rule of random marriage prevails, then the resulting age distribution of marriages should be the same, if marriage occurs randomly. It is also the distribution that would result in the single circle obtained by mixing the two circles in question. These two circles are said to be similar.

Addition of circles

Under the rule of random marriage, the distribution of marriages by the combined age of the spouses is the same for the sum of the marriages originating in two similar circles as for marriages originating in a composite circle made up by these two circles.

When dealing with the distribution of marriages by combined age of the spouses, it is possible to replace the large number of circles of each type and dimension by a set of circles of large size and of different types, i.e. with different age distributions. A theoretical study shows that as a first approximation, this set behaves as a single circle with respect to changes in the distribution of marriages by combined age of the spouses resulting from the vagaries of the age pyramid. In practice, this first approximation is still valid for troughs as important as the hollow cohorts born between 1915 and 1919.[3]

2 Marriages between first cousins

There are four types of marriages between first cousins: they can be the children of two brothers, of two sisters, or of one brother and one sister; the latter case is subdivided in two according to whether marriage unites a son of the brother to a daughter of the sister or, on the contrary, a daughter of the brother to a son of the sister. The following diagram summarizes these situations.

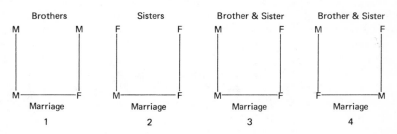

[3]Henry, Louis, 'Schéma de nuptialité; déséquilibre des sexes et âge au mariage', *Population* (1969), **6,** pp. 1067–122.

The term 'parallel cousins' is used in the two first instances and 'cross cousins' in the two others. To simplify, we designate them by numbers 1, 2, 3 and 4. The four types of marriages are not equally frequent as is shown by the three examples in table 17.1.[4]

Table 17.1 Distribution of marriages between first cousins of 4 types: selected countries

Country	Marriages of type				
	1	2	3	4	Total
Germany	21	29	23	27	100
Austria	18	33	21	28	100
Italy	22	28	21	29	100

Source: Hajnal, *op. cit.*

The children of two sisters marry more often than those of two brothers, and a woman marries the son of a sister of her father more often than a son of a brother of her mother. Various explanations have been offered, some of them borrowed from psychoanalysis. J. Hajnal has shown that it was possible to explain the direction and, at least in part, the size of these differences by assuming simply that the probability of marriage between two persons depends only on the difference between their dates of birth. The results that he obtained for a few values of the mean age difference between husband and wife are shown in table 17.2.

Table 17.2 Theoretical frequencies of marriages between first cousins by age difference

Husband older by	Marriages of type				
	1	2	3	4	Total
0 year	23·2	27·1	24·9	24·9	100
2 years	23·3	27·1	24·3	25·3	100
5 years	24·1	27·5	24·1	27·3	100
10 years	25·6	27·6	12·3	34·4	100

Source: after Hajnal, *op. cit.*

The difference in frequency between the two types of cross-cousin marriages results only from the age difference between spouses; it does not exist when the spouses are of the same age on the average. The other frequency difference, that between the two types of marriages between parallel cousins, prevails with any lag in age between husband and wife; but it is more pronounced when there is no lag, or when it is weak, than when it is strong.

Before any computation, it is possible to account for the direction of the observed inequalities. The age of marriage of men is more variable than that of women. It follows that the births of children of two brothers are more spread out in time than those of the children of two sisters; age differences between cousins that are such as to preclude marriage are more frequent. The sons of the sister of a woman's father are, on the average, older than she is if women

[4]These examples are drawn from: J. Hajnal, 'Concepts of random mating and the frequency of consanguineous marriages', *Proceedings of the Royal Society* (1963), **150**, pp. 125–77.

marry younger than men. On the contrary, the sons of her mother's brother are, for the same reason, younger than the woman is on the average. Therefore, she has a higher chance of marrying the former than the latter in the general case where the husband is older than the wife.

Let's demonstrate how to set up a computation of this type. To reduce the amount of computation, we abandon the civil year as a unit of time and replace it by a group of five years that includes dates ending either with 0, 1, 2, 3, 4, or with 5, 6, 7, 8, 9.

Table 17.3 gives simplified distributions of the differences in five-year birth periods between a father and his children, a mother and her children, a child and his younger brother and sister, according to observations relating to a rural population from the past.

Table 17.3 Differences in five-year birth periods between a man or a woman and their children, and between a child and its younger siblings

5-year periods	Difference between		
	father and children	mother and children	siblings
0			1
1			5
2			3
3			1
4	8	10	
5	20	24	
6	22	29	
7	18	22	
8	15	12	
9	10	3	
10	5		
11	2		
12			
	100	100	10

From these data, we must now derive the difference in birth periods between a man and his female first cousin. We suppose that the age of a man or a woman at the birth of their children is independent of that of his or her brothers and sisters at the birth of theirs. The data below permit us to obtain first the distribution of the difference in birth periods between a person and the children of a younger brother or sister. Table 17.4 gives the computation for the children of a younger brother.

In each cell of the table appears the frequency of the difference between a father and his children, multiplied by the frequency of the difference between a child and his younger siblings (thus 75 is the product of 15, frequency of 8, and 5, frequency of 1).

The sum of the numbers in the upward diagonal from left to right gives a number proportional to the frequency of the difference of birth period between a person and the children of a younger brother; 8 for the difference 4, 60 for 5, 146 for 6, etc. We operate in the same way for the difference between a person and the children of his sister. We obtain thus the two frequency distributions of table 17.5 (rounded and simplified to make the total equal to 100).

Let us now attempt to obtain the difference in birth periods between first

Table 17.4 Computation of the distribution of differences in birth periods between a person and the children of a younger brother or sister

Difference between father and his children (5-year period)	Difference in birth period between a child and his younger brother or sisters (5-year period)			
	0	1	2	3
4	8	40	24	8
5	20	100	60	20
6	22	110	66	22
7	18	90	54	18
8	15	75	45	15
9	10	50	30	10
10	5	25	15	5
11	2	10	6	2

Table 17.5 Per cent distribution of the differences in birth periods between a person and the children of his younger brother or sister

Difference (in 5-year periods)	Differences in birth period between a person and the children	
	of a younger brother	of a younger sister
4	1	1
5	6	8
6	15	18
7	20	25
8	19	23
9	16	16
10	12	7
11	7	2
12	3	
13	1	
Total	100	100

cousins born of two brothers. This is obtained by combining the distribution of the difference father-children and the distribution of the difference between a person and the children of a younger brother. Each cell contains the product of the corresponding frequencies: thus 48 is the product of 6, in the table below, and 8, frequency of 4 in the distribution of table 15.3. The table of products of frequencies is given in table 17.6.

The sum of numbers in a descending diagonal from left to right is proportional to the frequency of the difference in period of birth between a man's child and the child of his younger brother. The simplified distribution of these frequencies is included in column (1) of table 17.7. The difference is considered to be negative when the child of the older brother is born after the child of the younger brother.

We now take the sex of the children into account. One is male, the other

Table 17.6 Computation of the difference in birth periods between the children of two brothers (products of the differences between fathers and their children, and between the potential marriage partners)

Father-child difference in 5-year periods	Difference between a person and the children of a younger brother										Total of the diagonal
					5-year periods						
	4	5	6	7	8	9	10	11	12	13	
4	8	48	120	160	152	128	96	56	24	8	
5	20	120	300	400	380	320	240	140	60	20	8
6	22	132	330	440	418	352	264	154	66	22	44
7	18	108	270	360	342	288	216	126	54	18	138
8	15	90	225	300	285	240	180	105	45	15	320
9	10	60	150	200	190	160	120	70	30	10	591
10	5	30	75	100	95	80	60	35	15	5	917
11	2	12	30	40	38	32	24	14	6	2	1248
Total of the diagonal		2	17	70	190	396	682	1016	1337	1531	1493

Table 17.7 Distribution of the difference in birth periods between a man and his female first cousin in three instances

Difference in 5-year periods	(1)	(2)	(3)
−9			
−8		4	2
−7		14	7
−6	2	32	17
−5	7	59	33
−4	19	92	56
−3	40	125	82
−2	68	149	109
−1	102	153	127
0	134	134	134
1	153	102	127
2	149	68	109
3	125	40	82
4	92	19	56
5	59	7	33
6	32	2	17
7	14		7
8	4		2

female and we want to obtain the difference in birth period for a man and his first cousin. He may be the son of either the older of the two brothers considered, or of the younger one. In the first instance, we have the distribution in column (1), and in the second instance in column (2). Both distributions are symmetrical with respect to difference 0. The mean of the two (column (3)) gives the distribution of the difference in birth period between a man and a first cousin for all possible cases, the difference being negative, by convention, when the man is younger.

A similar procedure applies to the children of two sisters. For the children of a brother and a sister, two equally probable cases are encountered:

the brother is older,

the sister is older.

In each case, we draw up a table of products of frequencies and determine the distribution of these frequencies.

The next stage is to compute the mean of the distribution corresponding to the first case (when the brother is older) and of the distribution corresponding to the second case (when the sister is older); on the latter case, we include the difference as positive when the child of the younger brother is born before that of the oldest sister. The result is the distribution of the difference between the children of a man (whether or not he is older), and the children of his sisters; this difference is positive when the children of the man were born before those of his sisters. The latter computations are given in table 17.8.

Table 17.8 Distribution of the difference in birth periods between the children of a brother and a sister

Difference in 5-year periods	Difference in birth period between the children			
	of an elder brother and a younger sister (1)	of an elder sister and a younger brother (2)	$\frac{(1)+(2)}{2}$	
			per 10 000	per 1000
−9		10	5	
−8		54	27	3
−7	2	171	87	9
−6	21	397	209	21
−5	86	729	407	41
−4	235	1115	675	67
−3	489	1477	983	98
−2	833	1698	1265	127
−1	1219	1646	1433	143
0	1558	1305	1431	143
1	1708	825	1267	127
2	1563	401	982	98
3	1168	139	654	65
4	694	30	362	36
5	312	3	157	16
6	96		48	5
7	16		8	1
Total	10 000	10 000	10 000	1000

The difference of birth period between a man and a woman is taken as positive when the man is born first. Therefore, the distribution in the right hand column is that of the difference in birth period between a man and the daughters of a sister of his father. The difference between a man and the daughters of a brother of his mothers is symmetrical to the preceding one because of the change of sign.

All four distributions of differences are included in table 17.9.

Table 17.9 Computation of the frequency of marriages between different types of first cousins

Difference birth period between a man and his female first cousin (5-year period)	Cousins born of two brothers	Cousins born of two sisters	Cousins born of a brother and a sister. A man is the son of the brother	Cousins born of a brother and a sister. A man is the son of the sister	Difference* between the spouses	Products of (5) by $(5) \times (1)$	$(5) \times (2)$	$(5) \times (3)$	$(5) \times (4)$
	(1)	(2)	(3)	(4)	(5)	$(5) \times (1)$	$(5) \times (2)$	$(5) \times (3)$	$(5) \times (4)$
−8	2		3						
−7	7	1	9	1					
−6	17	6	21	5					
−5	33	19	41	16					
−4	56	45	67	36					
−3	82	81	98	65	10	8	8	10	7
−2	109	119	127	98	26	28	31	35	25
−1	127	149	143	127	208	264	310	297	264
0	134	160	143	143	364	488	582	520	520
1	127	149	127	143	215	273	320	273	308
2	109	119	98	127	115	125	137	113	146
3	82	81	65	98	36	29	29	23	35
4	56	45	36	67	13	7	6	5	9
5	33	19	16	41	7	2	1	1	3
6	17	6	5	21	4	1			1
7	7	1	1	9	2				
8	2			3					
Total	1000	1000	1000	1000	1000	1225	1424	1275	1318

*According to the observation given in table 17.3.

We must now compute marriages between first cousins, or at least numbers that are proportional to those marriages, under the hypothesis that marriages occur randomly between persons with a given birth period difference.

Consider such a group and call N the number of men or of women who make it up. We number the men from 1 to N, and select man number i. C_i is the number of his female first cousins in the group. To say that marriages occur randomly means that among N marriages which this man could contract, each of C_i marriages with a first cousin have as much chance to occur as any other. In other words, in N identical groups this man would marry a first cousin C_i times. This result is valid for the N men of the group so that out of N^2 marriages there would be $C_1 + C_2 + \ldots C_N$ with a first cousin.

The mean number per man of female first cousins present in the group is:

$$\frac{C_1 + C_2 + \ldots C_N}{N}$$

This we call $\bar{C}$.

Among N^2 marriages, we have $\bar{C}N$ marriages between first cousins. For the N which actually occur, we have on the average $\bar{C}$ marriages between first cousins, i.e. a number which is independent of the size of the group.

The result is valid for each type of first cousin and it remains to compute $\bar{C}$ in each case. Take for example the children of two brothers. Since remarriages are more frequent among men than among women, $\bar{C}$ varies from one type to another. There are, for example, more first cousins born from the brother of the father than from the sister of the mother. As a first approximation, however, it is possible to neglect these differences. It is then unnecessary to compute $\bar{C}$, since numbers proportional to the number of marriages of each type between first cousins will do.

Take the case of a man and the daughter of his father's brother and suppose that he was born 3 five-year periods before her. Since a woman marries a man with such an age difference, only 36 times out of 1000, the appropriate female first cousin will only be found 36 times out of 1000 in the group of difference + 3; the average number of first female cousins of the type considered (daughters of the father's brother of the man present in that group) is $0.036\bar{C}$. Since out of a total of 1000 boys, there are 82 who are born 3 five-year periods before a female first cousin of this type, the average number of marriages of type (1) between first cousins is proportional to 36×82 for the difference + 3.

By operating in the same way for each difference and by adding up products similar to 36×82, we obtain a number proportional to the number of marriages between first cousins who are the children of two brothers. These computations are made for each type in the right hand part of table 17.9.

By making the sum of the four totals equal to 100, we obtain the following distribution:

Type of marriage	
1	23·4
2	27·2
3	24.3
4	25·1
Total	100·0

We find the same result as J. Hajnal for a mean age difference between spouses of two years, a difference which is approximately that of the example.

Note: The model includes two distinct parts:

1 the estimation, under certain hypotheses, of the distribution of differences in dates of birth between a man and his female first cousin;

2 the computation of the number of marriages between first cousins under the hypothesis that the couples are formed randomly for each age difference.

If we had data from observation, we could replace the computed distributions by actual distributions. The model would then be restricted to the second part; that part, therefore, is the essential one.

Appendix I: Matrices and vectors

A matrix of the type (mn) is a rectangular table of numbers with m rows and n columns. When $n = 1$, we are dealing with a column vector. When $m = n$, the matrix is called a square matrix.

$$M = \begin{pmatrix} a_{11} & a_{12} & \cdots & a_{1n} \\ a_{21} & a_{22} & \cdots & a_{2n} \\ & \cdots\cdots\cdots\cdots\cdots\cdots & \\ a_{m1} & a_{m2} & \cdots & a_{mn} \end{pmatrix} \qquad V = \begin{pmatrix} a_1 \\ a_2 \\ \cdot \\ \cdot \\ \cdot \\ a_n \end{pmatrix}$$

M is a matrix with m rows and n columns, and V is a column vector. In what follows, we shall deal only with square matrices and vectors.

Multiplication of two matrices

The product AB (in that order) of two square matrices A and B of the same type (nn) is a square matrix C of type (nn) with terms c_{ij} that are equal to the sum of the term by term product of row i in matrix A and column j in matrix B.

$$c_{ij} = a_{i1}b_{1j} + a_{i2}b_{2j} + \cdots + a_{in}b_{nj}.$$

The product AV (in that order) of a square matrix of type (nn) and a column vector of n rows, V, is a column vector of n rows with terms γi (ith row or ith term) that are equal to the product, term by term, of line i of A by the first, and only, column of V.

$$\gamma_i = a_{i1}\alpha_1 + a_{i2}\alpha_2 + \cdots + a_{in}\alpha_n.$$

Example: Imagine a population distributed over three regions. Each column of matrix M refers to a region of origin (residence at the preceding census); it consists of the relative frequencies of the region of enumeration. In the column vector each row consists of the number of enumerated persons originating in a region. M and V are as follows:

	Region of origin				Residents		Region of origin
	A	B	C				
$M =$	0·80	0·20	0·10	$V =$	10 000		A
	0·10	0·70	0·20		25 000		B
	0·10	0·10	0·70		15 000		C

The product MV is the following V_1 vector:

$$\begin{pmatrix} 14\,500 \\ 21\,500 \\ 14\,000 \end{pmatrix}$$

computed as follows:

Region of enumeration

A	$8\,000 + 5\,000 + 1\,500 = 14\,500$
B	$1\,000 + 17\,500 + 3\,000 = 21\,500$
C	$1\,000 + 2\,500 + 10\,500 = 14\,000$

$$10{,}000 + 25{,}000 + 15\,000 \qquad 50\,000$$

In multiplying the matrix by the vector, we write the preceding table row by row. In current demographic practice, on the contrary, it is written column by column; the enumerated persons of similar origin are distributed by region of enumeration and the terms are added by row only as a last step.

Because of these differences, the conventions of matrix algebra may appear convenient to some, and inconvenient to others.

Appendix II: Expanding in a series

We have avoided resorting to more than elementary mathematics as much as possible; nevertheless we had to use expansions in series several times. These replace a function by a sum of ascending powers of a variable x, so that if its value is small, the function can be replaced by the first terms of the expansion when the total of the omitted terms is negligible. We can account in a simple way for the expansion used in the text:

$$\frac{1}{1+x}, \quad \frac{1}{1-x}, \quad (1+x)^k.$$

1) Expansion of $1/1+x$

The numerator 1 can be rewritten as

$$1+x-x$$

Therefore:

$$\frac{1}{1+x} = 1 - \frac{x}{1 \times x}$$

$-x$ in turn is rewritten as

$$-x(1+x)+x^2$$

Hence:

$$-\frac{x}{1+x} = -x + \frac{x^2}{1+x}$$

x^2 takes the form:

$$x^2(1+x)-x^3$$

Hence:

$$\frac{x^2}{1+x} = x^2 - \frac{x^3}{1+x}$$

and so on.
  It follows that

$$\frac{1}{1+x} = 1 - x + x^2 - x^3 + x^4 \ldots \tag{1}$$

Restricting the result to terms in x and x^2 gives exactly:

$$\frac{1}{1+x} = 1 - x + x^2 - \frac{x^3}{1+x}$$

and $x^3/(1+x)$ is the error resulting from replacing

$$\frac{1}{1+x} \text{ par } 1 - x + x^2$$

Examples:
a)
$$x = 0 \cdot 1 \qquad x^2 = 0 \cdot 01 \qquad x^3 = 0 \cdot 001$$

$$\frac{1}{1+x} = 1 - 0 \cdot 1 + 0 \cdot 01 - \frac{0 \cdot 001}{1 \cdot 1}.$$

Neglecting the remainder $0 \cdot 001/1 \cdot 1$ results in an error of less than 1 per thousand, which is negligible. Therefore:

$$\frac{1}{1 \cdot 1} = 1 - 0 \cdot 1 + 0 \cdot 01 = 0 \cdot 91.$$

b) $x = 0 \cdot 02$, x is very small and it is acceptable to stop at the term in x.

$$\frac{1}{1 \cdot 02} = 1 - 0 \cdot 02 + \frac{0 \cdot 0004}{1 \cdot 02};$$

By writing $1/1 \cdot 02 = 1 - 0 \cdot 02 = 0 \cdot 98$, the error is less than $0 \cdot 4$ per thousand.

2) *Expansion of* $1/1 - x$

A similar procedure can be used. It is simpler, however, to replace x by $-x$ in formula (1). That gives:

$$\frac{1}{1-x} = 1 - (-x) + (-x)^2 - (-x)^3 + (-x)^4 \ldots$$

or

$$\frac{1}{1-x} = 1 + x + x^2 + x^3 + x^4 + \cdots \tag{2}$$

Application: Compute $1 + a/1 + b$, for a and b which are small compared to 1. Neglecting the term in b^3, we write:

$$\frac{1+a}{1+b} = (1+a) \ (1 - b + b^2 + \cdots).$$

Multiply neglecting the term ab^2; this yields:

$$\frac{1+a}{1+b} = 1+(a-b)+(b^2-ab)+\cdots$$

$$= 1+(a-b)-b(a-b).$$

The error in this case is equal to

$$ab^2-(1+a)\frac{b^3}{1+b}.$$

Example: $a = 0\cdot1$ $b = 0\cdot2$
We write:

$$\frac{1+a}{1+b} = 1-0\cdot1+0\cdot2(0\cdot1) = 0\cdot92$$

The error is equal to:

$$0\cdot004-1\cdot1 \times \frac{0\cdot008}{1\cdot2} = -0\cdot0034.$$

3) *Expansion of* $(1+x)^k$

When k is a whole number, we have:

$$(1+x)^k = 1+kx+\frac{k(k-1)}{2}x^2+\cdots$$

by applying standard rules of multiplication for

$$(1+x)\times(1+x)\times\cdots\times(1+x).$$

To obtain the term in x we multiply each x by $(k-1)$ times 1. Since there are k separate x terms, this makes k times x, or kx. For the term in x^2, we multiply each x by another one, and the product by the 1's of the $k-2$ other parentheses. Since there are $k(k-1)/2$ ways of combining an x term with the $(k-1)$ others, this makes $k(k-1)/2x^2$.

We must now show that this expansion is valid for any value of k. In practice, it is sufficient to show it with k taking the form a/b, where a and b are whole numbers. We assume that expanding $(1+x)^{a/b}$ is possible; then it takes the form:

$$1+ax+\beta x^2+\cdots.$$

Raising $(1+x)^{a/b}$ to the b power gives $(1+x)^a$ as result, and we can write:

$$(1+ax+\beta x^2+\cdots)^b = (1+x)^a.$$

The two terms have whole numbers as exponents; we can apply the formula derived above to that case and write

$$1+b(ax+\beta x^2)+\frac{b(b-1)}{2}(ax+\beta x^2)^2+\cdots$$

$$= 1+ax+\frac{a(a-1)}{2}x^2+\cdots$$

The coefficients of equivalent degree terms are made equal, and this gives

$$b\alpha = a$$

$$b\beta + \frac{b(b-1)}{2}\,\alpha^2 = \frac{a(a-1)}{2}$$

or

$$\alpha = \frac{a}{b}$$

$$b\beta = \frac{a(a-1)}{2} - \frac{(b-1)a^2}{2b} = \frac{a(a-1) - a(b-1)}{2b} = \frac{a(a-b)}{2b}$$

that is to say:

$$\beta = \frac{1}{2} \cdot \frac{a}{b} \cdot \left(\frac{a}{b} - 1\right).$$

This confirms that, for any value of k, whole or fraction,

$$(1+x)^k = 1 + kx + \frac{k(k-1)}{2}\,x^2 + \cdots.$$

Further reading

This bibliographical sketch is intended for those who would like to pursue some of the subjects discussed in this book.

The student will be able to follow the most recent developments of the field of demography in the following journals: *Population Studies*, published by the Population Investigation Committee, London, and *Demography*, a publication of the Population Association of America. A third journal, *Population Index*, brought out by the Office of Population Research, Princeton University, provides current bibliography of the field.

There are many textbooks dealing with the sociology of population. Among them, for example: Judah Matras, *Population and Societies* (Prentice Hall: Englewood Cliffs, NJ, 1973); William Petersen, *Population* (3rd edition, Macmillan: New York, 1975); Ralph Thomlinson, *Population Dynamics* (2nd edition, Random House: New York, 1976). The interrelations of population with economic and social variables are also covered systematically in United Nations, *The Determinants and Consequences of Population Trends*, ST-SOA-SER A-50 (New York, 1971).

The emphasis of these works is not methodological. For a general discussion of demographic techniques, to some extent parallel to the treatment in the first part of this book, see the following: Mortimer Spiegelman, *Introduction to Demography* (Harvard University Press: Cambridge, Mass., 1968); Roland Pressat, *Demographic Analysis: Methods, Results, Applications* (Edward Arnold: London and Aldine-Atherton, Chicago and New York, 1972); Henry S. Shryock, Jacob S. Siegel and Associates, *The Methods and Materials of Demography*, 2 volumes (US Department of Commerce, Bureau of the Census, 1971).

For those who have been intrigued by Louis Henry's frequent references to historical demography, let us note that the subject is inspiring an increasing number of articles and books in English. For a discussion of methods, see: E. A. Wrigley (ed.), *An Introduction to English Historical Demography* (Weidenfeld: London and Basic Books: New York, 1966).

A selection of Louis Henry's own articles in the area of fertility models has appeared in: Louis Henry, *On the Measurement of Human Fertility* in *Selected Writings of Louis Henry*, translated and edited by Mindel C. Sheps and Evelyne Lappierre-Adamcyk (Elsevier: New York, 1972). On the subject of models, see also: Mindel C. Sheps and Jane A. Menken, *Mathematical Models of Conception and Birth* (University of Chicago Press: Chicago, 1973).

A wide variety of subjects related to analysis and models received advanced treatment in: Nathan Keyfitz, *Introduction to the Mathematics of Population* (Addison-Wesley: Reading, Mass., 1968).

Index